NEIGHBORS TO THE BIR

Fuertes' drawing captures the pintail's
rhythmic flight. *Laboratory of
Ornithology, Cornell University.*

ALSO BY FELTON GIBBONS

Dosso and Battista Dossi, Court Painters at Ferrara

Catalogue of Italian Drawings in the Art Museum, Princeton University (two volumes)

ALSO BY DEBORAH STROM

Birdwatching with American Women (as editor)

W · W · NORTON & COMPANY

NEW YORK   LONDON

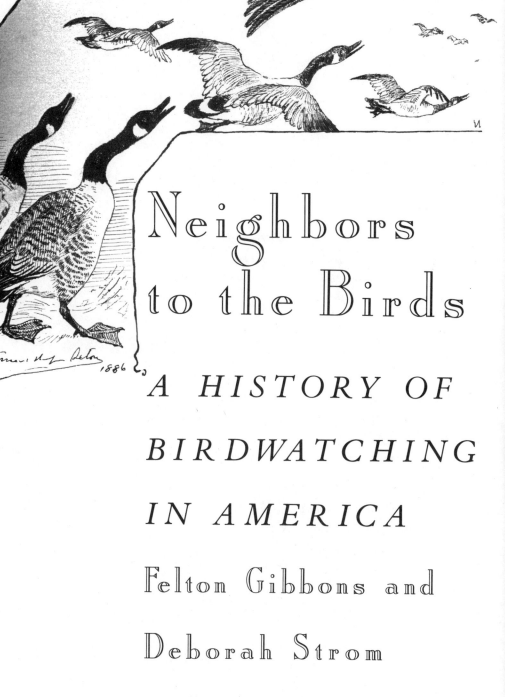

Neighbors to the Birds

A HISTORY OF BIRDWATCHING IN AMERICA

Felton Gibbons and Deborah Strom

Published simultaneously in Canada by Penguin Books Canada Ltd.,

2801 John Street, Markham, Ontario L3R 1B4.

Printed in the United States of America.

Photographs from the American Museum of Natural History and the

Southwest Museum carry the following negative numbers: p. 76 (30811); p. 89

(335696); p. 92 (14800); p. 211 (2A13049); p. 217 (2A4852); p. 327 (37292);

p. 334 (319650).

The text of this book is composed in 12/14 Bembo,

with display type set in Antique Open and Bembo.

Composition and manufacturing by The Haddon Craftsmen, Inc.

Book and Ornament design by Margaret M. Wagner.

Library of Congress Cataloging-in-Publication Data

Gibbons, Felton.

Neighbors to the birds.

Includes index.

1. Bird watching—History. 2. Birds, Protection of—

History. I. Strom, Deborah.   II. Title.

QL677.5.S77   1988   598'.07'234   88–1567

ISBN 0-393-02606-X

W. W. Norton & Company, Inc.

500 Fifth Avenue, New York, N. Y. 10110

W. W. Norton & Company, Ltd.

37 Great Russell Street, London WC1B 3NU

First Edition

1 2 3 4 5 6 7 8 9 0

IN MEMORY OF
GEORGE R. GIBBONS
AND
BARNEY O. STROM

Contents

Preface

*B*irdwatching is a seductive pastime. No one knows how many Americans are birdwatchers, but probably they number in the millions. Many birders start modestly in backyard or park but then become more and more committed to seeking distant species of birds they have yet to see. The authors of this book are sympathetic to fellow birdwatchers similarly caught up in an escalating addiction to this appealing pursuit. We too followed the birding urge farther and farther afield. First we canvassed New Jersey, then the New England and South Atlantic coasts. After detours to Western Europe, England, Scotland, and Greece, we went on to the Gulf Coast, the Southwest, and California. A weekend without at least one local birding jaunt was no fun and offered no escape from household or farm chores.

Birds, we found, echoing a thought from a great preacher of nature, John Muir, "are not just feathers of certain colors, numbers of a certain length . . . or of a group so and so." Muir instead watched birds because they "at heaven's gate sing." Myriad birders have come to agree with him in seeing birds at the forefront of the whole outdoor drama. They are active, often brightly plumaged, quick in perception, and sure of movement. They offer intelligible clues to their own complex personalities. Their behavior illuminates nature's linked interactions and warns of its increasing vulnerability to human assault. If in this age of environmental crisis, mankind is not prepared to read the signs the birds offer, natural disaster is sure to result. Birders know that the creatures they observe are the buoys and lighthouses of nature.

As both birdwatchers and historians, we became curious about the origins of this pursuit that could turn and pursue the pursuer. When and where in the history of America did the interest in birds begin? How, once the eating of wild birds became less necessary, did bird study grow into a recreation attracting millions? A search in the library for information was mostly fruitless. Books on birds are largely one of two types: either ornithological studies by and for scientists, or anecdotal travelogues by birdwatchers who tell of finding, for example, a rare wanderer from the Aleutians in a dump outside St. Louis.

We wanted to know not just about the mechanics of birding or the reasons for its pull toward Wanderlust or about its ecological lessons but also something of the social history of a beloved avocation. We wondered how birding related to human needs for outdoor recreation and how it grew to be a national sport. Our interest has concentrated on the amateur bird lover, not on the ornithologist, and our approach has been conventionally historical. But because of the broad scope of this subject, our survey of it is somewhat episodic. Studying birding's history opened our eyes to this activity's astonishing variety. First, the attraction of birds touched many talented men and women in the past, personalities like John James Audubon and Henry David Thoreau, John Muir and Theodore Roosevelt.

But birdwatching also introduces the participant to the long story of man's relationship to nature, seen in the ideals of the Audubon societies and the need to save birds from human predation, as well as in the American people's—and especially women's—return to nature for refreshment and inspiration after the closing of the frontier. Birds have also inspired writers and artists to esthetic perceptions of avian life and its place in nature. All these facets of the history of birdwatching came to us as a surprise. Birding, we found, offers more than fleeting glimpses of wing bars or beak forms.

To cover birding history as broadly as possible, we have approached it in two ways: summary descriptions of movements in birding and more focused studies of its early leaders. These include William Bartram, Alexander Wilson, accepted founder of American ornithology, Audubon, and two great Victorian naturalists, John Burroughs and John

Muir. Set against these portraits are chapters that survey the Audubon society movement and other campaigns for bird conservation, the contributions of women to birding, some famous controversies such as nature fakery, animal camouflage, and the introduction of alien birds to North America, the art and literature of birds, and how the sport of birdwatching is pursued today. Some readers may choose to follow the whole story as an unfolding narrative, while others prefer to sample chapters on pioneer birders or on past and recent trends in birding.

The appreciation of birds which enriched Audubon's and Thoreau's lives endures in today's birders who no longer try to shoot birds or study ornithology as a science. Instead they are content to wonder at the beauty of these intriguing creatures and their lively ways in much the same spirit that moved Thoreau nearly 150 years ago. But one question implicit in this book remains: why *is* birdwatching so popular? Surely the answer lies with the birds themselves. Their form and motion and the strangeness of their world astound us, and their behavior captivates our imaginations. Their comings and goings are apparently—but only apparently—haphazard, and every bird expedition becomes a wonderment and a stimulus to the birder's curiosity. When will the snow geese arrive at Brigantine sanctuary? How far south are the rough-legged hawks ranging from the tundra this year? Will the bluebirds return to the barnyard box once or twice, or not at all? The uncertain but always hopeful hunt for birds feeds the obsession of birdwatching as much as the charm of the creatures themselves.

An immediate appeal of birding is listing. Life lists, day lists, year lists, and Christmas counts satisfy painlessly and cheaply the human compulsion to collect. But the greatest reward of birdwatching is the opportunity to comprehend and absorb outdoor experiences. A quest for birds leads the watcher to discover hitherto unknown native paradises: barrier beaches dotted with sanderlings in January; Bosque del Apache Refuge, New Mexico, with sandhill and whooping cranes decked out in patches of snow during an early spring blizzard; Avery Island in Louisiana where the nesting egrets solemnly present their mates with sticks. These are places and sights unknown to most urbanites but on the beat of the avid birder. Birds bring one closer to a planet taken too complacently for granted and farther from the destructively crowded environment man has made for himself. Birds are among the most conspicuous wild creatures in our range of sight and by looking at them we can recapture a vital link with our roots. Hours spent watching birds can lead away from that quiet desperation which Thoreau saw as man's fate and toward a vision of freedom and joy.

We could not have undertaken this project without three magnificent libraries and their staffs: Firestone Library, the Marquand Library, and the Biology Library of Princeton University; the American Museum of Natural History Library; and Cornell University Libraries, especially the Laboratory of Ornithology. Special thanks are due the reference librarians of Firestone Library, especially to their head, Mary George, and to Joseph Consoli.

A number of people lent us their expertise with generosity and patience. They made our research particularly pleasant, and we offer our sincere gratitude to Dee Seton Barber and R. Dale Barber, Elizabeth Burroughs Kelly, Patricia Ledlie, Pamela Mack, A. Richard Turner and Deborah Warner.

For helping us to find photographs we would like to thank the archive at the American Museum of Natural History, Cornell University Libraries (Department of Manuscripts and University Archives) and its Laboratory of Ornithology, the libraries of the Gray Herbarium and the Arnold Arboretum of Harvard University, the Massachusetts Audubon Society, and the Leigh Yawkey Woodson Art Museum.

Many individuals provided us with photographs we include in this book. We offer special thanks to Patricia Boyer of the Jane Voorhees Zimmerli Art Museum of Rutgers University, Lauren Brown of the Connecticut Audubon Society, Jim Brett of the Hawk Mountain Sanctuary, Frances Collin, Pete Dunne, Lang Elliott, Steven Sibley, Samuel Grimes, Louis J. Halle, Frances Hamerstrom, Dorothy Healy of the Maine Women Writers Collection (Westbrook College, Portland), Diane Pierce, Arthur Singer, Bill Zimmerman, and especially Stephen Zimmer of the Seton Memorial Library at the Philmont Scout Ranch in Cimarron, New Mexico.

Barbara Kouts, Carol Houck Smith, David Gibbons, Lorna Mack, Lucille Allsen, and Lynda Emery helped us with their encouragement and expertise. To them we offer our lasting thanks. Finally, Helen Cruickshank has been a guardian angel to this project, providing precious information and photographs with good-humored generosity. We are particularly proud and grateful to have had her assistance.

. . . I found myself suddenly neighbor to the birds; not by having imprisoned one, but having caged myself near them. I was not only nearer to some of those which commonly frequent the garden and the orchard, but to those wilder and more thrilling songsters of the forest . . .

HENRY DAVID THOREAU,
Walden, or Life in the Woods

NEIGHBORS TO THE BIRDS

Chapter One

Bird Discoveries in the New World

*A*merica's colonists faced a world dominated by nature, and their survival depended on taming its forces and exploiting its useful products. The study of wildlife for the sake of knowledge alone was hardly conceivable in this time of practical demands, and natural history was seldom a concern until the late eighteenth century when, ironically, the wilderness was already receding westward. A new interest in American natural history arose with the surge of nationalism, but English initiative often took the first steps in this field. Mark Catesby, an Englishman, explored the Southeast in the second and third decades of the eighteenth century and produced an illustrated book of birds and flowers. The Quaker botanist John Bartram sent specimens of everything, including birds, to English and European scientists, and some even reached Linnaeus in Sweden.

Early, but sometimes fictitious, information on American birds went back to England with travelers in the late seventeenth century as shown in John Josselyn's *New-England's Rarities Discovered,* published in 1672. Josselyn, a junketing English historian, made two journeys to New England in 1663 and ten years later, and reported on its natural history writing "First, of Birds." Skeptical of other naturalists' totals, he believed that no more than 120 species lived in the area. He wrote of the "turkie" and the goose, a hummingbird that eats honey and hibernates, at least four kinds of "hawkes" and a small ash-colored bird that attacks them (kingbird), partridges, "grooses" and owls, "gripes" (which include eagles and vultures), a few field birds such as larks, wrens, swallows and starlings (meaning red-winged blackbirds), and quite a few shorebirds, some accurately and some quaintly named: "hookers" or swans, teals, "old wives" and "shoflers," knots, loons, bitterns, and kingfishers. Josselyn was interested in the usefulness of birds for food or, it may seem surprising today, as medicinal remedies. The goose and the turkey of course make good dishes and, according to Josselyn, so do most of the waterfowl except cormorants, which only Indians eat, after catching them while asleep and wringing their necks. Even snow birds (juncos) and "turkie buzzards" (vultures) are good to eat, and of course thrushes with red breasts, or robins.

Josselyn's recipes for the curative powers of birds were based more on folklore than on proven efficacy. Did anyone even then use an osprey's beak to clean the teeth, or drop owl's eggs in liquor as a cure for drunkenness, or apply an eagle's skin to warm a gassy stomach? The writer seemed to give way altogether to legend in describing the "pilhannow," king of birds, bigger than an eagle and sacred to the Indians. Josselyn mixed these quaint stories about birds with some good ornithological observations. Concerning the chimney swift, or "troculus," he noted correctly that it has horny tips on its wings to help it roost vertically in chimneys, but added the fiction that when finally leaving the nest it drops a chick down the chimney in thanks for the hospitality. Josselyn was aware that the female bird of prey is generally larger than the male, and like many other observers he was astounded at the passenger pigeon flocks. It is remarkable that he seemed alert to conservation problems, noting that pigeons were much diminished because the English netted them, and turkeys were rarely seen because they were hunted by both Indians and colonists. A largely inaccurate list of birds not native to New England closed his account. Josselyn revealed an enthusiasm for birds and a body of information on them that, however reliable, exceeds what other early travelers could offer.

The first contribution to American bird study in the eighteenth century, by Mark Catesby, aspired to a more rational level than Josselyn's quaint notes. Catesby was an English naturalist, not a colonial, who traveled in America and returned to England to publish his findings. He was primarily a botanist but included birds and animals with his plants because of a naturalist's enthusiasm for unexplored territory. Catesby's survey of vertebrates in the southeastern colonies resulted from two visits, from 1712 to 1719 and from 1722 to 1724, the first reaching as far north as Maryland, the second based in Charleston. After years of work at home in England between 1729 and 1747, which included learning to do his own engravings, he recorded his second American trip in *The Natural History of Carolina, Florida and the Bahamas.* Catesby's illustrations of 113 birds, though at times awkwardly drawn, were his central contribution to natural history. Linnaeus adopted seventy-five of his American species, one-third of those he listed from this continent. Jefferson based his Virginia list on Catesby and Alexander Wilson studied his book. So did Audubon, who adopted and dramatically developed Catesby's method of placing portraits of birds and plants together on a page.

Mark Catesby was able to put knowledge of American birds on firm ground because he was one of the first naturalists to insist on personally

Mark Catesby's study of the wood stork includes a separate sketch of the head and bill.

observing his objects of study. In contrast to Wilson and Audubon in the next century, he did not depend for financial support on soliciting subscriptions to a promised book, but earned his way by collecting American specimens and selling them to sedentary English naturalists eager for novelties from the New World. Among these were Sir Hans Sloane, founder of the British Museum, William Sherard, and later Peter Collinson, who also employed John Bartram as a field agent. Catesby was constrained by these relationships, as well as by choice, to keep in contact with the everyday objects of the natural world. He was an acute and patient observer of nature and his clarity exemplified the prevailing rationalism of his time. Although he recounted the old tale of a rattlesnake charming a bird, Catesby honestly added that he had never witnessed this event. Reflecting on the notion that swallows hibernate, he observed that swifts leave and return to the southern colonies at the same times as in England, probably after migrating as far south as Brazil. Catesby tried to replace folklore with observation and reason, which allowed him to open new doors to a sound ornithology.

Catesby believed that his 113 recorded species omitted only a few birds in the area he explored, but the claim was of course premature measured against later counts. His Latin nomenclature, with which his learned English patrons sometimes helped him, was wordy and lacked the conciseness of Linnaeus's system. This did not prevent American bird students from using Catesby's names long after the Linnaean names prevailed.

Catesby succumbed to a few other bird legends: that America had fewer birds because they had trouble finding this distant continent after the biblical flood; that the turkey vulture located carrion by smell, a point which Audubon disproved; and that the nighthawk made its boom with its mouth, not its wings. These few assertions of folklore still traditional in the early years of Catesby's work do not negate his contributions.

Catesby's work was taken up by a brilliant naturalist who was also a courageous traveler in the South, William Bartram. Like Catesby he was a warm lover of nature's wonders who gathered his field experience in a single book, his *Travels through North and South Carolina, Georgia, East and West Florida,* published in 1791. Bartram's explorations in the 1770s followed Catesby's by about fifty years, showing the slow pace of discovery during initial phases of American natural history. Bartram, like Catesby—and later in some degree Thoreau and John Muir—, was first a botanist, a field to which his father had introduced him in their early journeys together. But in the manner of his time William absorbed nature in most of the fields today kept separate by specialization and included in his accomplishments original contributions to knowledge of American birds.

The Bartrams were Quakers, living just outside Philadelphia, and their way of life was unadorned. They believed in freedom and tolerance for all God's creatures, whether black slaves, Indians, or wildlife. William's life seemed without any drama, with the crucial exception of his five-year journey through the south, made mostly alone. John Bartram, William's father, was a learned farmer and constant reader, who often acted as agent to some of the leading naturalists of Europe, sending them specimens of plants, birds, and any natural objects he found intriguing. In 1728 John built a stone house a few miles west of Philadelphia on the Schuylkill River near its confluence with the Delaware. He designed and built his home himself in a style that is both grand and vernacular. Between the house and the river on a southern slope he established Bartram's Gardens, a botanical garden in part still extant today.

William, born in 1739, received a classical education. From youth he loved to dream over birds and plants and to draw them laboriously. His father's principal patron in London, the Quaker merchant and amateur botanist Peter Collinson, praised Billy's drawings done at age fourteen. A few years later the young naturalist was working on commission for the British ornithologist George Edwards. Directed by his father toward a medical career, William instead opened a store in Cape Fear, North Carolina, with the aid of an uncle living there. He had already traveled as a boy of fourteen with his father on a collecting trip to the Catskills. When the store failed in 1765, John Bartram, backed by Collinson's patronage, took his son to explore the botany of Georgia and Florida. William chose to stay on in Florida to start a rice and indigo plantation on the St. Johns River. But this failed too for lack of good local labor. In 1773 he abandoned commerce and farming for nature studies and launched his major solo voyage, five years of wandering in the American South, his own chosen land.

William Bartram's journey followed no linear route as he meandered back and forth in leisurely contemplation of all things natural and of native life as well. He went along the coast to Charleston and Savannah, then hiked inland to Augusta, returning two years later to north Georgia in search of Indian lore. Once he went west across Alabama to the Mississippi, passing through Tallahassee and Mobile and turning back at Baton Rouge. But he preferred most of all to tour in Florida. From St. Augustine he sailed by dinghy up and down the St. Johns River to Orange Lake and hiked inland as far as the Alachua Savannah near Gainesville, which struck him as an engaging pastoral paradise.

Like his father William Bartram benefited from English patronage in the form of an annual salary of fifty pounds from Dr. John Fothergill, a physician and horticulturist, in exchange for all plant specimens collected. Fothergill wanted Bartram to travel northward to find hardy plants that might grow in England, but Bartram was too deeply attracted to the semi-tropical environment of the South with its rich flora and refused the request. On every page his *Travels* corroborates his love of the lush and exotic. He was so absorbed in Florida's natural plenty that often he forgot for months to send material to his patron, who did not find Bartram's field services faultless.

His great quest ended, William returned home to find that both his uncle in Cape Fear and his father had died and that his brother was proprietor of Bartram's Gardens. He settled at the family home, took over supervision of the garden, and slowly turned the journal of his trip into the *Travels*. He did little else for the remainder of his long life. When offered a chair in botany at the University of Pennsylvania he expressed his gratitude but declined. President Jefferson asked him to join the Lewis and Clark expedition as field naturalist, but William said no, since by then he suffered from old age and poor eyesight. The truth is, William Bartram in late years simply wanted to cultivate his garden. He had become a sage of nature, as John Burroughs and John Muir would later be, and the world came to his door by the Schuylkill. Washington, Hamilton, Jefferson, Madison, George Mason, and Benjamin Rush stopped to pay homage to the gentle Quaker botanist and traveler, while younger naturalists like Alexander Wilson and Thomas Say were his informal pupils. Always a dreamer, as much a romantic as a scientist, Bartram was content with memories of his early journey to a distant paradise.

William Bartram's feeling for nature was paradoxical and nearly mystical. With one ear attuned to rational deism and the other to the yearning music of romanticism, he would let the beauty of a plant or bird entrance him and in the next breath describe it with analytical exactitude. So far the only other naturalist capable of fusing such warmth of appreciation with intellectually sound observation was the English vicar Gilbert White. White's influential letters on the natural history of his village meadows were published two years before Bartram's *Travels*. This coincidence is a double milestone often taken to mark the beginnings of a modern approach to nature study. But White's parish did not reach beyond the gentle slopes of Hampshire, and his daily observations were correspondingly limited, while Bartram ranged through an exotic wilderness full of little known creatures.

Bartram's love of pure nature sustained him while alone in a wild land and supported his disciplined study of daily minutiae. His mode of living redeemed a debt to his Quaker heritage. He was practical and curious, genial and enthusiastic, eager to enjoy life esthetically and sensually while accepting its intellectual challenges. Enlarging on Quaker ideals, he believed that animals were rational and intelligent and had been granted freedom by God. Even plants, he felt, had volition and a kind of intelligence, while slaves and Indians also deserved liberal consideration. One of Bartram's purposes in travel was to study Indian life, to which he devoted a portion of his book. Throughout his journey he never experienced hostility from Indians, and his empathy for them gave an enduring authority to the anthropological aspect of his work. His interest in a native life unspoiled by civilization—the frontispiece of his book reproduced his portrait of Mico Chlucco, "King of the Siminoles"—as well as in distant horizons placed him among the early romantics. His link to this movement, at least in England, contributed to that country's literary history. Bartram's *Travels* intrigued Coleridge first, then Wordsworth, Shelley, and Carlisle. English romantic poetry often reflected his tales of wondrous places in a far land. The fountain in Coleridge's "Kubla Khan," for example, derived from one in Florida described by Bartram.

Ostensibly William Bartram went into the wet southern country to find plant specimens for Dr. Fothergill, his patron. His deeper goal was to see, to study, and to learn. In this search the rationality of his time served him as a working method, and his perceptions of the southern landscape opened his mind to intellectual discovery. His most beloved elysium was the Alachua Savannah in north-central Florida. This topographical feature, factually described, sounds ordinary enough: an approximately round sunken area fifteen miles across, often swampy in the center and bounded by natural berms, located a few miles south of Gainesville. But Bartram saw the savannah as a paradise charged with nature's bounty, and in his journal wrote warmly of Alachua's birds:

> The prospect is greatly beautified by the prodigious number of wild fowl of various kinds, such as cranes, herons, bitterns, plover, coots. There are also vast herds of cattle, horses, and deer which we see far distant in detachments over the vast plain. The upper regions of the air contribute to this joyful scene. The silver-plumed herons early in the morning hastening to their fisheries, crowd to the watery plain. The sonorous stork and whooping cranes proclaim the near approach of the summer heat and descend from the skies in musical squadrons.

Such a vision flows from William Bartram's Arcadian longings, the inspiration that fed his working scrutiny of nature. His daily observations of birds were not usually so lyrical but sought after scientific information. Bartram had a broad sense for the sweep and flux of nature as well as familiarity with two environments, Florida and the Middle Atlantic states. So it is reasonable that he should see the birds as creatures in motion, following the seasons like the plants and stars. Migration is the theme of William's extensive passage on birds in the *Travels*. He began by saying that most of the birds he knew had been recorded by Catesby and Edwards, who did not grasp the grand design of their movement which tied them to the flow of nature. Bartram pointed out that the priests and philosophers of the ancient world studied the passage of birds, just as they did the stars, for clues to seasonal change and aid in regulating agriculture.

Failure to perceive the dynamics of the bird world, Bartram felt, led to superstition and error. He cited the old belief that attributed the swallows' winter absence to their hibernation under the mud of lakes and rivers. As Catesby did, he corrected this fallacy by exposing it to the light of reason:

> This notion, though the latest, seems the most difficult to reconcile to reason and common sense, respecting a bird so swift of flight that it can with ease and pleasure move through the air even swifter than the winds, and in a few hours time shift twenty degrees from north to south, even from the frozen regions to climes where frost is never seen, and where the air and plains are replenished with flying insects of infinite variety, its favorite and only food.

The basis of Bartram's remarks on birds was his list of 215 American species, nearly twice Catesby's total. Following the usual order at that time, he began with owls, vultures, and raptors, and went on to crows and woodpeckers, then to the field birds, with waterfowl at the end. Each species bore a Latin name of two to six words and a laconic English description. But the innovative element in Bartram's list reflected his view of birds as living, mobile creatures. Taking his native Pennsylvania as a pivotal point for observing birds in migration, he designated the migratory habit of each species by a typographical symbol beside its name indicating one of five patterns of movement: birds which come to Pennsylvania in spring from the South; those which arrive there in the fall from the North and winter over or continue farther south; birds which arrive in the South in spring, breed, and turn southward again, never reaching middle latitudes; permanent residents of the South; and residents of Pennsylvania.

Bartram made some supplementary remarks about the migration of several species and raised a few questions about song and taxonomy. He considered that the pied ricebird (bobolink) demonstrated the connection between migration and feeding patterns. It passes through Florida in early April during a grasshopper glut, not leaving until this food source is exhausted. It reaches Pennsylvania six weeks later in mid-May, when May flies and certain locusts abound and feasts energetically on these. The bobolink had been thought to migrate in flocks of males only, but Bartram found evidence in some captive birds in Charleston that a confusing spring moult makes the sexes look similar when they travel together.

Bartram took Catesby to task for underestimating the vocal virtuosity of the catbird, which the English naturalist said had only one note, presumably because he never heard its brilliant medley in breeding season. And he criticized Catesby, and Linnaeus, for classifying the yellow-breasted chat among the pipits when its traits, carefully observed by Bartram, indicated another genus (which, however, he did not specify). These sensible observations attest to Bartram's commitment to rational analysis. His concern with migration led him to dissect bird specimens in order to study their gonads, in the hope that information about their sexual state might offer clues to the migratory impulse. This hypothesis puts Bartram's thinking in a remarkably modern light, since ornithologists have only recently begun to study possible links between hormonal change and migration. Bartram's remarks about the bill of the

Florida "crying bird," as he called the limpkin, indicate his precision in zoological description:

> The bill or beak is five or six inches in length, arched or bent gradually downwards, in that respect to be compared to one half of a bent bow. It is large or thick near the base, compressed on each side, and flatted at top and beneath, which makes it appear foursquare for more than an inch where the nostrils are placed, from whence to their tips, both mandibles are round, gradually lessening or tapering to their extremities, which are thicker for about half an inch than immediately above, by which the mandibles never fit quite close their whole length. The upper mandible is a small matter longer than the under; the bill is of a dusky-green color, more bright yellowish about the base and angles of the mouth.

Expanding this microscopic view, Bartram remarked that the limpkin was not related to cranes or herons, as previously believed and, though comparable to "Spanish curlews" (white ibises?) it must belong to a separate genus. It has been so classified ever since.

Minute observation leading to immaculate deduction formed the basis of William Bartram's ornithological insights. Yet he was a man who could sing a rhapsody beyond everyday experience, and beyond grammar too, while looking at a magnolia tree. Coleridge preferred to think of Bartram as a simple traveler who could admire the fish glinting in the water before he ate them. Bartram's pragmatic side was harder to see: the underlying Franklinian good sense, his sensitivity in observation, and the rational pursuit of fresh conclusions.

None of the bird students after Bartram achieved his personal synthesis of devotion to nature's mysteries with a capacity for analytic insight. For example few, if any, showed awareness of migration. The writers of state histories around 1800 had more pragmatic purposes than Bartram. These historians flourished at a time when the newly independent states were eager to survey and promote their assets. The early state histories, mostly factual and businesslike in tone, sought to describe every local feature—human, industrial, and natural. They generally included an inventory of birds known in the state, sometimes with brief discussion; but the authors, mostly political figures and some clergymen, were amateurs in natural history without the lifelong experience of

Bartram. The writer who takes first place among the state historians, in intellectual capacity if not chronologically, is Thomas Jefferson.

Jefferson wrote his *Notes on the State of Virginia* in 1781 and expanded them the following year. The modest title *Notes* came from a plan to circulate the publication privately in France, where it was published without the author's permission in 1785. As an agricultural theorist and country squire, Jefferson was much interested in natural history and especially in birds. He included in his *Notes* a list of birds known to him in Virginia but without commentary on individual species. It is characteristic of Jefferson that he based his list on published sources, for he was a scholar by instinct and practice. He took Catesby, the only source available to him, as the starting point of his inventory and adopted Catesby's Latin and common names. To cover all fronts, he also included Linnaeus's Latin names and a reference for each species to Buffon, the great contemporary French writer on natural history (whose knowledge of North American birds, however, was limited and second-hand). He considered Catesby's drawings "better as to form and attitude than colouring, which is generally too high."

The principal list of ninety-three birds in the *Notes* is ordered roughly in the usual eighteenth-century pattern, starting with hawks, then the corvidae, orioles, and woodpeckers. Elsa G. Allen, the recent historian of ornithology, found Jefferson's knowledge of classification accurate for predators, woodpeckers, and finches but, as was typical at that date, less so for smaller passerines such as warblers that were not so well known then. Jefferson supplemented Catesby by adding a group of thirty-two species of his own. These included some common birds and some given traditional quaint names, such as the gray eagle, wet hawk, whistling plover, water witch, and water pheasant, and well known if sometimes generically designated species or families like the swan, loon, and nighthawk. The *Notes* modestly end with a demurral common to the early listers and also made by Bartram: "doubtless many others . . . have not yet been described and classed."

The earliest bird list in a state history occurs in Samuel Peters's *General History of Connecticut,* published in 1781. Peters, poles apart from Jefferson, was an Anglican cleric, a Tory, and a witty, irreverent writer. With his short list of birds, often eccentrically named, he offered a few wry comments, but it is not always possible to tell if he was relating inherited folk tales or inventing fantasies to amuse the reader. A bird delicious to eat is the dew-mink, he said, making his own transliteration of chewink, the towhee. He seemed quite taken with a shorebird called the humility, an odd name he was not the only writer to use. The humility could not fly high and could outrun a pursuing dog without flying; it was very alert to gunners and was the size of a blackbird. No one has convincingly decoded this early name, which could refer to a willet, a greater yellowlegs, or perhaps a killdeer. Peters's comments on the whippoorwill, by which he meant the nighthawk, are patently facetious, for he said its boom means "Pope" and forewarns of a storm or, it may be, a change of religion that will give fright to Protestants and disbelievers. Peters's fables recall Josselyn's guide, which placed birds in roles from folklore; but the seventeenth-century traveler wrote from honest ignorance, while the Connecticut divine tried to beguile the reader with a self-conscious interpolation of legend.

In New England, where a longer past fed local knowledge, more state histories appeared than elsewhere. New Hampshire and Vermont were the subjects of reports after the Revolution by Jeremy Belknap and Samuel Williams, respectively. Belknap was a minister and historian, governor of his state and a serious intellectual, though not on Jefferson's level. His local bird list in *The History of New Hampshire* of 1784 totaled 133 species in categories of his own invention. He supplied Latin names, but the question mark that often accompanied them indicates doubt about his innovative scientific designations. His often picturesque common names included the speckled and swallow woodpeckers, the cherweke (towhee), tomteet, and hang-bird (a widespread nickname for the oriole, which hangs its nest). Belknap interspersed his list with anecdotal descriptions of a few familiar New England species such as the goose, swan, snow bird (dark-eyed junco), and crossbill. He accepted the theory that swallows hibernate without any of the reasonable doubts offered by Catesby.

Samuel Williams, also a clergyman, published *Natural and Civil History of Vermont* in 1794. In his preface Williams displayed some learning by criticizing Buffon for his sketchy knowledge of American fauna. He omitted the usual list of birds in favor of an extended discussion of individual species, roughly by category. His grouping of the birds recalls Bartram's method but is by no means as complete. First he correctly observed that ample water and wooded hills full of bugs make good breeding grounds that attract the birds to Vermont in spring and summer. Some can survive the winter there, too, and in this category Williams mentioned the crow, the red-headed woodpecker, and the blue jay among others. These contrast in behavior to the birds of passage, the swallow and martin, the snow bird and Canada goose. He granted all these species more or less extended descriptions, which touch, for example, on the flying ability of the goose and the several types of swallows. He mentioned the nesting habits of "house," cliff, and bank swallows and offered some evidence to show that they hibernate, wintering in large numbers in a hollow tree.

Other groups Williams discussed are the song birds, which thrive when man clears and cultivates the land—suggesting a paradox in conservation—and birds that he could fit into no category such as eagles, kingbirds, plovers, and wild turkeys. Williams's survey of Vermont birds mentioned fifty-seven species, some only in generic terms. Ornithologically his study is hardly well informed, with the swallows still consigned to winter sleep, but he shows some analytic insight into birds with his schematic division by seasonal behavior.

Only one early state history came out of the South, as might be expected from the well-established civilization of South Carolina. John Drayton published *A View of South Carolina, as Respects her Natural and Civil Concerns* in 1802. Drayton gave an unadorned list of eighty birds and added a single comment at the end. His compilation was for the most part straightforward, although a few local common names crept in. These include the blue linnet (probably meaning the indigo bunting), the fishing hawk for the osprey, the purple jackdaw instead of the grackle, and the large white-bellied woodpecker, which could be the pileated. In his one discursive comment Drayton noted that many birds in his state are in passage, including geese, a variety of ducks, pigeons, and the snow bird.

Another student of state birds has found a place with the amateur historians, although his background and approach were more scientific than theirs. Benjamin Smith Barton, M.D., of Philadelphia, professor of botany and medicine at the University of Pennsylvania, is ranked as America's first professional scientist in natural history. As his work showed, he was a friend of William Bartram. In 1799 Barton published an incomplete book called *Fragments of the Natural History of Pennsylvania*. Barton suffered from poor health and died of tuberculosis at forty-nine, leaving many projects unfinished. Had he lived longer, he might have advanced knowledge of American fauna to new levels of sophistication.

Barton's work on Pennsylvania natural history is typical of his unrealized projects in that it failed to exploit the disciplined methodology he commanded to attain full results. His treatment of Pennsylvania birds was promising in format but sketchy. He followed his friend William Bartram in separating the birds by seasonal passage or permanent residence, with further notes on "occasionals" and "accidentals," terms he invented which are still used today. Based on his own observations, which he noted alongside flowers that bloom simultaneously, he listed ninety-eight migrant birds in Pennsylvania in spring and summer, thirty-one in winter, and thirty-nine year-round. Despite his professional approach Barton liked to throw in amusing asides about bird life. In a discussion of the migration of the Carolina parakeet, he said Dutch settlers twenty-five miles north of Albany were so astounded to see a flock of these colorful birds that they took it as a warning of the end of the world.

The work of Benjamin Smith Barton is of interest as a foil to the uninformed and unsystematic state histories and as confirmation of William Bartram's perception of an ever-changing bird world. Barton's vision of birds related to the rhythms of the weather was a kernel of ecological insight that took many years to mature.

*T*he early explorers of the American West, pushing into an unmapped wilderness, had a more expectant point of view than the state historians compiling information about better known lands. The travelers to the West took it as one of their tasks to report on the natural phenomena that surrounded them so abundantly. The earliest of these explorers were often members of military missions, who had no more expertise about natural history than the state historians. They too employed colloquial names that are confusing today and took to heart the folk tales they heard about birds.

In the late eighteenth century the western frontier reached no farther than Kentucky and Indiana. After the Louisiana Purchase explorers trekked farther west, into the Arkansas Territory and across the Mississippi, up the Missouri to the Columbia and the Pacific. The early nineteenth-century expeditions spearheaded by that of Lewis and Clark were usually under army aegis and consequently well organized. Their purposes were strategic, commercial, and geographic, and their staffs often included naturalists charged to collect and study specimens of flora and fauna.

In the last decade of the eighteenth century several individual officers published accounts of their journeys which included passing remarks on bird life. The first was Thomas Anburey, a British officer and author of a series of travel letters entitled *Travels through the Interior Parts of America* (1789). Anburey's few remarks on birds are more engaging than precise but show some sympathy for them. He recorded the firebird, yellow and larger than a sparrow (the female scarlet tanager), and the orange hanging bird or oriole, describing its unique nest and making the surprising claim that its young can be tamed and taught. He admired the plumage of the bluebird, and like many of these early writers, who frequently mentioned the hummingbird and the eagle, he treated the hummer with familiarity. He described its anger in dispute over territory despite its tiny size, and how it conceals its nest in moss. To obtain an unspoiled specimen of the hummingbird Anburey charged his gun with sand but was unsure whether the bird was killed by that or by the blast.

Another military explorer of Anburey's time was Gilbert Imlay, an American officer of the Continental Line from Monmouth County, New Jersey, who traveled to the frontier after the Revolution. An adventurer and early novelist, Imlay is best known for his love affair in Paris with Mary Wollstonecraft, the prominent English feminist, whom he abandoned after she bore his child, who later married Percy Bysshe Shelley. Imlay's *Topographical Description of the Western Territory of North America* came out in 1792. It contained a simple list of 109 species, supplemented by twenty more, a longer inventory than any to that time except in Bartram's *Travels,* published in 1791. Like most other early students of birds, Imlay followed Catesby's nomenclature, the most authoritative available. He offered few extended remarks about the birds except for the naive observation that the ivory-billed woodpecker's bill is in fact made of ivory.

Another wanderer to the eighteenth-century frontier was Jonathan Carver, who recounted his journeys to the upper Middle West in *Three Years Travels through the Interior Parts of North America,* dated from 1778 to 1796. His primary interest was Indian life, but he included many remarks about birds, as usual mingling valid observation with legend and familiar names with colloquialisms. Carver listed the eagle, hawk, nighthawk, and fish hawk among others and described each in a short paragraph, along with more problematic species such as the wakon bird, the whet-saw (saw-whet owl?), and the nightingale, perhaps meaning the mockingbird. The nighthawk, he said, flies higher and higher in the moments before a thunderstorm, and the "whipperwill" was called the *mackawiss* by the Indians because that is how they hear its call—an early instance of the difficulty of translating bird calls into words.

Carver slid into inaccuracy when he called the loon a species of dabchick (pied-billed grebe) that is shorter than a teal, confusing this large diver perhaps with the much smaller grebe, and when he claimed that the fish hawk can drop oil from a sac to lure its prey. The wakon bird may derive from an Indian legend that identified it with the Great Spirit. Carver's description of this mythical bird is explicit as swallow-size, brown and green with a purple tail three times its body length, but no species corresponds to his account.

Lewis and Clark's expedition of 1804 to 1806 served as a model for the later large-scale explorations beyond the Mississippi. This heroic trek had long been a dream of President Jefferson, who took a deep personal interest in it for the harvest of knowledge it would bring and as celebration of the nation's expansion to the continental limits following the Louisiana Purchase. Jefferson instructed the captains of the expedition to gather all data in the realm of natural history, but unfortunately the expedition staff, unlike its successors, did not include a naturalist, and the amateur captains, or sometimes their sergeants, could undertake observations of the natural world only in spare moments. Meriwether Lewis, the better educated of the leaders, was more adept at recording what he saw, and he wrote most of the entries in the official journal on birds as well as an appendix giving a wealth of sightings. For the most part the Lewis and Clark bird records are no more than a list of species spotted, and a few highlights of these observations will suffice here.

Early in the trip on June 4, 1804, a "nightingale" that sang all night disturbed the camp; it was probably a mockingbird, if not a catbird. On the Lolo Trail near the Columbia River the expedition found pheasants, blue jays, a small white-headed hawk (Mississippi kite?) and a larger one, crows, and ravens, as well as a mystifying species somewhat larger than a robin, bluish brown on the back, with a black tail and black head stripes but brick red neck, breast, and belly. White pelicans particularly intrigued the explorers. Joseph Whitehouse records in his journal that Captain Lewis shot one having a pouch that held five gallons. This occurred near a pelican island roost with 5,000 to 6,000 birds.

The trip journal also contains thorough descriptions of the white heron (that is, the great egret), the avocet, and the *pica pica hudsonica,* the common western magpie designated with its nearly correct specific name. Cranes, wood ducks, and brant were frequent, a semi-palmated plover was sighted, and blue-winged teal seen daily were often gathered for a first-rate dinner. The journal contains some entries that tantalize the modern bird student, such as the listing of a "white turkey" and

Clark's description of a "corvus bird" the size of a kingbird, which could have been a gray jay or the nutcracker later named for him.

Lewis's appendix augmented the expedition's official journal with a rapid listing of many more bird species. These include "blue cranes" (great blue herons), swans, a sitting whippoorwill, cedar birds, killdeer, bald eagles, lark woodpeckers (flickers?), and "white brant" (snow geese). Alert to migratory behavior, Lewis gave some dates of arrival and departure. However cursory, these brief seasonal notes were valuable as the first from western lands.

Despite the thousands of pressing tasks in leading the expedition, Lewis and Clark found time to collect specimens, which they brought east for study by more expert eyes. President Jefferson ordered these deposited in Charles Willson Peale's museum in Philadelphia, a central location convenient for students. Lewis and Clark had not recognized any unlisted species among their bird specimens. But Alexander Wilson, just starting work in bird study and soon to be known as author of the ambitious *American Ornithology* (see Chapter Two), studied the western skins in the Peale Museum. Equipped with more expertise than the explorers, Wilson found three new species among their specimens. Appropriately he named them Clark's crow (now called Clark's nutcracker), Lewis's woodpecker, and the Louisiana tanager (now the western tanager). After some dispute with Peale about the right to publish these discoveries, Wilson drew them for the third volume of his *Ornithology*. This resolution honored him, Peale, Jefferson, and especially the courageous expedition leaders. But it is regrettable that, in the realm of birds, little else resulted from Lewis and Clark's awesome journey. Peale and Wilson, in going over their bird skins, found that the return journey had been too demanding for these delicate souvenirs. Methods of specimen preservation had not been available, and little that was discernible remained of their skins.

Of the expeditions that followed several were significant for findings in natural history. The best known and best organized were those led by Major Stephen H. Long, an Army officer and lifelong explorer of the West sector by sector. Long crossed the Mississippi and trekked northwest to the upper Missouri in 1819, and in 1823 went northwest from Chicago to the top of Lake Superior. On both journeys a naturalist attached to his staff, Thomas Say of Philadelphia, dealt with daily biological questions. Say was a disciple of his great-uncle William Bartram, an acquaintance of Alexander Wilson, and a specialist in entomology. While he followed Bartram's lead in studying all facets of nature, his lack of expertise in birds limited his ornithological contribution to Long's expedition. Say was paid two dollars a day during his service to Long, who warmly acknowledged his courage and good humor throughout the journey in its official journal. After his final return Say retired to the intellectuals' commune at New Harmony, Indiana.

Say's list of birds on the second Long expedition contained fifty-three species, not a large number but including some less well known birds than those found by Lewis and Clark. White pelicans again stood out in the foreground, one group rising so high that it seemed to dissolve in the sky, and masses of passenger pigeons flocked everywhere. The list named many western types such as curlews, sandhill cranes, cow buntings (cowbirds), an unidentified tern, a bald eagle on its nest, and Bartram's sandpiper, the early name for the upland plover, honoring Say's mentor. A rarer sighting was two "swallow-tailed hawks" (kites?). The Indians provided some exotic bird lore: once they cooked a fine dinner of swan, and a brave paid a visit wearing a live kestrel on his head as an ornament.

Captain John R. Bell wrote the official journal of Long's 1819 trip to the Rocky Mountains, when Say was also along as naturalist. Here information on birds is sparse, although Say added a species not yet noted by any explorer, the prairie chicken. Bell described the friendly curiosity of a barn swallow that followed the group for miles and the behavior of cow buntings so bold that they hopped under horses' hooves and rode about on buffaloes' backs.

An expedition differently organized and with another goal was led by Nathaniel Wyeth in the early 1830s up the Missouri, across the Rockies, and down the Columbia to its mouth. Wyeth, a Bostonian, was a courageous, adventuresome, but sometimes incautious leader, a private entrepreneur intending to establish fur and other trading businesses. He staffed his expedition with more talent in natural history than any of the others, taking along John Kirk Townsend of Philadelphia, an ornithologist, and Thomas Nuttall, a British botanist and bird student who had been director of the Harvard botanical garden. Townsend and Nuttall were the first naturalists to cross the Rockies and reach the Pacific.

Townsend was young, eager, and clear-headed, but his career after his western journey was disappointing. Though he worked as a government ornithologist, his health had been undermined by the strain of his

Early naturalist: William Bartram as portrayed by his
friend Charles Willson Peale. *Independence National
Historic Park Collection.*

travels and he published little. Liked by all, Nuttall was a blithe English-man, oblivious to outdoor hardships and to everything but the plants which obsessed him. Sometimes, while collecting in the mountain mead-ows, he absentmindedly wandered so far that he had to be collected himself. At the time of the expedition he published a thoroughly scientific *Manual of Ornithology of the United States and Canada.* Nuttall's journal of the trip with Wyeth is lost, but Townsend's records the two naturalists' bird discoveries. The number of unusual species they spotted indicate that bird study on the western trails was reaching professional status.

Starting out from Independence, Missouri, the two scientists saw abundant field birds in the rolling countryside: yellow-headed black-birds, pipits, larks and lark sparrows, chestnut-collared longspurs, bobo-links, and ravens. Nuttall soon found a mourning sparrow, which Audubon renamed Harris's sparrow after his friend and sponsor. On the Platt River springtime brought long-billed curlews, Bullock's oriole, the western tanager and kingbird, and at the Laramie River a red-shafted flicker. Townsend recorded the familiar huge flights of passenger pi-geons, as well as pileated woodpeckers and golden plovers that blanketed the ground by the thousands and gave him a tasty dinner. He also saw brilliant flocks of Carolina parakeets, screaming with no fear of expo-

A daguerreotype of Thomas Nuttall, versatile naturalist. *Archives, Gray Herbarium Library, Harvard University.*

sure and too easy shooting to challenge the gunner, and concluded that to bring them down would be nothing but murder.

On the Wind River Range Nuttall discovered a new small goat-sucker, Nuttall's poorwill (now called the common poorwill), while Townsend evened the score by finding a mountain mockingbird. Familiar western species appeared: sage hens in the plains, the western marsh wren and their predecessors' namesakes, Clark's nutcracker and Lewis's woodpecker. The two naturalists managed to see such rarities as a violet-green swallow, an arctic towhee, and a western veery in the mountains. At Fort William, the expedition's trading post on the Willamette River, Townsend discovered Vaux's swift and a subspecies of hairy woodpecker known to Audubon. There were also Traill's flycatchers, chestnut-sided chickadees, bush tits and Bewick's wrens, solitary vireos and the black-headed grosbeak.

Once they reached the mouth of the Columbia River, the tireless naturalists did not rest but took ship for Hawaii, on the journey enhancing their lists with seabirds and pelagics including guillemots, black shags, the brown albatross, tropic birds, petrels, puffins, and small auks. While the time in Hawaii was recreational and not recorded, Nuttall returned to the California coast to take up the quest. Still persistent, he found among others a new kind of magpie near Monterey and at Santa Barbara a black pewee (that is, the black phoebe), the tricolored blackbird, and a nesting yellow-crowned hummingbird. At San Diego he boarded the *Alert* for home via the perilous rounding of the Horn. On board was a young Harvard acquaintance named Richard Henry Dana, a fellow adventurer. Dana, later the author of *Two Years before the Mast,* said that Nuttall on a calm night used to "spin a yarn" with the young sailor during his trick at the wheel.

*T*he traveling bird student, the state historian, and the expedition naturalist experienced the bird world as random discovery, noting species as they came upon them. Mark Catesby, the first naturalist to study American birds systematically, undertook a complete survey of them but fell far short of his goal without ever realizing its scope. Starting in the nineteenth century, however, bird study entered a new phase. In his *Ornithology* Alexander Wilson tried to include every American species, not just those he happened upon but each one diligently pursued and studied.

Alexander Wilson in traditional pose of
melancholy from Gosart's *Poems and
Literary Prose of Alexander Wilson,* 1876.

Chapter Two

Alexander Wilson, Pioneer Bird Student

Alexander Wilson earned an honorable title: the Father of American Ornithology. What did Wilson do to deserve this honor? Here was an immigrant Scot of modest background, sketchily educated, first a weaver, a peddler, and an untalented poet, later in America a village schoolteacher and an encyclopedia editor. What impelled this restless man to seek out nature and focus intently on bird life? From what resources did he gather the momentum to produce a fully illustrated, nine-volume work? His *American Ornithology,* published between 1808 and 1813, was more elaborate than any book yet produced in the United States, and it surveyed with fresh results a field to which the author brought less than ten years' experience.

Wilson was born in 1766 in Paisley, the western Scottish textile center. His father made a good enough living in the local trades of weaver, distiller, and smuggler; his mother died when Alexander was ten, and his father soon remarried. The boy left school after the elementary grades. Perhaps his father and step-mother detected his intellectual abilities, for they intended to prepare him for the ministry and briefly put him to study with a divinity student. These ambitions for him failed, and like most youths in Paisley he was apprenticed to a weaver, his brother-in-law William Duncan. Although he served out his three-year indenture, Alexander, a restless, sometimes even disturbed young man, still searching for some firm grip on life, abhorred being tied long hours to the loom. So he took to the road as a peddler, his pack filled with cloth from the home looms.

In these itinerant years he was also writing poetry, popular in mode and dialect, similar to that of Robert Burns. Wilson's most successful Scottish poem, a folk comedy about a marital spat called "Watty and Meg," was published anonymously and came to be widely attributed to Burns, an error Wilson let pass uncorrected. Along with Paisley cloth Alexander carried subscriptions to his poems and tried to sell them too. Throughout life a tireless wanderer, Wilson enjoyed touring Scotland and took in its sights along the way. But his peddling business was a failure. From time to time need drove him home to bind himself again to the loom.

Wilson had fleeting glimpses of the joys of intellectual life but lacked the education or money to pursue them. His friends Thomas Crichton, his Scottish biographer, and David Brodie, a fellow weaver who had some classical education, treated him as an intellectual equal, and their talk stimulated him to read. He had far reaching hopes for his poems, a volume of which he had published prematurely in 1790. Wilson hoped to find his intellectual place through his poetry, even though it was seldom better than mediocre. Later in America he pursued his verbal talent by teaching himself German, and the descriptions he wrote for his *Ornithology* reflect his self-education as a writer. As often happens, Wilson's letters are more spontaneous and moving than his stilted verses. The letters to Crichton and Brodie written on the Scottish peddling trips cry out with melancholy. He wrote to Brodie in January 1791:

> All the stories you have read of garrets, tatters, unmerciful duns, lank hunger, and poetical misery, are all sadly realized in me. The neglect of an unrewarding world has blasted all those airy hopes that once smiled so promisingly, and I find the dream of my fate running thus—Renounce poetry and all its distracting notions, descend to the labourer's vale of life, then attend the dictates of prudence, and *toil or starve*.

Such thoughts leave no doubt that Wilson was frustrated with his failure to master the intellectual life. His failed ambition led him into the characteristic melancholic depression of the unfulfilled genius. Similar letters to friends during the lowest point of his American career, when he taught for more than five years in provincial schools, his mind on the birds and not on his pupils, suggest he was suffering from a recurrent onslaught of melancholy.

Alexander Wilson demonstrated another trait consistent with the typical melancholic genius. He had a trenchant wit, which could shade over into stubborn impatience, even perverseness. He exercised his wit in genre poems like "Watty and Meg" as well as sparingly in his letters. The most amusing of his letters were reserved for a young lady, perhaps his fiancée, Sarah Miller, for whom he painted vivid pictures of life's crudities on the Kentucky frontier:

> Yet I don't know but a description of the *fashions* of Kentucky would be almost as entertaining as those of London and Paris. What would you think of a blanket Riding Dress, a straw side saddle, and a large mule with ears so long they might almost serve for reins . . . ? Or what would you think of a beau who had neither been washed or shaved for a month, with three bands of blue cloth wrapt around his legs by way of boots, a ragged great coat, without coat, jacket, or neckcloth, breathing the evil perfume of corn whisky? Such figures are quite fashionable in Kentucky.

Wilson was also able to turn his wit against himself in his boisterous description of a failed chase after a nuthatch in winter, which resulted in cold wet clothes and mud to the waist:

> I started this morning, by peep of dawn, with a gun, for the purpose of shooting a nuthatch. After jumping a hundred fences, and getting over the ancles in mud (for I had put on my shoes for lightness), I found myself almost at the junction of the Schuylkill and Delaware, without success, there being hardly half an acre of woodland in the whole neck; and the nuthatch generally frequents large-timbered woods. I returned home at eight o'clock, after getting completely wet, and in a profuse perspiration, which, contrary to the maxims of the doctors, had done me a great deal of good; and I intend to repeat the dose, except that I shall leave out the ingredient of the wet feet, if otherwise convenient.

He could also be sharply critical, particularly in his youth. He is said to have struck up a correspondence with Burns, then sent the poet an untactfully frank criticism of one of his works. He received a rap on the wrist from Burns and never heard from him thereafter.

Political beliefs were as deeply meaningful to Alexander Wilson in

America as they had been in Scotland. In America his sympathies were liberal and democratic, and his patriotic feelings for the new nation were warm and spontaneous. One of his two American heroes was Thomas Jefferson; the other, William Bartram. The elders of Milestown, Pennsylvania, asked him to give a patriotic speech for Jefferson's first inaugural in 1801, which he called "Oration on the Power and Value of National Liberty." This was published and brought him some fame. He twice approached President Jefferson by letter and once went to visit him. Wilson sealed his new loyalty to the United States by becoming a citizen in 1804, and later asserted his leftward leanings by paying a visit of homage to the aging Tom Paine in New York in 1808.

Once Wilson's strong-minded politics led him astray. In his early Scottish years, in a harsh land harshly ruled, he was politically radical. During a time of unrest among the weavers, whose craft was threatened by industrialization, Wilson twice wrote bitter attacks in verse on mill owners, only half concealing their names. The second time, he foolishly sent an owner his libelous poem with an anonymous extortionary letter that contained a threat to circulate it and demanded money not to. The mill owner was highly respected in the community and the law struck back swiftly. Wilson was convicted of libel and extortion and spent several short periods in jail while his friends scrambled for bail. Finally he had to burn the offending poem on the jailhouse steps.

Soon after this sorry setback Alexander Wilson understandably enough determined to escape to America. He spent four months weaving non-stop to earn his passage and sailed from Belfast in June 1794 as a deck passenger with his nephew. They landed in July at New Castle, Delaware, and from there walked to Philadelphia, the center of Wilson's life during his remaining nineteen years.

On his second day in America on the road to Philadelphia the future ornithologist spotted a bright bird in the woods, which, he was surprised to find, everywhere covered this new land. He shot it, and it proved to be a red-headed woodpecker, stridently colored in red, white, and black and thus somewhat resembling the American colors. But years of distraction were to pass before Wilson could turn a serious eye to birds. Penniless, he first had to find work, and finding none as a weaver, he got a job with an engraver. Later a weaver north of the city took him on but, repeating his earlier pattern of restlessness, Wilson soon put together a pack of goods and resumed the life of a peddler, wandering through New Jersey and Virginia.

Though he now made an adequate living, it occurred to him that schoolteaching was a more socially acceptable pursuit which might also afford some time to study on his own. Wilson took on a motley succession of village schools, mostly just north of Philadelphia, but the fees and the physical facilities were far from adequate, and this new career brought no more satisfaction than his other efforts. At some of these posts he stayed only a term, though once at Milestown near Bristol he lasted five years, until one night he fled in the dark, it is thought, to escape an incipient scandal involving an unidentified married woman. A more promising post followed at Gray's Ferry on the Schuylkill, a few miles from central Philadelphia.

At first this post promised no more than the better teaching conditions Wilson sought, a living salary and a sound building. But he soon discovered that a near neighbor was William Bartram, America's senior and beloved naturalist. Bartram was by then a semi-recluse, but with constant visitors to the charming early Georgian house that his father had built on a slope above the Schuylkill and to Bartram's Gardens, a famous and enchanting specimen nursery of native and exotic plants. The Bartrams were devoted to botany, but, following the generalist approach to nature in this time, they studied birds too. Alexander Wilson's fortunate discovery of William Bartram about 1803, then a calm and kindly Quaker with wispy white hair, changed the younger man's life. Bartram became his mentor, a genial spirit that presided over Wilson's conversion to natural history.

Internal reasons, as well as William Bartram's guidance, contributed to Wilson's continuing interest in birds, which he was beginning to draw. Alexander Lawson, a fellow Scottish immigrant, became important in Wilson's life after 1800. Lawson was to become the principal engraver of illustrations for Wilson's *American Ornithology,* a huge task he reluctantly undertook but saw through with devotion. Even in the more congenial teaching position at Gray's Ferry Wilson became depressed at the burden of routine that kept him from escaping to the woods and birds. Bartram and Lawson advised him to stop studying books and playing melancholy Scottish airs on his flute and instead to take up drawing as a distraction, suggesting that he draw the birds he saw and shot. Wilson followed this advice, which turned out to make history. In several letters to Bartram in 1803 and 1804 Wilson referred to his growing collection of bird specimens and drawings. He also sought Bartram's criticisms of his draughtsmanship and, revealingly, his identification of the birds. The father of American ornithology still had a good deal to learn in 1804, only four years before his *Ornithology* began to appear.

Like any tyro birder Wilson, always a persistent autodidact, learned from the available ornithological books, which in his time were few. The principal ornithologies he used were Thomas Bewick's *British Birds,* which he owned; William Turton's 1806 revised version of Linnaeus; John Latham's *A General Synopsis of Birds;* George Edwards's two books, *A Natural History of Uncommon Birds* and *Gleanings of Natural History;* and above all Catesby's *Natural History of Carolina, Florida and the Bahama Islands.* Most of these books except Catesby's concerned European or exotic species and were of little help to an American ornithologist. Most of them described the birds schematically, without life histories, an approach which Wilson was to improve radically. The illustrations in these books were all too obviously based on dead, limp, or propped up skins, shadows of the live bird. Edwards, for example, who had never crossed the Atlantic, illustrated his American birds mostly from specimens shipped him by John Bartram. Only Catesby knew local birds firsthand and, though he usually showed them in stiff profile views, he let a flavor of his direct knowledge filter through in the bold big format and the confident coloring of his illustrations.

Latham was important to Wilson as a guide to phylogenesis, or family tree, of birds. Since his *Ornithology* presented the birds in no rational order but only as he came across them, Wilson compensated for his casualness by prefacing his first volume with a phylogenetic table of birds drawn from Latham. Wilson had nothing but scorn for the French naturalist Comte de Buffon's ignorance of American bird species, and he justly ridiculed Buffon's thesis that they were mere debilitated off-spring of their European cousins. In learning to draw birds, Wilson chose Catesby's illustrations as his models. Indeed the drawings in *American Ornithology* hardly exceed Catesby's visual perceptions of seventy-five years earlier. Like Catesby, Wilson was usually content to draw his subjects according to a rigid formula of viewpoint, most often a profile only occasionally enlivened by a stiff turn of the head.

A critical student of books by his predecessors, Wilson became acutely aware that knowledge of American birds had been largely based on the study of dead skins. Misconceptions about behavior, color, and anatomy inevitably resulted from sedentary scrutiny in the laboratory. Wilson came to believe that the ornithologist must spend as much time as possible in the field, studying birds in their chosen circle of nature. This creed allowed him to step ahead of his predecessors and to anticipate Audubon and all of modern bird study as it advanced into the age of binoculars and the camera. In the preface to his second volume Wilson claimed that "the greatest number of the descriptions, particularly those of the nests, eggs, and plumage, have been written in the woods, with the subjects in view, leaving as little as possible to the lapse of recollection." At the head of the sixth he wrote, "From these barren and musty records [earlier ornithologies], the author of the present work has a thousand times turned, with a delight bordering on adoration, to the magnificent repository of the woods and fields—the Grand Aviary of Nature. In this divine school he has studied no vulgar copy."

To any bird student travel in the field is essential. Wilson's travels —prolonged, strenuous to the point of destroying his health, courageous, and sometimes obsessive—were the core of his American life. He plunged into the wilderness beyond the reach of roads, mostly on foot, sometimes riding, once rowing and drifting down 440 miles of the Ohio River in a skiff, occasionally by schooner or punt. But mostly he walked. Wilson undertook five principal American journeys, beginning in 1805 when the *Ornithology* was conceived and continuing during the publication of most of its volumes. His trips were to upper New York State and Niagara Falls; two to Albany and New England as far as Portland; one south by a coastal route to Savannah; and the longest— west to Pittsburgh, Louisville, through Kentucky and Tennessee, and along the Natchez Trace across Mississippi to New Orleans. In the last years of his work devoted to shorebirds, Wilson made a number of short trips to the area of Great Egg Harbor, New Jersey, to collect specimens, sometimes accompanied by his follower George Ord. The aim of these travels was twofold: to collect new species of birds in their various habitats and to sell subscriptions to his book.

Alexander Wilson's travels have an historical significance beyond ornithological research. Enroute he wrote long letters narrating what he saw to friends at home, often to Bartram (whom Wilson several times urged to go along but who was too old to accompany him), Lawson, and William Duncan, his brother-in-law. These letters almost never mentioned birds, as Wilson reserved his observations on them for his *Ornithology;* but they were rich in lively descriptions of frontier and town life in the new United States, seen by Wilson's bright, occasionally scornful eyes and assessed by his acute intelligence. He recorded his earliest trip to Niagara, when he visited a farm near Lake Cayuga which he and Duncan had bought, in a long poem, "The Foresters." The stunted cadences of this, his major American poem, provide little more than a banal record of his walking trip and no foretaste of the eloquence of the later prose letters from the South and West.

An incident on the way to Niagara instigated Wilson's debut as an ornithologist. In the New York woods he shot a bird he was unable to identify, a twelve inch gray-backed, black and white capped songbird, which he thought might be an unrecorded species. Later he sent a drawing of it to President Jefferson, who included birds among many interests. Jefferson replied at length, though unable to pin down the bird, which was later identified as a gray jay and well enough known. He in turn asked Wilson about a woodland ground bird he'd often seen but was not able to name, which turned out to be a towhee.

Wilson undertook his subsequent journeys to New England, the South, and West for financial reasons as well as birdwatching purposes, because his book's future depended on selling advance subscriptions. His task was difficult, as he worked alone and had to justify the necessarily high price of $120 for the projected ten illustrated volumes (later reduced to nine, including one that was posthumous). In moments of discouragement he wondered if he had undertaken a project too elaborate for the young republic. Though he showed sheets or a sample volume to anyone interested, sales often went slowly, disheartening the author. But when they went well his spirits soared. Stopping at Princeton on his first New England trip, he called on "the reverend doctors of the college" in "this spacious sanctuary of literature." They entertained him courteously but mentioned no cash. Furthermore, when interviewing the professor of natural history, Wilson discovered to his astonishment that the man "didn't know a sparrow from a woodpecker."

In burgeoning commercial New York and throughout towns to the northeast he garnered praise for his work but few commitments to buy it. He returned to Philadelphia with forty-one subscriptions and with an opinion of New England as tightly wrapped in poverty and devoid of culture. Leaving immediately for the South, Wilson again met disappointing setbacks but was boosted by the kind reception of the president, who had subscribed to the book on first advertisement. Despite freezing weather, river crossings without fords or bridges, primitive accommodations, and the scarcity of birds in winter, the southern journey achieved financial success—250 subscriptions, enough to finance the whole book and to enlarge the first volume's printing from 200 to 500.

The western trip, launched in late winter of 1810, was more demanding yet, an adventurous gamble of endurance through hundreds of miles of frontier wilderness. The walk to Pittsburgh was uneventful, and Wilson sold a satisfactory number of subscriptions in the already gritty industrial city. His bold decision to float down the Ohio to Louisville in a skiff, christened *The Ornithologist,* despite local advice against attempting it alone, eased and sped that leg of the trip. In Louisville by purest chance Wilson met a fellow bird artist when he stepped unannounced into Audubon's store. Both looked over the other's drawings, and Audubon started to subscribe to Wilson's book but changed his mind when his business partner spoke against it. This conjunction of birding greats was an historic moment that quickly became strained and later clouded in controversy. In the days following, Audubon claimed he helped Wilson find new species in the field but Wilson denied this. In any case Wilson soon left by foot for Lexington and Nashville where, as he pushed farther into the wilderness, he found living conditions primitive and intolerable. "Science and literature have not one friend in this place," he reported, speaking of Louisville but summing up his whole frontier experience.

His final test was the Natchez Trace, some 400 miles of uninhabited trail from Nashville to the Mississippi through an endless forest that was home only to Choctaws and Chicasaws. Despite warnings to the contrary, the Indians proved friendly. But Wilson almost didn't make it. Toward the end he contracted dysentery from bad food and water, the disease that was to kill him three years later. Too weak to sit a horse, he eased his pain by eating raw eggs and strawberries. He stumbled on to the river and was able to reach New Orleans after recuperating at the home of a hospitable aging planter named William Dunbar. The elite of the Natchez plantations and of New Orleans were generous with subscriptions to his book. Robert Cantwell, one of Wilson's recent biographers, summarizes the western trip this way: in six months he covered 3000 miles, spent $455, found a dozen new species, and returned with two Carolina parakeets in his pockets and six painted buntings in a cage.

Wilson's final trip to New England in the fall of 1812 during the last year of his life was necessitated by financial difficulties and was mainly devoted to adding a few subscriptions and collecting on old ones. Its sole contretemps occurred in Haverhill, Massachusetts, when he was denounced as a Canadian spy by some citizens jittery about the war with Britain. He was arrested but released immediately with apologies.

Alexander Wilson's energy and his commitment to see his ambitious book through become evident when it is understood that in the midst of his strenuous travels production of the volumes moved ahead, too, and with growing momentum. The first volume appeared in 1808, then the pace increased to two volumes a year, and in the author's last months let up again. Since he could not collect on subscriptions by contract until the end of the year when each volume reached its buyer, Wilson was under growing pressure to produce in order to catch up on lagging finances. When he was traveling he sent back his drawings to Lawson, and he worked up his field notes into draft descriptions of species to revise in final form on his return. When in Philadelphia, he devoted long days and nights to the book.

Nominally in these last years Wilson was assistant editor of Rees's *Encyclopedia,* a well-paid job offered him in 1806 by its publisher Samuel Bradford, which he accepted as a welcome release from the curse of school teaching. Even more of a blessing, Bradford and his partner Inskeep agreed to undertake the hazardous venture of publishing *American Ornithology.* But as the pace of bringing out the great bird book increased, they complained that Wilson was giving it all his time and shirking his job on the encyclopedia. He had to quit that post, his sole source of income, and devote every moment to his own beloved project. This brought him no money for himself, since its income was plowed back into coming volumes, and it is unclear how Wilson lived in his last years. As hard up as ever and seeking suburban peace, he often lived at Bartram's Gardens.

Wilson was plagued by the technical difficulty of maintaining quality in hand-coloring the etched plates—a problem which Audubon also encountered in his *Birds of America.* The work was monotonous, and the colorists, poorly paid, came and went. They had to rely for guidance on skins which tended to fade and lose the crisp borders of nature. Wilson alone knew the birds first-hand and was obliged constantly to monitor the coloring, with which he was often dissatisfied. Eventually all his assistants drifted away and he had to take over the task himself. His compulsion to keep up quality heaped another burden on the harried author, already trammeled by poverty, travel exhaustion, and pressure to accelerate the pace of producing his book in order to finance it. Despite his devotion, the freshness of the illustrations noticeably diminished in the later volumes. By the time the seventh came out and the eighth was largely done in the shop, Wilson was exhausted. He contracted dysentery again and died quickly in August 1813, at age forty-seven. His follower and executor George Ord searched for instructions about finishing the *Ornithology*'s ninth volume as well as for any worldly goods to distribute, but found nothing. A wealthy and irascible amateur, more applied than good-willed, Ord was well enough acquainted with Wilson's wishes and methods to complete the volume, to which he added the first biography of its author.

American Ornithology is a nine volume work, five for field birds and the last four covering shore birds, the first survey exclusively of American birds, the first to do justice to their richness. It presents 264 species, compared to 440 eastern American birds in a standard modern field guide. Of these, forty-eight, forty-five, or thirty-nine, depending on which authority is followed, were new discoveries by Wilson. He often used an outmoded nomenclature that prevents an exact count of these new species, but they include such familiar birds as the sharp-shinned and broad-winged hawks, fish crow, field, song, and swamp sparrows, the white-eyed "flycatcher" (vireo), and the bay-breasted, Tennessee, Kentucky, prairie, Connecticut and Cape May warblers. Of course there are patent errors in Wilson's pioneering book; for example, the flycatchers, often the birder's stumbling block, and the terns are much jumbled. But by any estimate Wilson's contribution was immense, especially given his poor working conditions, modest personal background, and the lack of ornithological precedents.

He illustrated every bird presented in *American Ornithology* on plates interspersed in the text near the corresponding description. Four birds on average occupy each plate in sizes approximately proportioned to life. Only the bald eagle, the ruffed grouse, and the "great-footed hawk" (peregrine falcon) occupy a plate by themselves. The birds appear almost without setting, supported only by a minimal twig or stone. In this regard Wilson seems to step back from Catesby's magnificent floral settings, a device further developed by Audubon. An untalented draftsman, Wilson was unable to animate his birds to any extent, but like Catesby mainly stuck to a standard profile view. Wilson occasionally portrayed birds in appropriate action, for example, his characteristically oblique nuthatches in Volume I and his hummingbirds in the next volume.

Alexander Wilson was a self-taught and amateur artist without

Audubon's flare for visual excitement, but he was innately a builder with words. His descriptions of the birds are the strong core of his book. He gave them authority but avoided formality, and each bird's plumage receives an exact description probably based on a skin. Even more original are his remarks on behavior, breeding, song, and eating habits, obviously products of direct field observation and an aspect of the book that looks forward to modern behavioral methods of bird study. Here, for example, is his trenchant paragraph on the diet of the national bird:

> The appetite of the Bald Eagle, tho' habituated to long fasting, is of the most voracious and often the most indelicate kind. Fish, when he can obtain them, are preferred to all other fare. Young lambs and pigs are dainty morsels, and made free with on all favorable occasions. Ducks, Geese, Gulls, and other sea fowl, are also seized with avidity. The most putrid carrion, when nothing better can be had, is acceptable; and the collected groups of gormandizing Vultures, on the approach of this dignified personage, instantly disperse, and make way for their master, waiting his departure in sullen silence, and at a respectful distance, on adjacent trees.

This fresh sense of the birds' actuality was a major contribution, based on Wilson's willingness to wander with eyes and notebook open, and also on his independent reaction to the dry, classifying bird books of the eighteenth century. Unlike them he mostly omits taxonomic controversy in order to say what the birds look like and do. Some of his essays, such as that on the barn swallow, are discursive and quite literary; some are laconic due to a lack of information, especially those for the sea birds, which he researched at the end of his life. All evidence, including his informal prefaces to each volume, his stress on behavior, and his personal effort to obtain widespread subscription to the book, shows that he had in mind a work of popular appeal.

In person Alexander Wilson was spare, average in height with dark hair. His face was thin and bony, with angular cheekbones; his nose aquiline and prominent. His eyes were large and dark and like an owl's shone with intelligence and curiosity. He had no known deep relation to a woman, despite one biographer's fictive efforts to make him a lover. In thought and character he tended to be withdrawn, and at times he declined into melancholy. Reflecting loose ties to his parents, he sought

OPPOSITE. Typical profile portraits of a goldfinch, blue jay, and northern oriole from Wilson's *American Ornithology.*

independence in his movements, in religion, and in the critical turn of his mind. He was impatient and outspoken with others' foolishness, and his critical acumen could be barbed, as in his astute remarks to Bartram about the vagaries of bird nomenclature. Wilson was no genius, unlike Audubon who wore his talent on his deerskin sleeve, but the Scot had a probing, skeptical intelligence. He floundered through four decades of his short life before finding in birds the means of making a contribution and of attaining the fame he longed for. A gutsy Scottish persistence saw him through constant obstacles.

Despite cantankerousness and self-imposed isolation, Alexander Wilson partook of ideas widespread in his time. Three ruling ideologies guided his thinking: rationality, deism, and patriotism—all trends of thought dominant after the French Revolution and during American federalism. Instances of Wilson's rational intelligence—or, better, his intolerance of irrationality—have been cited: his criticisms of Buffon and of confusing bird nomenclature. His determined self-education showed his faith in the mind's expandability, and he several times cried out against slavery as a waste of human resources. Wilson had little conventional religion, as few intellectuals did in his time, but he subscribed without qualms to the liberal deism of the day, which saw God not in structured theology but in the panoply of nature, a sweeping universe reflecting His unfathomable creativity. In his second prefatory essay Wilson wrote that the diversity of birds "overwhelms us with astonishment at the power, wisdom and beneficence of the Creator" and "leads us to the contemplation and worship of the Great First Cause, the Father and Preserver of us all." With the open-eyed enthusiasm of the new arrival Wilson, perhaps from the moment he shot the red-headed woodpecker, developed an intuitive faith that America, above other nations, was blessed by God's prodigality in nature.

Politically aware, enthralled with the liberalism of Jeffersonian democracy seen against the suppression of his radical experiments at home, he was grateful he had chosen a land of plenty, which was daily celebrated by the bird songs and movements in the treetops. Wilson looked down on the European bird scholars as bookish systematists who never enjoyed the action in the field, and he refuted Buffon's insulting assertion that American birds were merely the weaker strains of continental families, immigrants driven into exile. He sought to know and make known the birds of the new nation. He could not have foretold the troubled story of how far it was to this goal, but he knew that he must seek it by keeping faith with his intellect, his deistic beliefs, and his love of this new land. It is also pleasing to know that Wilson finally received some mundane rewards in the last year of his life when he was elected both to the Columbian Society of Philadelphia Scholars and to the American Philosophical Society.

Alexander Wilson's fame cannot stand up to Audubon's, which was nourished internationally by tales of frontier heroism. They were the two founding fathers of American bird study and in their work made similar contributions, yet in character and thinking they stood poles apart. While Wilson sometimes strained to realize his ambitions, Audubon soared to easy fame on a balloon—surely at times self-inflated— of charismatic artistic genius and spontaneous charm. Wilson, poor from start to end, lacked advanced education or a cultural background as well as the confidence these bring. The younger Audubon came from a wealthy background and claimed that he studied with the first master of France, Jacques Louis David. In America ostensibly in training for a mercantile career, he was free to watch birds, draw, dance and skate, and to court the well-off young woman in the magnificent columned house next door, his future wife, Lucy Bakewell.

With these opposite backgrounds it is not surprising that Wilson and Audubon had contrasting personalities. Alexander was silent, lonely, stubborn, and somewhat plodding. With only diffuse native talents he suffered through long years of unfocused striving toward an aim in life. John James was a gregarious extrovert, athletic, restless, quick of mind, and welcome at any level of society. He was able to nurture his facile talent from an early age, but he too suffered through years of struggle, traveling incessantly to sell and find material for his book, without income, away from family and unable to support them. But he bore these burdens as fortuitous challenges to his insouciant energy.

While Wilson and Audubon were personally far apart, their working careers had some evident parallels. Both first undertook mercantile pursuits at different levels, and both failed, preferring to watch birds. While neither had the heart to sell goods, both were effective in selling the work dear to their hearts. Both took to the woods after birds with an almost spiritual fervor; both were driven to travel to the point of exhaustion. Wilson felt some fear at pushing into unexplored areas and a little disgust at frontier crudeness, whereas Audubon seemed to love nothing better than an adventure with backwoods people that served to make a good anecdote. Both men observed birds with an acuteness unequalled before and seldom since. The difference lies in how they conveyed this knowledge. Wilson's forte was verbal description, and his straightforward illustrations were supplementary. Audubon praised the birds almost entirely in his famous rollicking plates, as personal in style as they are insightful in ornithology, and not in his text, which was completed by an amanuensis and printed separately. To summarize this comparison in a word, after all Wilson was a Scot and Audubon a Frenchman, but it would be more meaningful to remark on the differences in their generations. Wilson, the deist, patriot, and youthful radical, was a man with scientific aspirations in the age of revolution, the late eighteenth century. Audubon, the driven genius, the master of a personal expressive style, was deeply committed to art and romanticism.

It is little wonder that these two disparate personalities, when they met in Audubon's store in 1810, started off on a somewhat strained footing; or that frequent later interpretations of this scene have failed to resolve the differences in how the participants later reported it. Wilson called to sell his book, and Audubon was inclined to subscribe until stopped by his partner, Ferdinand Rozier. Wilson then showed Audubon his drawings, and Audubon offered to show the visitor *his*. It would be hard to guess which artist was more dismayed at this threat of competition in so narrow a field. But Audubon, realizing that Wilson was well into publishing his book, gracefully retreated by saying he sketched for fun. Audubon then lent Wilson some of his drawings and offered to take him birding. So the meeting ended, but it would have its reverberations.

Wilson reported the incident with laconic disinterest in his journal, without calling Audubon by name, but did say they went out together two days later and found sandhill cranes and pigeons, species well known to him. If this entry seems cool and ungrateful, Wilson compounded the discourtesy by noting on his departure from Louisville that he had "neither received one act of civility from those to whom I was recommended, one subscriber, nor one new bird." Audubon read that inaccurate statement years later and chose to reply in an elaborate defense, published in 1831, which was a good deal less accurate than Wilson's journal entries. Audubon asserted that he had helped Wilson find birds he had never seen, that his guest had not only borrowed some of his drawings but, against his wishes, had used at least one without acknowledgment in his *Ornithology*.

Audubon's riposte was in turn refuted by George Ord, who was assiduous in defending Wilson's interests at any cost. Ord had published fragments of Wilson's western journal, including the portion on the Audubon meeting, but his pro-Wilson, anti-Audubon bias was so strong that he was suspected of editorial manipulations. Before the American Philosophical Society Ord claimed, with good reason, that the borrowing ran the other way, that it was Audubon who had lifted several bird motifs directly from the plates of *American Ornithology*. These comprised the cerulean warbler and redwing blackbird, both shown in flight and thus appealing to Audubon's sense of animation, two perched birds, the flicker and the Mississippi kite, and others less obvious. Chronologically Wilson's versions certainly came first, and the cited birds in their stiffer earlier style fit awkwardly with Audubon's vivid foreshortenings.

Meanwhile, to compound the confusion, Audubon had retracted his claim of having helped Wilson, admitting that they were together only briefly and "that nothing worthy of his attention was procured." Thus the actuality of the first encounter between the founders of American bird study is clouded in a comedy of poorly remembered self-serving assertions. An interchange of motifs between artists was not in itself considered reprehensible, especially in the European tradition from which Audubon came. It is likely that the two bird artists did not take this matter as seriously as did their followers.

Wilson and Audubon met once again briefly about a year later in Philadelphia. This time Audubon called on Wilson and was received politely. They did not speak of birds but Wilson suggested they go together to see the paintings of Rembrandt Peale. Audubon reported that he began to feel uncomfortable and soon left. Such were the uneasy relations between the two men who, in their different ways, did the most for American bird study in the early nineteenth century. But the consensus of historians is that Wilson's visit to Audubon in Louisville played a role in inspiring the younger artist's emerging commitment to his masterpiece, *The Birds of America*.

A portrait drawing of Audubon late in his life.
Massachusetts Audubon Society.

Chapter Three

John James Audubon, Pioneer Bird Artist

*F*ame like death arrives inexplicably and suddenly, and so it did with John James Audubon when he went to England in 1826 to seek patronage for publishing his bird drawings. Taking the part of a romantic frontiersman, he spoke picturesque Frenchified English and wore long ringlets and sometimes his deerskins. In Liverpool and Edinburgh the gentry lionized him until he was exhausted, and thereafter most doors in England opened for him, though he found Londoners cooler than provincials. He was proud to record that he was welcomed by a bevy of peers, by Sir Walter Scott, and by leading artists like Thomas Bewick and Sir Thomas Lawrence, as well as by a number of scientific colleagues. He cultivated support at court and eventually attained the patronage of King George IV, who endorsed *The Birds of America* but never paid for his copy.

Audubon's popularity in England arose from British romantic longings, followed him back to America, and grew steadily as it still does today. Formal memorials to him mark principal sites of his career: at his grave near his last home in New York; at Henderson, Kentucky— site of his worst early failures; in New Orleans and at Oakley Plantation in West Parish, Louisiana. Conservation societies across the nation, hospitals, streets, dry cleaners, and gas stations bear his name. In his later years he dined on wild turkey with President Jackson, who ate milk toast, won the support of Edward Everett and Henry Clay, called on President Sam Houston of Texas in his log-cabin capitol, and was taken about Florida and the Gulf of Mexico in U.S. Treasury ships.

Audubon's fame did not come just from seizing a chance in a meandering life nor from the welcome of English society. A number of factors contributed to it: the brilliance of his artistic genius; his devotion to his art, to nature, and to his adopted America; his patience through years of struggle to find recognition for his work; and the support of friends, young assistants, his two sons, and above all his wife Lucy. Lucy was a human clue to John James' inner life. She had every faith in his destiny even though she often had to support their family, and the demands of her employment as governess and teacher sometimes prevented her from joining her wandering husband. In addition to these solid advantages, Audubon, an effective self-publicist, fed the growth of his own fame by recounting his acquaintance with Daniel Boone, his apprenticeship under the great revolutionary painter Jacques Louis David, and even by implying descent from the French royal family. His biographers have dismissed all these claims as longings of a wishful imagination.

John James Audubon's life story is eventful, complex, and tinged with the color of the frontier. Like a migratory bird he had inexplicable urges to move on. For example, in New Orleans in 1821, destitute and scratching out a living with occasional portrait commissions, he persuaded a reluctant Lucy to join him with their sons but left for Natchez two months later. All his ceaseless peregrinations cannot be described here. After leaving his father's estate in Pennsylvania, Mill Grove, he spent the first half of his life mainly on and near the two great rivers he loved, the Ohio and the Mississippi, that bore him west and south to the wilderness and to Louisville, Henderson, Ste. Genevieve, Cincinnati, and New Orleans. Then came the English visits, with a trip to Paris. While *The Birds of America* was in production in London he commuted regularly between supervising its progress there and the sites of more bird drawings in America. He migrated with the birds to the New Jersey marshes, the Poconos, Maine, New Brunswick and Labrador, his beloved Louisiana, and the Texas Gulf Coast. He usually spent winters at the Reverend John Bachman's in Charleston. On his final journey after publication of *The Birds of America* Audubon went up the Missouri by steamboat in 1842 to gather specimens of mammals for his and Bachman's *Quadrupeds of North America.* Only the limitations of age and travel prevented Audubon from realizing an old desire to see and cross the Rockies. Modern biographers recount his movements along the lines summarized here, stressing the picturesque unfolding of an appealing life. What they lack is an effective analysis of Audubon's art and of his contribution to bird study and natural history in America.

A good deal about John James Audubon's vivid genius relates to his parental background. His father was Jean Audubon, a French merchant and naval captain based at Nantes at the mouth of the Loire. He invested in a plantation near Les Cayes, Santo Domingo (now Haiti) as well as in a handsome Pennsylvania farm, Mill Grove. Twice imprisoned by the British before and during the American Revolution, Captain Jean joined the French navy and his ship stood off Yorktown where he was pleased to witness Cornwallis's surrender. John James's mother had a more shadowy role since her son was illegitimate. He and his descendants took pains to invent for him an upper-class Creole mother with aristocratic connections in Louisiana, who gave birth to him at a plantation on Lake Pontchartrain. His mother was in fact a rural French girl named Rabin, who went out to Santo Domingo in domestic service. In any case Jean Jacques Audubon was born near Les Cayes on April 26, 1785. His mother died a few months later, and his half-sister, Rosa, was born of another woman two years later. Hardly had the two Audubon children learned to walk than their father's foothold in the Caribbean colony was threatened by slave insurrections. In 1789 he sent them to France, also torn by revolution, and three years later the Audubon Santo Domingo plantation, the naturalist's first home, was seized by natives.

At this point in John James's childhood Anne Moynet, his father's wife, nine years older than he, became the dominant figure. She was a complacent and kindly woman of some means, an inheritance from her first husband. She promptly took his two illegitimate children to her bosom and legally adopted them. Under Mme. Audubon's indulgent eye Jean Jacques's early education was sketchy at best. What he liked most to do after school hours, or during them if he could, was to wander in the fields, collect birds, bugs or plants and draw them. He turned his bedroom into a natural history cabinet, a project his father praised. Nevertheless Captain Jean, during one of his brief returns from sea, hauled Jean Jacques off to a naval school, which had little effect on his immunity to discipline.

The formative change in young Audubon's life came in 1803 when his father sent him to Mill Grove, hoping to avoid his conscription into the Napoleonic armies. Mill Grove was a working farm graciously set above Perkiomen Creek near the Schuylkill River, not far from Norristown. While the setting was charming and offered an enticing introduction to America, it was not clear to the Audubons nor to their local agents what John James was to do there, a question which the pleasure-loving teen-ager resolved for himself. His months at Mill Grove, as he liked to recall, were the most idyllic of his life. He danced and skated and rode, but best of all he coursed through the woods hunting birds for the table and as specimens.

His pursuits seemed frivolous to his family, but like many youthful experiments they indicated paths toward meaningful interests. He found some phoebes living in a cave, caught a few and tied colored thread to their legs to see if they would return to the same home in another season (they did). He was thus probably the first to study bird movements by banding. He invented the method of posing birds for their portraits when he realized that he could prop up a limp, newly shot bird in any pose by inserting wires into its body. One can imagine young Audubon waking up early one morning with this thought, excitedly throwing a saddle on his horse and galloping off to Norristown to buy wire. The device seems simple but it was new and opened a vision of the living bird which Audubon pursued throughout his life. And it was at Mill Grove that he met the Bakewells, an English family living in the mansion next door. He quickly courted the eldest Bakewell daughter, Lucy, and they married after he had returned from France with his parents' approval. Audubon then opened a store in Louisville, where they made their first home. During these frontier years the young Frenchman took the oath of United States citizenship on July 4, 1812, in Philadelphia. Like his fellow birder Alexander Wilson, he had an immigrant's ardor for America where nature's riches ignited his patriotism.

The store, despite the conscientious efforts of Audubon's partner, Ferdinand Rozier, was a failure. Audubon detested being caged behind the counter and spent every moment in the field with his gun, justifying his outings as supplying fowl for the table. As Audubon's business tottered his portfolio of bird drawings grew. It had not yet occurred to him that he might turn his drawings to profit. Then the encounter already described—one such as novelists imagine—occurred when Alexander Wilson stepped into the Louisville store. Although Audubon at that meeting said he drew for fun, it is likely that from this moment he no longer did and that the encounter implanted in his restless mind the vision of a bird book larger and richer than Wilson's.

A subsequent hostile exchange of charges between the younger bird artist and Wilson's coterie in Philadelphia obfuscated the impact of the Louisville meeting. When the rancor between the two men is put aside, no doubt can remain about Audubon's debt to the Scot. It is clear that Audubon repeated four or more of Wilson's bird motifs in *The Birds of America*. When he made his first long journey down the Ohio and Mississippi to New Orleans to seek birds, he carried with him seven volumes of Wilson's *American Ornithology* and in Louisiana searched for the other two. He could hardly have afforded to ignore Wilson's innovative work. While the Scot is not as well known today as Audubon, John James himself acknowledged Wilson as the founder of American ornithology. Audubon took his place as its brilliant first son, bringing to bird study a vibrant new life formed of personal empathy and artistic genius.

John James Audubon's failure as a merchant in Louisville was soon compounded in Henderson, Kentucky, and in Ste. Genevieve, Missouri. Audubon and Rozier inexplicably moved their store to Henderson, although Louisville was then a good-sized town and Henderson only a settlement of a few houses. It may be that Audubon instigated the change with his usual migratory urge and love of the wilderness. Harder to understand was their push westward to Ste. Genevieve undertaken in mid-winter with the rivers still full of ice and foraging for food a hardship. During this hazardous trip Audubon was overjoyed with the long delays in camp when he could chase birds or hunt with the local Indians, while Rozier was so miserable that he wrapped himself in his blanket day and night. The move to the Missouri frontier turned out to be fortunate for both men: Rozier was content to join the French community of Ste. Genevieve and became an established merchant there, while Audubon broke away, dissolved the partnership, and returned to his family and the old store in Henderson. There, struggling to recoup losses, he moved with fateful momentum toward failure. On the river he built a mill too large for the area's needs and also a steamboat, which was stolen, driven to New Orleans, and disappeared. Plagued by debt and with it shame, he sank to the low point of his life when he attacked the thief of his steamboat with a knife.

The Henderson debacle forced the artist and his family into years of poverty until his book began to repay the superhuman work put into it. His failure at commerce reinforced Audubon's determination to undertake the book and left him no alternative but to offer his special talents to the public. Once the commitment was made, he brought to its pursuit focused energy, powerful determination, and a competence in managing the myriad details of production that any businessman would admire. The making of *The Birds of America,* the largest book ever produced, was a heroic enterprise. It involved negotiating with a supporting cast, which included Robert Havell, the highly talented engraver in London who made the plates, and the colorists who hand-colored the illustrations, a monotonous task which demanded constant checking.

Another essential team member was William MacGillivray, a young ornithologist in Edinburgh, who polished the supplementary text of the book called *Ornithological Biography.* He added scientific information and smoothed out Audubon's Gallic English, but his work demanded a steady flow of copy. When Audubon returned to America to draw more birds, as he periodically had to do, he relied on his son Victor to oversee the unruly operation but showered him with fussy instructions by letter. Audubon's daily concerns were complex: the financing of the project and simultaneously its artistic oversight and the need for new material. He funded the book by selling advance subscriptions which he solicited himself, occasionally aided by agents. Subscribers were to pay for each number of five plates when issued and delivered whether in Great Britain, France, or America. This method led to the juggling of intractable variables. The number of subscribers kept changing as Audubon found new ones, and old patrons defected because of the high price of the work. The appearance of the numbers was not regular, since much handwork was involved. The production of *The Birds of America* generated an unsteady cash flow, and so the completion of the work was a triumph, not just of art and the love of nature but of John James Audubon's, and Havell's, organizational ability.

Among book connoisseurs *The Birds of America* is called the double elephant folio. This unique classification honors its mammoth dimensions, for no other work can claim such a designation. Why did Audubon conceive his *Birds* on such a scale, inflating cost and problems of production? It was not just that he thought in grandiose terms, but from the beginning he obsessively insisted that every bird be portrayed life-size. Audubon was committed to ornithological truth, and like a Renaissance artist he drew his models against a gridded backdrop to assure accurate proportions. This method endowed his bird portraits with nature's own range of scale. He showed birds such as the whooping crane and the great egret bending their heads to the ground to fit on the 39½ by 26½ inch pages, while the field and wood birds, engraved on a much smaller plate, floated on the white paper as if in ample space. The first plate in *The Birds of America* was the wild turkey, Benjamin Franklin's choice for the national bird, which amply filled its large sheet. William Lazars of Edinburgh engraved it, but Audubon was forced to drop him when a strike closed his shop.

The initial prospectus for the *Birds* envisaged eighty numbers comprising 400 plates, priced at two guineas a number, purchasable separately. The whole work in five volumes cost a thousand dollars, an imposing sum for a book then and now. Toward the end of the project Audubon learned of some new species which he insisted on including, notably the western birds found by Thomas Nuttall and John Kirk Townsend, the first naturalists to cross the Rockies. After frenzied negotiations he managed to obtain duplicate specimens of the Nuttall-Townsend birds thanks to funding from his friend Edward Harris. He added these at the end of his book but had to break his rule by crowding several species to a page.

When the last plate was pulled on June 30, 1838, *The Birds of America* comprised 435 plates illustrating 489 species in 1,065 bird portraits. The extra drawings allowed the artist to show both sexes, immatures, and repeats in various poses. Audubon's 489 American birds compared to Wilson's 264 and to a modern estimate of just under 800. Each plate of the *Birds* bore the current Latin and common names of the subject and to the left "Drawn from life and Published by John James Audubon," followed proudly by the initials of his scientific societies and on the right the engraver's credit line. The plates appeared in a random order imposed by the availability of specimens and sometimes by esthetic considerations. Aware that this presentation would not satisfy taxonomically minded scientists, Audubon commissioned MacGillivray to do a systematic index to the book. Issued separately, this reordered the birds into families and genera and added two species.

Scholars have traced and catalogued every extant complete set of *The Birds of America,* but an unknown number of copies has been broken up for sale as separate prints. The author also sold single sheets during the years of publication. Audubon by no means enlisted the number of subscribers he had hoped for; always buoyant, he once projected as many as 500 but he ended with eighty-two in America and seventy-nine in Europe, enough to support production and clear a modest profit. Allowing for gift and reserved copies, experts believe that Havell printed just under 200 complete double elephant folios. The technique used for the plates, usually for convenience called engraving, was a sophisticated mixture of etching, aquatint, and line engraving in combinations adjusted to each subject.

The story of Audubon's life, well publicized by him and others, proves that he was first and always an artist, for he struggled above all for success in art. A more delicate question is how serious a bird student he was. Was he a reliable observer, and did he merit recognition as a scientific ornithologist? Or was he no more than an enthusiastic amateur turned on by the beauty of birds? As an appealing and controversial naturalist, John James often faced attacks on his scientific ability. These seem petty and irrelevant today, for their bite has been dulled by his fame in the years since.

In identifying birds Audubon did make some errors that marred his book and the *Ornithological Biography*. Some of these were simply due to the limits of ornithological knowledge at the time. "Small-headed flycatcher" was the label given by both artists to a design which Audubon claimed Wilson had pilfered from his portfolio, but ornithologists have never found the species. Audubon was often fooled by immature birds, which he sometimes incorrectly called a separate species. For example, he considered the sandhill crane the young of the whooping crane, an error Wilson and others also made. More egregious was the case of his notorious "Bird of Washington," a tan eagle which Audubon first shot on the winter trip to Ste. Genevieve. Throughout his life he stubbornly insisted that it was a third species of American eagle in the face of irrefutable advice that it was a young but full-grown bald eagle still in immature plumage. Like many naturalists in the post-Linnaean age John James suffered from an urge to discover new species even when sufficient grounds were lacking. But the majority of the birds he first recorded are still on the books today.

Audubon sometimes went astray as well in the short articles he wrote in England to help build his reputation there and gain entry to scientific societies. Some of these essays are exemplary and incorporate well-founded observations on bird life that go beyond anything to date. His articles on the swallows, for example, buried for all time the old notion that these birds hibernated in the mud of ponds, and his discussion of whether the turkey vulture finds its food by sight or smell was cogently reasoned on the basis of field experiments. But in his description of the behavior of the rattlesnake, a unique American species which aroused fascination abroad, Audubon hit a snag. One of his more famous drawings showed a nest of mockingbirds invaded by a rattlesnake which had climbed up for its prey. Some doubted that a rattler could climb a tree, and claims on one side or another flew back and forth across the Atlantic by packet. Audubon, harried and defensive, went so far as to assert that rattlesnakes also coil around animals and stifle them like a constrictor. This claim wiped out his credibility on snakes, and before the controversy receded rattlers, which never did stifle, were also denied their license to climb.

Audubon's mistakes, much touted by his rivals, seem negligible today and not worth dwelling on. The astounding accomplishments of his life are more than enough to pull a discrete veil over a few missteps. The *Ornithological Biography,* done hand in hand with the picture book, was also a revealing testament to his stature as a bird student. Here, aided by MacGillivray's editing and scientific material, Audubon described the subjects of the engravings species by species. Topics under any bird might cover habits, range in various seasons and in migration, diet (Audubon was evidently in the habit of checking the stomachs of birds he shot), reaction to predation—in short any aspect of bird behavior observed during years of experience in the field. Happily the *Biography* does not read like a scientific bird book, for its approach is anecdotal, informal, lively, and engaging. Audubon wrote it rapidly under the pressure of producing *The Birds of America* and with no chance to expand his field notes. It is a personal outpouring of all his years in the woods and fields, enriched with his spontaneous love of nature. The *Biography* might well have been called *Affectionate Anecdotes on American Birds.*

Dozens of examples from this book show Audubon's brilliance in translating field experience into description. His telling of how the summer families of Canada geese gather in flocks as ice first covers the streams, of how they rise, circle, and line up in their V-shaped traveling formation with a cacophony of warning honks makes a picture not only ornithologically precise but evocative of the rhythmic flux of nature. "Should one of the young feel fatigued, his position in the ranks is changed, and he assumes his place in the wake of another who cleaves the air before him. The parent bird may fly by his side for a while to encourage him." Audubon gives a precise picture of the duck hawk (or peregrine falcon) hunting a snipe. It "will alight on the highest branch of a tree near the marshes favored by the Snipe, move its head as if counting every little space below, and, if he spies a Snipe, will dart like an arrow, rustle his wings loudly, seize the bird and fly with it to the woods." Particularly valuable is Audubon's description of the ivory-billed woodpecker, because it is probably extinct in the United States. The author's mastery of detail is seen in this account of the bird's nesting, which occurs in early March:

> The hole is, I believe, always made in the trunk of a live tree, generally an ash or hackberry, at a great height. The birds pay much regard to the tree's location and to the slanting of its trunk, preferring retirement and wishing to protect the opening from access to running water during beating rainstorms. To prevent the latter, the hole is generally dug immediately under the junction of a large branch with the trunk. It is first bored horizontally a few inches, then directly downwards (in depth) sometimes not more than ten inches, at other times nearly three feet downward.

The mated ivory bills work together at the nest excavation, one waiting on the trunk outside to relieve the other when the first is fatigued. Audubon's observations are appealing for wide-eyed freshness and the sense of on-the-spot insight. His reports make us feel the flow of wilderness life around us, the caress or bite of the weather and the shift of the seasons.

Imaginative and passionately devoted to nature, with a quick eye but little patience, John James was not as cool or scientifically minded as Alexander Wilson. It is instructive to compare their remarks about one species. Here is Audubon on the whippoorwill and its song:

> The Whip-Poor-Will continues its lively song for several hours after sunset. Then it remains silent until the first dawn of day, when its notes echo through every vale and along the mountain valleys until the rising sun scatters the darkness. I have often heard hundreds in a woodland chorus, each trying to outdo the others. The fact that this bird may be heard at a distance of several hundred yards will enable you to conceive the pleasure felt by every lover of Nature who may hear it. A fancied resemblance of its notes to the syllables *whip-poor-will* has given rise to its name, but an

accurate description of its song is impossible, not to mention the feelings it excites in the listener. . . .

Immediately after their springtime arrival, their notes are heard in the dusk and through the evening in all the thickets and along the edge of the woods. Clear and loud, they are to me more interesting than those of the Nightingale.

Of the same bird Wilson says:

These notes seem pretty plainly to articulate the words which have been generally applied to them, *whip-poor-will,* the first and last syllables being uttered with great emphasis, and the whole in about a second to each repetition; but when two or more males meet, their whip-poor-will altercations become much more rapid and incessant, as if each were straining to overpower or silence the other. . . . At these times, as well as at almost all others, they fly low, not more than a few feet from the surface, skimming about the house and before the door, alighting on the wood-pile, or settling on the roof. Towards midnight they generally become silent, unless in clear moonlight, when they are heard with little intermission till morning.

Wilson provides more solid information on the behavior of the whip-poorwill, but Audubon evokes the bird as a romantic symbol of his own longings. Its song offers him "the pleasure felt by every lover of Nature."

Audubon's chosen means of communication was not the medium of words but drawing. Another great deposit of bird lore lies on the sheets of *The Birds of America.* Dazzled by the color and life of these designs, the observer finds it hard to believe that Audubon based every bird on a real specimen which he had studied for hours. As with the *Biography,* the naturalist veils the supporting ornithological data behind his artistry, but a few examples of how Audubon used his field experience in the *Birds* will suggest what lay behind his performance. The anhinga, Florida's skinny cormorant cousin, perches above the mangrove swamps, spreads its wings to dry them, and wiggles its snaky neck to look around, just as Audubon wittily portrayed it. The dipper teeters half awkwardly, half acrobatically on the rocks of mountain streams in a way that Audubon has captured more trenchantly in his silhouetted double portrait than words could. The artist's wit and the joy in life he sees and shares with the bird world shines out from his depiction of the home life of house wrens, shown nesting in a battered tophat. Audubon brings an even subtler acuity of vision to his portrayal of brown-headed cowbirds. The curving outlines of the pair make a harmonious design, but the invention is nature's and the artist only an interpreter, since cowbirds do feed in pairs with backs arched and heads lowered. Through

innate empathy with nature Audubon saw the details of bird life with singular insight. The fascination of his masterpiece lies in its visionary sweep but behind this lay daily study of birds he knew and loved.

Another question arises: was Audubon committed to the problems of

The house where Audubon stayed in Key West. *Massachusetts Audubon Society.*

conservation which have more and more concerned the ornithological world? It is well known that he was an habitual hunter and a crack shot, and that he killed birds in huge numbers for sport, for the table, and as specimens. For example, one morning in Florida in December 1831 he set out to "procure" twenty-five brown pelicans in order to select a single male to draw. It must be understood that he worked without a telescope and that the only way he could study a bird closely was to prop it up before him. In Audubon's time unregulated hunting of anything edible was universal. The uncounted hordes of birds, such as the passenger pigeons which Audubon and his contemporaries described, were such a familiar sight that no prophet could foresee the speed of these flocks' decimation.

In his writings called Episodes, stories of American life interspersed with his bird biographies, Audubon hinted that he had some idea of the conservation problems his country would face. Yet in the several tales involving conservation issues his attitude showed less than full commitment to the cause in all but one case. His story "The Live Oakers" related how teams of men live in the woods to harvest these noble southern trees. Audubon's first reaction to this scene was admiration for the lumbermen's prowess. Only then did he add that it was a shame to see the great trees fall, killing their own saplings on the way, and he expressed some concern that their future might be threatened by such cutting.

Telling the history of the ill-fated passenger pigeons in the *Ornithological Biography,* Audubon narrated their slaughter in uncounted numbers with all the horrifying particulars his practiced eye could gather. He reported a communal butchering near the Green River in Kentucky that lasted a day and a night, when thousands upon thousands of birds were knocked down with poles. Their overcrowded perches collapsed, killing the pigeons in them and those below, 300 pigs were driven in to fatten on the remains, and after the most edible corpses were gathered up the last scraps were left for every sort of mammal predator as well as for hawks, eagles, and vultures. Passenger pigeons flocked in numbers vast enough to create a legend in eighteenth- and early nineteenth-century America. Audubon recorded that a man in Pennsylvania took more than 500 in a net one day. The bird artist did not foresee this populous species' destruction by man's predation but feared only environmental incursion. "Persons unacquainted with these birds might naturally conclude that such dreadful havoc will soon put an end to the species. But I have satisfied myself by long observation that nothing but the gradual diminution of our forests can accomplish their decrease. They not infrequently quadruple their number yearly, and always at least double it."

Audubon was once angered by a crime against conservation which he recounted in the episode "The Eggers of Labrador." While on that coast in 1833 John James saw shiploads of men invade the nesting colonies, especially of black guillemots, and gather some eggs while destroying the rest, the chicks, and the parent birds. Audubon was profoundly disgusted with the eggers and wrote an uncharacteristic puritanical diatribe against them, not only because bird life was being threatened and wasted but because the eggers were shiftless and drunken criminals. Except in such a blatant case, Audubon lived too early in the history of conservation to make a full commitment to this cause. Binoculars had not yet replaced the gun. Across frontier America hunting was still a necessary way of procuring food, and even the artist's bird study depended on it. On occasion Audubon revealed a premonition that his adored wilderness paradise might someday retreat before other forces. He had an intuitive but unformed understanding of the issues of conservation based more on the spirit of his relation to nature. It is still fitting that a principal agency of this cause, the National Audubon Society, bears his name.

However unique Audubon's genius or dramatic the turnings of his career, he still remained a man of his times. The bird artist, as his work announces unmistakably, lived in the decades of romanticism's dominance. He contributed to bird study on many levels: from taxonomy to behaviorism in the *Ornithological Biography* on to a style of bird art like nothing before, the pinnacle of his achievement. The energy, force of wit, and movement in his art are inconceivable outside the context of romanticism.

In other ways besides bird study Audubon was a child of early nineteenth-century America, when the frontier was still king. In his later urban years he never failed to remind himself and others that by choice he was a woodsman. Unlike Wilson, who was obsessed only with birds and never too happy on the trail, Audubon had a broad sense of the whole environment, its people as well as its wild creatures. This breadth of interest founded an American tradition continued by such naturalists as Henry David Thoreau, John Burroughs, and John Muir. Wilson offered first-hand commentary on the American scene but only in letters published some years later. Audubon placed his appealing vignettes of contemporary life, his Episodes or Delineations, right among his bird biographies. These are only pocket tableaux of what he did and saw but are so freshly observed and new in subject that they reveal the touch of a talented historical reporter. His juxtaposition of them with the bird biographies reinforces Audubon's aim of dealing with creatures that live in real places.

The Episodes teem with life drawn from the breadth of his experience and the parade of people he knew. There are sketches of notable personalities such as Daniel Boone, the flamboyant portraitist John Jarvis, and Samuel Constantine Rafinesque, the eccentric naturalist obsessed with splintering off new species. There are descriptions of natural disasters—floods, fires, hurricanes, a surprise earthquake in Kentucky, and what it's like to be becalmed for days on the Gulf of Mexico. There are stories that uncover the underworld of life beyond civilization: one about wreckers in Florida who live off stranded ships and sometimes cause them to strand, about squatters in Labrador and in the South, and about how the itinerant author was nearly done in by a family of murderous thieves in a lone cabin. By good luck help arrived in time and frontier justice took over.

Audubon painted word pictures of places like Natchez and Niagara Falls, which he considered too overwhelming to portray. He described creatures like the perch, opossum, and cougar, and scenes of fishing and hunting for cod, raccoons, deer, and moose. There is a vignette of the authentic native scene of sugaring-off the maples, which suggests a parallel to Currier and Ives's prints of American life. A man with a quick eye and an immigrant's adulation for his new land, Audubon took nature for his mistress, but the customs and vagaries of man were in his sights too.

John James Audubon's relations to the world he knew were mostly wholesome and direct. But his life seems more touching if one realizes that he was torn by a number of conflicts. His father expected him to enter trade, but he failed so disastrously that he had no choice but to make his avocation of drawing birds a profession. He valued the apprentices who helped him with his drawings, George Lehman and especially Joseph Mason, his companion through lean months in the lower Mississippi region. But pride prevented Audubon from giving Mason the credit he deserved, and the young artist ended by turning against his master. Audubon loved his Lucy with all his heart but often he could not support her and their two sons. When they were united he tended to run away from them again, and in absence he developed a disturbing pattern of pleading with Lucy to join him, then reneging in fear that he could not take care of her as she expected. Audubon's sons, Victor Gifford and John Woodhouse, were drawn willy-nilly into their father's enterprises, doing administration and assisting with the drawing. They never seemed able to break away from his demands or live their own lives.

Like any artist Audubon experienced a conflict in balancing commercial goals with artistic freedom, but once the publication of *The Birds of America* was assured, a more confident Audubon showed resourcefulness in managing both aims. More often in his early years than later when successful, John James tended to tumble into a disabling despondency, and then in reaction he would leap back with an energy that surpassed most men's capability. Audubon, a genius as artist and naturalist, showed signs of what in his day was called the melancholic temperament. Yet despite obstacles of inner conflict, he became an astute field ornithologist, a brilliant romantic artist, in maturity a man of business and an engaging reporter of his times. The personal conflicts he overcame made his achievement all the more heroic.

John Burroughs photographed in
the year of his death by Charles Lummis.
Southwest Museum.

Chapter Four

John Burroughs, Hudson River Naturalist

*J*ohn Burroughs, the white-bearded sage of Slabsides, his Hudson River retreat, became "Mr. Nature" for late Victorian readers. The studies of this most beloved writer embraced all fields, but it was his love of birds that invited him to enter every corner of the outdoors. One hundred years ago every literate American knew Burroughs's name; today it seldom evokes any response. Now even bird students ask who John Burroughs was. Like the other great priests of nature, Audubon of the Ohio and Mississippi woods, Thoreau in riparian Concord, and Muir in the Sierra, Burroughs is intimately identified with one locale, the Catskill foothills on the Hudson's west bank. From this base he wandered outdoors every day without focused purpose, immersing himself in nature and absorbing whatever lessons it happened to lay before him.

Burroughs shared his empathetic, almost mystical sense of nature in over two dozen books. He often fleshed out his outdoor impressions by distracting the reader from his first love with comments on thinkers or contemporary issues. John Burroughs wrote consciously without scientific discipline. He expressed a dispassionate but genuine appreciation of nature but he did not seek to analyze its secrets. Burroughs's essays, couched in direct language with not much claim to style, were accessible to a wide readership, which in turn brought him much fame. But

Burroughs was more than just a naive, self-propelled writer who treated country values. To understand this successful essayist, beloved teacher, and national figure requires some thoughts on the opening question of who he was.

John Burroughs was an unassuming man with homespun values of moral probity and an intellect limited by his background. As a farmer's child he had to seek out his own education. From the first a country person, he took nature as his guide, the source of bodily and spiritual health and the focus of his daily labor outdoors and at the writing table. Burroughs, much like Thoreau in Concord, was bound by deep sentiment to a half-acre of nature. He never felt at ease anywhere but in this undemanding corner, but as a young man he had his years of journeying, working in Washington in the civil service, traveling to England, and then in New York State as a bank examiner.

When writing had brought him fame as an older man, he was cajoled out of his reluctance to leave his home ground and went to Jamaica, to Alaska with the Harriman expedition (during which he once tried to jump ship), to California and the Southwest. He spent his middle years in peace at Riverby, the fruit farm he established on the Hudson at West Park, just across from Hyde Park. In the later years he often lived at Slabsides, the famous woodland retreat he built two miles up the hills from the river.

John Burroughs had strong cultural ambitions, born of deprivation, which led him to worship some of the top minds of his time: Walt Whitman above all, Emerson, Thoreau, Theodore Roosevelt; Wordsworth, Carlyle, and Darwin; and later on Bergson, to mention only some of his eclectic favorites. Even before his civil service years, while a school teacher in his middle twenties, Burroughs began writing. He first found an historical model in Dr. Johnson, he studied Emerson with devotion, and in 1861 he met his principal god, Whitman. He wrote copiously and unpretentiously during the quiet middle years at Riverby. Later he broadened his observations of nature into speculations on evolution and geology as well as homilies on his spiritual quest and literary or biographical criticism that included two books on Whitman and sketches of Audubon and Roosevelt.

The total of Burroughs's books reached two dozen. His patient studies of God's creatures, digestibly reported, had influence beyond expectations, thanks to new ideas of the time. He guided the country's thoughts to outdoor pleasures and to the potentials of the new national parks. In

1887 he was pleased when a Chicago teacher asked to use his *Pepacton* as a reader, a practice soon adopted elsewhere. Today Burroughs's books, once on every parlor shelf, are hardly known at all. His voice now seems a distant echo of Victorian sentiment.

John Burroughs was born into a family of dairy farmers near Roxbury in Delaware County, New York, amidst the rolling hills below the Catskills. As a boy he did his share of farm chores and came to know the local wildlife as a matter of course. He grew up with his own insights into nature free of bookish knowledge, an approach absorbed from a farm childhood and nurtured throughout life. When at last he found an urban audience, he left his country family behind. With chagrin he later recorded that no member of his family had ever read one of his books.

To Burroughs his home farm was not only beloved but sacred. His ties to the land and to his family went beyond sentiment, for his whole spirit was deeply rooted in nostalgia. It has been said that, when bereavement struck the Thoreau family, Henry bore his grief stoically, but when Burroughs's parents died his grief was unbearable, nor did it ever fade. Burroughs spent most of his mature summers on the old farm in a second family home there, Woodchuck Lodge, almost as closely associated with him as Slabsides.

In his late teens John Burroughs began to move out into the world and find experiences that helped form him. Always intellectually ambitious, like other autodidacts such as Alexander Wilson, he turned to school teaching. Between teaching appointments he enthusiastically spent his savings on a few academic courses at nearby educational institutions, but he was too poor for the extended program of study for which he longed. This smattering of education did more to whet his appetite for learning than to fulfill his needs. It may be significant that the courses he took, offered by local seminaries, focused on religious values. His first published article, "Vagaries vs. Spiritualism," written in 1856 at age nineteen, reflected this emphasis, and so by implication did much of his later writing.

Burroughs's teaching, once requiring him to travel as far as Illinois, broadened his contacts with people. Nearby in New York State he met a young woman colleague, Ursula North, and after his Illinois appointment he married her at the early age of twenty. From the start their marriage was uneasy, though it endured. They often lived apart, since John had a need to live outdoors while Ursula preferred the ease of town life. Burroughs's meeting with Walt Whitman in New York inspired him to write with growing momentum that led to an early high point in his best known poem, "Waiting" of 1863. At this time John also met Emerson, who was lecturing at West Point; he had already studied the Concord sage's essays in depth. Unexpectedly he found in the military academy library a giant book of bird prints by John James Audubon, and over this he pored for hours. Clearly the revelation of Audubon was no less than formative.

During the Civil War Burroughs went to Washington to seek a job in which he could serve the Union as a civilian exempt from the military. A gentle idealist, he hated machines, war, and violence, even though in his early years he occasionally went hunting and for decades carried on a gunning war against the woodchucks which besieged his garden. He was often with Whitman in Washington, and together they sought release from a hectic world by taking nature walks. Burroughs's 1866 book on Whitman, his first, vigorously backed the poet's unconventional and poorly appreciated works.

Burroughs found an undemanding post in the Treasury Department as guard of a vault. He simply stood before it all day at a high desk, and so had ample time to review his experiences in nature and even to write. Here, before his country's stacked reserves of money, John Burroughs wrote his first nature book, *Wake-Robin,* published in 1871 and devoted mainly to birds. It is his warmest paean to the birds and may have accounted for his nickname, John O'Birds.

Burroughs's Treasury service led to an unexpected reward when the department sent him to England on business in late 1871. England's neatly divided fields, hedgerows, narrow roads, public footpaths, and sonorous birds inspired Burroughs's love, especially during later more leisurely visits. On this trip he managed to see Oxford and Stratford and, spurred by his characteristic hero worship of leading intellectual figures, he even called on Carlyle. On his return he took a job for income as a New York State bank examiner and surprisingly became successful and respected at this task over the next ten years. At the beginning of this period he moved to Riverby and settled into his tranquil life there, dividing his time between bank work, fruit farming, and the labor of writing.

John Burroughs focussed on birds in *Wake-Robin,* for he saw them as heralds announcing nature's wonders. The pioneering bird students like Wilson and Audubon had devoted years of intense study to American species, but their approach to birds and the reports of their investigations were patently different from Burroughs's. John O'Birds was even more a self-taught student of birds than his predecessors, yet without the guidance of many books he was still able to acquire a thorough knowledge of eastern American birds. He could describe the traits and actions of obscure species, and he could communicate the sighting of a bird with freshness by linking the seeing to the telling of it in direct recall. Burroughs was well tuned to bird song, unquestionably an innate sensitivity, which Audubon and Wilson did not so much display. He could enhance his characterization of a bird by describing its song, although his direct transcriptions of calls, like most such efforts, were not always clear. He recorded the song of the hermit thrush thus in *Wake-Robin:*

> ... I detect this sound rising pure and serene, as if a spirit from some remote height were slowly chanting a divine accompaniment. This song appeals to the sentiment of the beautiful in me, and suggests a serene religious beatitude as no other sound in nature does. ... It is very simple and I can hardly tell the secret of its charm. 'O spheral, spheral' he seems to say; 'Oh holy holy! O clear away, clear away! O clear up, clear up!' interspersed with the finest trills and most delicate preludes.

His report of his second trip to England, *Fresh Fields* of 1884, compares the songs of British and American birds and notes a slight preference for his native flock. Burroughs was equipped with all the capabilities—honest field work, patience in tracing action, and an ear for song—to make him a paragon of bird appreciation. But the tone of his writing—genial, bland, intimate, always thankful for nature's bounty—was different from the viewpoint of bird students earlier in the century. Burroughs speaks with Victorian sentiment, remote from the early empirical exploration of American birds. Some of his ways of thinking about nature derive from mid-century transcendentalism and from Thoreau, and so too from Thoreau's teacher, Emerson, but Burroughs's search for guidance seldom needed to turn back earlier than the Concordians.

When John Burroughs described a bird, the reader could feel the sensitive looking that lay behind the words. Burroughs always scrupulously respected the actuality of his subject, and he allowed no distracting embellishments in his prose. He strove assiduously for honesty and avoided too much style. But Burroughs could not escape the conventions of his time, and he often projected into a bird description some personal sentiment which was more a poetic invention than a reality of nature. He seldom described a bird completely but told just enough to unveil the feelings suggested to him by the wild creature. What he wrote of the bald eagle in "Wildlife about my Cabin," published in *Far and Near,* is typical:

I want rather to feel the inspiration of his presence and noble bearing, I want my interest and sympathy to go with him in his continental voyaging up and down, and in his long elevated flights to and from his eyrie upon the remote, solitary cliffs. . . . Dignity, elevation, repose are his. I would have my thoughts take as wide a sweep, and I would be as far removed from the petty cares and turmoils of this noisy and blustering world.

Burroughs in a thoughtful moment at his Slabsides retreat. From *Bird-Lore.*

Burroughs does not anthropomorphize here, though he occasionally employed that device with tact. Instead he traces a flight of human sentiment in a late romantic vein, inspired by gratitude for the revelation of a wild creature and by yearning to identify with its prowess. Burroughs specifically endorsed this humanizing approach in "A Sharp Lookout" from *Signs and Seasons:* "Man can have but one interest in nature, namely, to see himself reflected or interpreted there, and we quickly neglect both poet and philosopher who fail to satisfy, in some measure, this feeling." Or at the start of his career in the introduction to *Wake-Robin:* "If I name every bird I see in my walk, describe its color and ways, etc., give a lot of facts or details about the bird, it is doubtful if my reader is interested. But if I relate the bird in some way to human life, to my own life,—show what it is to me and what it is in the landscape and the season, then do I give my reader a live bird and not a labeled specimen."

Neither Wilson nor Audubon permitted any such subjective overlay in their bird descriptions. They simply sought to tell all they could about the bird without adornment of feeling. Burroughs's approach is literary, since it flows less from the object in nature than from within his intellect. His aim is to derive new meanings from his outdoor experiences which can stimulate insights when filtered through memory of observed reality. Throughout life Burroughs viewed the world in literary terms. One of his first memories of self-education was of making a list of new words learned, and he even reduced his love of birds to a literary exercise in an essay from *Birds and Poets* of 1877, where he drily catalogued the usage of birds in poetry.

John Burroughs's long experience in the field leads to a summary question: what contribution did this prolific writer make to bird study? On the negative side, Burroughs was no scientific ornithologist, nor did he wish to be one. He kept no systematic records of bird sightings other than a selective journal. While his daily experience led to much knowledge of local birds, he had no instinct for new scientific discovery, only for what he loved to see again and again. Had I "studied the birds?" he wrote. "No, I have played with them, camped with them, gone berrying with them, summered and wintered with them, and my knowledge of them has filtered into my mind almost unconsciously."

Nor was Burroughs, in contrast to John Muir, committed to the conservation of nature, then gaining national attention. John O'Birds, with boyish curiosity, thought nothing of reaching into a woodpecker's hole and pulling out the nestlings to see what they looked like, or of drowning a cowbird chick caught freeloading in a Canada warbler's nest. Burroughs confessed that in the fall of 1876 while hunting grouse he saw a lone passenger pigeon in a tree. "I killed it, little dreaming that, so far as I was concerned, I was killing the last pigeon." It is not easy to explain this casual attitude toward conservation in a man to whom nature was all. Perhaps from childhood Burroughs retained something of the farmer's hard feelings that wildlife was apparently plentiful and sometimes a nuisance. More likely Burroughs felt that, while species come and go and populations rise and fall, nature in the end must balance out its losses and reassert its wholeness. Something of a hermit, he joined few organizations, disliked politics, and never entered the activist sphere of the conservation movement.

No one can doubt that Burroughs inspired a vast popular awareness of birds and all of nature in the decades when the modern affinity for the outdoors emerged. His essays taught their lessons gently and sweetly, and as white hair came he slid into the role of nature guru, the beloved sage of Slabsides. His books, expressed in direct and easy language, were suitable for school use and readable by all ages in the stuffy parlors of late Victorian America. One can guess that a result of an evening reading might be a family walk in the country on Sunday.

The appeal of Burroughs's essays is not easy to perceive today. They relate events so simply and immediately that their content seems deceptively minimal, presented with a distilled, almost mystical purity. Enlarging on Wilson's and Audubon's methods, he narrated behavior as seen close up and after long acquaintance, as more recent birders do through binoculars, but with his own eye. John O'Birds told just how a turkey vulture lands on a post, holding its wings extended for a second or two until balance is sure, and he described how a species that economically builds a quick flimsy nest in the South will spend weeks making a windproof home in the North. John wrote that he sought "to see no more and no less than is actually before you; to be able to detach yourself and see the thing as it actually is. . . . In short, to see with your reason as well as your perceptions, that is to be an observer and to read the book of nature aright." The writer most akin to Burroughs, one often mentioned by him, is the Reverend Gilbert White, the astute English parish naturalist, who could as well have written the words above.

Burroughs did not seek out certain birds, as Audubon and Wilson did in Louisville, but sauntered forth, to use Thoreau's term, on his daily nature walk, anticipating the enjoyment of whatever he found. After his day's field sightings he jotted them in his journal in rough spontaneous annotations unlike the literary polish of Thoreau's daily records. Burroughs's day book, put aside for an interval, served to aid his memory and provided themes for the nature essays. This process sought to guarantee fidelity to first observations. Above all there is an overlay of good feeling in Burroughs's writing, of sympathetic human sentiment, which is the foundation of its appeal.

Burroughs's personal, vaguely symbolic writing influenced other essayists of his time, such as Dallas Lore Sharp and Bradford Torrey (see Chapter Twelve). All these writers, and especially John O'Birds himself, traced a line of inspiration to one font, Henry David Thoreau. Burroughs wrote two essays on Thoreau, one in 1889 published in *Indoor Studies,* and some extended afterthoughts at the end of his life in *The Last Harvest* of 1922. In addition, his literary executor and biographer, Dr. Clara Barrus, explored the relationship between the two naturalists, and a description of this interaction may enhance perceptions of both men. Viewing Thoreau and Burroughs together defines the paradox of their relationship. As personalities they were as different as an eagle and a sandpiper, but they shared many attitudes about nature.

In his two essays, Burroughs saw Thoreau as a prickly, cold, judgmental New Englander, petulant in politics, intolerant of everyone except plain outdoor men, an inward person with an aggressive wit, who could observe astutely and think profoundly, but mostly for his own uses. Thoreau could be silly, obsessively hoeing his seven acres of beans and measuring stumps; he could be an extremist like his hero John Brown. His radical idealism was both admirable and exaggerated; as a writer he was neither nourishing nor convincing but he stimulated by arousing exasperation.

Burroughs may have described Thoreau harshly because he himself shared none of these austere traits. Where John was tolerant, complacent about men and the world, a sweet and gently ideal writer, Henry was distant, proud, and tough-minded. He went to Harvard and continued to read in its library, while Burroughs's education was hit-or-miss. Both were practical men and good at farming, but John, something of a sensualist, adored the month of April when nature delicately came to life again, while Henry liked winter so that he could see the shape of the land. Both men shared a curious practice when observing birds, one that may jolt modern birders obsessed with listing. When Thoreau or Burroughs saw a bird they often would describe it with affectionate detail but not bother to identify it. This slight rebellion against the demands of science was one small way of expressing their worship of nature, not as an outdoor laboratory full of biological queries but as a single interlocking whole, structured like a vertebrate animal vastly enlarged. Both men took a precocious stance that looked to ecology before its time, Thoreau as an astounding prophet whose intellect reached toward the next century, Burroughs as a parish preacher about nature, persuading with a quiet earthy lyricism.

Confronting Thoreau, Burroughs seemed trapped in his own anti-intellectual intolerance, which accepted only the most simplistic values. Just as he perceived that a bird was lovely but declined to investigate it, he was only able to see Thoreau as a fellow nature worshipper but unable to reach the demanding heights of Concord idealism. Burroughs saw Thoreau as a thoughtful browser along rough trails which led to untamed nature, but he felt this wilder landscape now needed to be trimmed to suit a more indulgent age. Burroughs, passively loving nature as it is, could not grasp Thoreau's intellectual rebellion from traditional natural history.

The two naturalists in their own ways looked to the same teacher, Ralph Waldo Emerson. Burroughs wrote two tributes to Emerson, first in *Birds and Poets* of 1877 using an Emersonian style, then in *The Last Harvest* in 1922, a retrospective view of a sixty-year-old relationship. In 1860, when Burroughs at twenty-three wrote one of his first essays, "Expression," he used Emerson's style so convincingly that James Russell Lowell, editor of the *Atlantic Monthly,* had to check it for plagiarism before accepting it. Burroughs looked upon the Concord essayist as the distant priest of idealism, always positive, pure, removed from the brute world, and a selfless guide to the sweet wholeness of the universe. Emerson's vision of nature's unity gripped the young Burroughs's mind most potently. This aspect of transcendental thought reinforced his secular perception of nature, while the puritanical and ethical concerns of the Emersonian essayists had less appeal. Burroughs enjoyed the sensual side of nature as well as its objective study and so could not follow Emerson and Thoreau in all their moral commitments. As a writer Burroughs outgrew Emerson as model. He found his master's dry wit and calculated verbiage inappropriate for outdoor musings and with a little more maturity he gained the confidence to publish in the spontaneous epistolary style that in time attracted readers nationwide. Burroughs characteristically looked up to Emerson as a man more than he admired the thought in his essays. Burroughs' views of great minds were self-reinforcing, and so he found merit in Emerson's mode of probing with pointed spiritual insights but without the need for a doctrinal framework.

John Burroughs was attracted to another great figure in his time, Charles Darwin. His late essay on Darwin appeared in *The Last Harvest,* and its title, "A Critical Glance into Darwin," prepares the reader for some conservative hesitation about evolutionary theory, asserted with a country naturalist's reductive intuitions. Burroughs was unhappy about Darwin's doctrine of natural selection because he conceived nature as perfect in order and constant in purpose, ruled by a universal intelligence. Darwin's natural selection is touched off by random struggles, a concept Burroughs found intolerable because it violates the ideal of nature's ineluctable wholeness. Burroughs did not perceive nature as always benign and without pain. But his natural world, unlike the Darwinian one with its genetic lottery, is overlaid by patterns forming a whole that makes every act meaningful, whether bitter or joyful. The Darwin whom Burroughs could personally embrace was not the systematic thinker of *The Origin of Species* but the young naturalist in *The Voyage of the Beagle.* It is not surprising that Burroughs found more to admire in this observant traveler—a paragon for himself—passively opening his mind to the breadth of nature and allowing its pantheistic interrelations to emerge. As he did in assessing Emerson, Burroughs spoke more as a humanist than as an intellectual, and was quick to admire Darwin's personal virtues but cautious in accepting his theories.

Burroughs showed a similar pattern of feelings for his friend Theodore Roosevelt. The two men, diametrically opposed personalities, struck it off in genial comradeship from the beginning. Their relationship focused exclusively on their appreciation of nature. Burroughs wisely avoided discussing politics with the president, who in turn put that interest aside when with John O'Birds. Roosevelt invited Burroughs to accompany him as nature consultant on a trip to Yellowstone Park in April 1903. The president was attacked in the press prior to the trip about his alleged plans to shoot big game in a national park. But T.R. renounced his hunting plans before departure and wisely took along America's prime nature lover to attest his innocence. The only animal the president killed in the park was a field mouse, caught in his

Theodore Roosevelt ready to explore the outdoors. *Department of Library Services, American Museum of Natural History.*

hands with the help of his hat, neatly skinned and sent back to Hart Merriam at the Biological Survey in hopes it might be a new species (it wasn't, but it had never been reported at Yellowstone). Burroughs and Roosevelt birded continuously and located a Townsend's solitaire, a new species for both, and a pygmy owl.

Afterward T.R. occasionally invited Burroughs to the White House for birding on the grounds or in Rock Creek Park, and after Roosevelt's Washington years they met at Sagamore Hill. Once the two birders spent a weekend at Pine Knot, the president's cabin in western Virginia. Together they tallied seventy-five birds, two of which T.R. had not known before—the swamp sparrow and the pine warbler—and two the president identified for John O'Birds, Bewick's wren and the prairie warbler. Both identified a blue-gray gnatcatcher, and their score was even. For some years Roosevelt urged Burroughs to record this occasion in an article, writing him with comradely chiding, "Don't forget I showed you the blue grosbeak and the Bewick Wren and almost all the other birds I said I would." Burroughs's memorial of the Pine Knot weekend appeared in one of his last books, *Under the Maples,* published two years after Roosevelt's death.

The mutual respect of the two men emerges from statements each made about the Yellowstone visit. The president wrote:

> One April I went to Yellowstone Park, when the snow was still very deep, and I took John Burroughs with me. I wished to show him the wild game of the Park, the wild creatures that have become so astonishingly tame and tolerant of human presence. . . . In April we found the elk weak after the short commons and hard living of winter. Once without much difficulty I regularly rounded up a big band of them, so that John Burroughs could look at them. I do not think, however, that he cared to see them as much as I did. The birds interested him more, especially a tiny owl the size of a robin. . . . I was rather ashamed to find how much better his eyes were than mine in seeing birds and grasping their differences.

And John Burroughs in *Camping and Tramping with Roosevelt* says: "Throughout the trip I found his interest in bird life very keen, and his eye and ear remarkably quick. He usually saw the bird or heard its note as quickly as I did—and I had nothing else to think about. . . . Of course, his training as a big game hunter stood him in good stead, but back of that was his naturalist's instincts, and his genuine love of all forms of wild life." It is amusing that each of these experienced birders gave admiring credit to the other's eye.

Burroughs in his natural way spoke for the best of American values as his times saw them. He was not as jingoistic as Wilson and Audubon, new immigrants who declared their love for America in the public square, and from the Civil War onward he avoided joining causes because a private life seemed more fruitful to him. Yet Burroughs, a farm boy, carved out a field through his own talents and offered another confirmation of the Lincolnesque values of honesty, the patient pursuit of personal ideals, and devotion to work despite obstacles. In later life Burroughs was granted a number of honors that culminated his long career, including honorary degrees from Yale, Colgate, and the University of Georgia. More personal recognition came in invitations to camp with Theodore Roosevelt in Yellowstone and with Thomas Edison, Henry Ford, and Harvey Firestone in the Great Smokies. These companions stood for the core of American values, and that Burroughs took his place among them tells its own story.

Another honor invested John O'Birds as the patron saint of birders. Frank Chapman, a key figure in the ornithological world as curator of birds at the American Museum of Natural History, formed the habit early in his career of calling on Burroughs at Riverby, and they frequently met for field trips thereafter. In 1899 Chapman founded *Bird-Lore,* soon to become the organ of the National Association of Audubon Societies, and asked Burroughs to write the lead article in the first issue, entitled "In Warbler Time." Chapman reported in his autobiography that once when he called on Burroughs, the older naturalist characteristically saluted the younger expert with a modest statement of a birder's curiosity: "I'm glad you've come, Chapman. My son has just shot a duck I don't know. I wish you would come in the house and tell me what it is."

John Muir photographed in 1901 by
Charles Lummis. *Southwest Museum.*

Chapter Five

John Muir, Mountain Naturalist

*A*s a totally rounded naturalist John Muir was curious about everything in the outdoors, from mountain ranges and their geology to minuscule alpine wildflowers, and he of course included birds as well as mammals and trees in his sweeping view of nature. He also had a vast influence on modern attitudes toward the environment, and his importance as an early and eloquent conservationist earns him a place in any discussion of American nature, whether it concerns birds or any of Muir's other far-ranging interests.

John Muir like Audubon was a patent genius. He was an intense explorer of nature who preferred to go alone, he was a daring mountaineer, a botanist and horticulturalist, a geologist who was influential for his studies in glaciology, a forester, and from youth to old age a lover of birds and animals. Wherever Muir focused on the world, he perceived it in a way that was fresh, thoughtful, or radically innovative. Throughout life but especially later on his vigorous and delightful writing most often served the cause of conserving the wilderness he knew from a lifetime's experience.

Muir's life, like Audubon's, followed a rising curve of commitment and discipline. In youth he was beset by poverty, hesitance, and the tyranny of chance; then he reveled in a time of self-discovery during ten years at Yosemite and in the Sierra Nevada before settling down to marriage, fatherhood, farming, and writing, along with continued travels. Like Audubon, too, Muir was something of a prophet whose vision projected from his own time into ours. He directed the transcendental view of nature toward a philosophy of the outdoors that is accessible today. A practical man as well as a visionary, in 1892 he helped to found the Sierra Club, one of the largest conservation groups in America, and served as its first president for twenty-two years until his death in 1914.

Muir's youth had parallels with both Alexander Wilson's and John Burroughs's. Like Wilson he came from a small Scottish town, Dunbar on the Firth of Forth. John, the third of seven children, was born in 1838. Eleven years later his father, Daniel, decided to emigrate to Ontario. Finding no suitable land in Canada, the immigrants went to southern Wisconsin and staked out a farm near Fountain Lake. John, as he glowingly recounted fifty years later in his memoir *The Story of My Boyhood and Youth,* was enchanted with the wildlife of this untouched land. But he never had much time to enjoy it. Daniel Muir was an obsessive religious fundamentalist who read only the Bible and had no time from his devotions for farming. He became a lay circuit preacher and eventually, to his family's regret, sold his farms and moved to Portage.

Meanwhile the burden of the farm work fell heavily on John as oldest son, and, with his younger brothers, he worked daily from before dawn to dusk to support the family. Throughout life John Muir had heroic strength, and his Wisconsin farm years tested his physical prowess. But they deprived him of the exploratory leisure, either outdoors or in, which most encourages learning. Daniel Muir permitted no recreation, only backbreaking field work and Bible study. John at least drew from his youth a good knowledge of the Bible, to which he referred throughout his writings, even, it may be, finding stylistic inspiration there.

Young John did find time at home for one game by secretly shortening his sleeping time. Using only materials found lying around the farm, he made witty and fantastic machines. Friends urged him to display his inventions at the state fair in Madison, where they were a popular success. Several admirers then persuaded this bright but raw farm youth to enter the state university. Muir ended by spending five terms at the University of Wisconsin, supporting himself during occasional leaves by schoolteaching or work on the home farm.

Several intellectual experiences at the university were crucial to John

Muir's development. The first involved two teachers, Professors James Davie Butler and Ezra Slocum Carr, who introduced him to New England transcendentalism. Both Butler and Carr remained lifetime friends, especially after the Carrs moved to Berkeley. Jeanne Carr was perhaps Muir's most intimate patron and his inspiring correspondent. A chance event at the university was an odd and seemingly ephemeral happenstance. As Muir and a fellow student, M. S. Griswold, emerged from a class in botany in the spring of 1863, Griswold pulled a twig from a locust tree and remarked that it was related to the pea. John was astounded but soon convinced of the unexpected connection. This off-hand moment marked the beginning of Muir's lifelong pursuit of botany. Thereafter he always botanized while traveling and soon began to travel in order to botanize.

Muir's talent for mechanical design seemed the most likely means to a livelihood after his studies. After two years in Canada working in a broom factory, while collecting plants in his spare time, he then migrated south and found work with a carriage parts firm in Indianapolis. There chance again visited him when a piece flew off a machine belt and wounded his right eye. For weeks he lay in a darkened room with his eye bandaged, wondering if he would lose its sight but wondering beyond this about his future, weighing his love for the outdoors and plants against an engineering career. Divining his own destiny during this time of enforced introspection, he decided in favor of the ideals of nature rather than likely material success in manufacturing. His eye recovered, and, acting on his resolve, he formed a demanding plan to walk to the Gulf of Mexico. He took the train from Indianapolis to Louisville, walked rapidly through that city and on into the southern countryside, new to him and promising unknown plants, forests, and mountains.

Muir vividly recorded the adventures of his trip in a journal, edited posthumously by his biographer William Frederick Badè as *A Thousand Mile Walk to the Gulf.* Like Thoreau's travel records, Muir's are more than just a day book, for the movement is stopped from time to time by thoughtful essays inspired by new surroundings. Muir's most insightful moment during the journey came while camping under giant live oaks in the Bonaventure Cemetery outside Savannah. At this low point in his walk he was starving, living on a cracker or two a day, while awaiting a delayed shipment of money from home. In the shadowy place of death he chose for shelter he was awakened each morning by a lively tumult of birds that "chattered and scolded in half-angry, half-wondering tones," a small crowd swelling to a large one. So he found irrepressible life in the presence of death and, meditating on both with echoes of transcendentalism filling his mind, he experienced a revelation about the oneness of all life. The insight presaged much of what he was to learn from the mountains of California. He noted his sense of world unity in the address he wrote in his southern journal: "John Muir, Earth-Planet, Universe."

The second crisis of his walk caught up with him in Florida. During his final leg of 155 miles across the peninsula from Ferdinanda to Cedar Key, he found little appeal in the muddy swamps and tangled growth of this semi-tropical environment where he had to sleep on damp

"Oh no, not for me," said John Muir when he first saw Yosemite. This view appeared in William Cullen Bryant's *Picturesque America*.

hammocks, eat stale food, and drink dark swamp water. On arriving at his goal, Cedar Key and the Gulf, he was half dead of malaria. A kind family on the island, the Hodgsons, took him in and nursed him. Though still convalescent he planned to pursue his journey to Cuba and South America. He took passage on a schooner bound for Cuba. But he realized in outings there that his health was not yet good enough for strenuous travel along the Orinoco and the Amazon.

So he ended his southern adventure and sailed for New York, then to Panama and on to San Francisco. Again chance had redirected Muir's steps. Thirty years old when he arrived in San Francisco, he did not know that he was near the end of years of wandering in search of a personal ideology. During his next decade in the Sierra Nevada the answers to his spiritual search unfolded with a grace of which a farm boy from Wisconsin could never have dreamed.

After docking in San Francisco Muir walked rapidly through that city, as always driven to escape the urban scene, asked a stranger the way to the country—any way, any country—and hiked right on to Yosemite Valley. Overwhelmed by the scope of this landscape, he first reacted by muttering, "Oh, no, not for me." Stunned reluctance soon gave way to considered appreciation, then to inspired and profound love. "I have crossed the Range of Light," he said in *My First Summer in the Sierra,* "surely the brightest and best of all the Lord has built; and rejoicing in its glory, I gladly, gratefully, hopefully pray I may see it again," as he did, again and again, always more perceptively. And, writing to the Carrs, he said he was "bewitched, enchanted, and tomorrow I must start for the great temple to listen to the winter songs and sermons preached and sung only there."

For Muir the Sierra was a religious vision, his cathedral and his shrine. His father was a fundamentalist fanatic, driving John to rebel against an excessive dose of Christianity. Instead he formed a cult of nature worship just as intense. In the context of Muir's perception of his Range of Light the smaller events of his mountain years fade in significance, including his work as shepherd, miller, and guide, undertaken as support while his ever longer treks through the Sierra fanned out from Yosemite.

John Muir gained knowledge of the Sierra first of all by placing one foot before the other. Through total immersion in the mountains, he sought physical and spiritual identification with them. He believed in traveling light, and had a sensual faith in his body's toughness. He was ready to climb out of the valley dressed in boots, "tough old clothes, gray like the rocks," and an open white shirt; with one pocket full of dried bread (to avoid mold), in the other a packet of tea, his notebook, tin cup, and perhaps with a book tied to his belt, sometimes the Bible or *Walden*, the Bible of American naturalists. No impediments must intervene between this land of rocks and firs and his sensing of it. Nothing stopped his intense longing for every possible—or sometimes impossible—experience of this unfathomable miracle of nature.

As Muir took up life in the Sierra his devotion to botany persisted, but in response to this environment he added geology and the study of trees, birds, and animals to his interests. Geology, and especially his work on glaciers, was a central avenue to finding the richer meanings in nature which the mountains promised. Geologists in the nineteenth century were concerned with discovering the origins of Yosemite and other unusually abrupt Sierra valleys. When Muir arrived there the accepted explanation was that at some cataclysmic moment the bottom of Yosemite Valley had dropped, carving its vertical cliffs and admitting the Merced River. The hypothesis of a cataclysm had no appeal to Muir, who saw nature as subject to a slow evolving flux of forces. From his first sight of Yosemite he felt that the gradual friction of glaciers must have carved its rounded peaks, the vertically cut valley, and steep subvalleys.

Muir of course had come to know the Sierra more intimately than anyone during his strenuous explorations. In October of 1872 he was transported to ecstasy when he discovered a living glacier between the Black (now called Madera) and Red mountains in the Clark Range southeast of Yosemite. As soon as the euphoria passed he set out to drive stakes into the ice, placed so that he could sight along them to survey the glacier's movement. On repeated visits he watched the ice mass flow with inexorable slow rhythm. Muir went on to find numerous active glaciers concealed under the snows of the Sierra. Through a mass of evidence Muir earned universal acceptance for his remarkable single-handed demonstration of the glacial origins of the Sierra Mountains.

John Muir experienced another burst of ecstasy when he saw the green ice next to Black Mountain for reasons that went beyond the collaboration of his glacial theory. He also sensed the presence of a powerful force that embodied his vision of a protean nature without boundaries, always changing, in constant flux. This was the nature perceived by Emerson and the transcendentalists and by Darwin, whose theory of evolution Muir accepted without hesitation. The glacier like the wind gathered the energy of nature in an action that forcibly brought new forms. Glaciers, storms, and earthquakes were nature's plows and axes, far more relentless in shaping the earth than man's designs. An earthquake once taught Muir a living lesson in how nature writes its changes on the earth's face. As he watched a mountainside ground to a talus before his eyes, Muir described his thoughts in his journal in this way: "There are no harsh, hard dividing lines in nature. Glaciers blend with the snow and the snow blends with the thin invisible breath of the sky. So there are no stiff, frigid, stony partition walls betwixt us and heaven. There are blendings as immeasurable and un-traceable as the edges of melting clouds. Eye hath not seen, nor ear heard, etc., is applicable here, for earth is partly heaven, and heaven earth."

John Muir's observations of flux in nature were directly in line with the philosophy of his times, formulated in New England transcendental-ism and given voice by Emerson. Long before his years in the Sierra Muir had studied Emerson's ideas, above all the essay *Nature*. Now he was granted the chance to meet the Concord philosopher on Muir's chosen ground in Yosemite, when Emerson visited the valley in May 1871. Muir at first was shy about presenting himself to the great man, but each was longing to meet the other, and once the ice cleared their greetings were warm. John invited the elderly visitor to see his home-made cabin. Emerson came and even climbed a ramp to Muir's sleeping loft, his "hang-nest," as he called it, cantilevered over a stream to provide a pleasant background noise and equipped with skylights for observing the mountains and the sky. Emerson called on Muir every day of his visit, but John longed to take the sage of nature camping in the wilderness so that they could immerse themselves in this glorious land-scape. Teddy Roosevelt later jumped at the chance to camp with Muir, but Emerson, sixty-eight years old, heeded his companions' admonitions about his health and declined. Muir was much disappointed. He rode a ways with the New England party as it departed, waved a shy good-bye to Emerson's hearty one, and went on to sleep under a sequoia.

Afterwards the two men corresponded extensively, and Emerson persistently urged Muir to leave the wilderness and work from a civi-lized base, as did Mrs. Carr. The philosopher's visit to Yosemite and their resulting relationship made Muir realize that his ties to nature were more intimate than the transcendentalist's. Emerson's concept of nature was an artifice constructed in the study; no absorption in the landscape was needed to formulate the cool ethical epigrams of *Nature*. Muir began from a pragmatic base, first identifying with his wilderness site, then allowing the more objective strains of his thinking to emerge organically from his subjective feelings. Muir's viewpoint was that of a second-generation transcendentalist, reflecting Emerson's thought, yet experiential and driven by a deep urge to open the soul romantically to nature's caress.

More far-reaching in effect was Muir's adamant belief that nature was not designed to serve man but had its own inner rhythms. His position was based on a moral stance from which he confronted the still virulent American urge to hunt and eat animals, to knock down woods and plant more profitable cornfields, and to take nature as an endlessly renewable gift. In these convictions about nature's vulnerability lies the seed that grew into Muir's dedication to conservation; it is one of the first breaths of the movement anywhere. Muir, like Audubon and Burroughs, described the vast flocks of passenger pigeons, and on their demise he needed only to quote "some smug practical old sinner" who flatly asserted that the birds "were made to be killed and sent us to eat." As early as the *Thousand-Mile Walk* Muir was aware of the confrontation between using nature and letting it be: "Now it never seems to occur

Muir's family home near San Francisco is now a museum.

to those far-seeing teachers that Nature's object in making animals and plants might possibly be first of all the happiness of each one of them, not the creation of all for the happiness of one. . . . The world, we are told, was made especially for man—a presumption not supported by the facts." For Muir nature existed in its own realm, neither hostile to man nor available for exploitation.

These ideas inspired John Muir's commitment to conservation and it would be unjust to write of him without mentioning his dedication to preserving nature. His first concern was the sorry state of the forests, an asset pathetically vulnerable to rapacious commercial use. In 1874, his survey of Yosemite done, he began agitating for a national commission to look into the setting aside of forest reserves. Congress formed such a commission in 1876, and Muir went along as a consultant when its members inspected forests. The subsequent history of the struggle to create forest reserves was tangled since politics clouded the issue. During the government's backing and forthing Muir often wrote passionate appeals to protect the trees, the most famous being his article "The American Forests" in the *Atlantic Monthly,* republished as the closing of *Our National Parks:*

> Any fool can destroy trees. They cannot run away, and if they could, they would still be destroyed—chased and hunted down as long as fun or a dollar could be got out of their bark hides. . . . Throughout all the wonderful, eventful centuries since Christ's time—and long before that—God has cared for these trees, saved them from drought, disease, avalanches and a thousand straining leveling tempests and floods; but He cannot save them from fools —only Uncle Sam can do that.

John Muir's most opportune moment to influence conservation policy came in 1903 when he was notified that President Roosevelt wished to visit Yosemite and go camping alone with John O'Mountains, as Muir was often called. Muir and the president spent a long weekend hiking and camping in the Mariposa sequoia grove, on the rim of the valley and in it. Since no one was with them, nothing is directly known of their conversations—Burroughs thought these two irrepressible talkers would clash in a contest of loquacity. But it is telling that the president soon after trebled the acreage of federal forest reserves and created sixteen new national monuments including the Grand Canyon.

John Muir enlisted early on as a prime mover in the campaign to protect great natural sites as national parks. His books and the series of articles "Studies in the Sierra" undertook to educate the public about these unique assets. In 1889, fourteen years before the Roosevelt visit, Muir led a Yosemite tour for Robert U. Johnson of *Century* magazine. Muir and Johnson then issued a call to make the Yosemite area a park, adding the same appeal for King's Canyon and the sequoia region to the south. Their voices reached Congress, which authorized a Yosemite park the following year. Muir, founding spirit and first president of the Sierra Club, played a major inspirational role in initiating the national park movement and in setting up what became the national forests. He deserves, more than anyone, to be designated the father of American conservation.

Where in John Muir's thoughtful scheme of nature do birds fit? He mentioned them often with heartfelt appreciation, but he did not follow Burroughs in looking upon them as the summoning heralds of nature. Muir saw the birds as absorbed organically in the landscape, as another link in a whole interacting universe. Wherever his explorations took him, he observed and recorded the birds as part of the picture, just as with impartial interest he surveyed the flowers, trees, the rocks, and weather. At his frontier home in Wisconsin he was enchanted by the American birds new to him, which he described at length in *The Story of My Boyhood and Youth*. He noted the kingbird, admirable fighter not even shying from hawks, the whippoorwill and nighthawk and their trick of feigning injury to protect their nests, and the bobwhites which did not always make it through the winter. On his thousand-mile walk he gave a list of birds at Cedar Key, even though he was ill at the time, including white pelicans which lined the shores like foam, the beloved clever mockingbird, quail and crows "with a foreign accent" (fish crows perhaps). At Twenty-Hill Hollow, his first outpost in California, he recorded seeing larks distinct from the eastern ones, blue and white herons, burrowing owls, killdeer, a sparrow hawk, and a golden eagle that was hunting hares.

In the Sierra he quickly found the water ouzel (dipper), to Muir the most treasured bird of all and the one he wrote most about, also "blue cranes" (herons), log-cocks (pileated woodpeckers), hummingbirds, linnets, Steller's jays and the wily Clark's crow (Clark's nutcracker), flickers, "cheery confiding canaries" (goldfinches), mountain quail and blue grouse, and the gray (golden) eagle. As he rowed down the Sacramento River Muir saw brant, curlews, sandpipers, killdeer, buzzards, wood ducks, great blue herons again and sandhill cranes.

Evidently Muir did not make such cursory lists for scientific purposes but only to sense the patterns of nature in an environment. He did not always bother with exact identifications; he sometimes used generic terms like woodpecker or hummingbird, or confusing European ones like linnet (probably the redpoll, or perhaps the purple finch), or he might observe well but without a conclusion as in "crows with a foreign accent." Recalling those other generalists, Thoreau and Burroughs, he seemed to appreciate a bird more for not knowing what it was. Once in the Sierra he heard a musical flute-like night bird that "I would gladly lie awake a week to know, very soft and sweet, yet brave, cheerful and clear." Or he saw a tiny bird emerge from the bushes and "in one moment that cheerful confiding bird preached me the most effective sermon on heavenly trust that I have ever heard through all the measured hours of Sabbath, and I went on not half so heart-sick, nor half so weary."

Despite retaining an amateur's affection for birds, Muir could not help exercising his acute intellect on whatever he saw. When he commented on bird behavior, it was with pungent accuracy, as in describing the loon's haunting scream; or how the blue grouse in winter moved up into the trees to eat buds and seeds while the mountain quail migrated vertically down the slopes to the foothills. He observed the confrontation of a golden eagle and a hare, which stood calmly in the mouth of its burrow confident that it could duck in faster than the predator could strike. Alert to how the birds adapted to their habitats, Muir often mentioned their feeding habits. He entertained Emerson by describing how the pileated woodpeckers eat acorns, preferably wormy ones, and store them against the winter in the bark of trees like squirrels.

John Muir had a favorite bird, the dipper, a mountain dweller like him, as were his preferred animals, the Douglas squirrel, the mountain sheep and the grasshopper. He wrote frequently and lovingly of the ouzel, to him a symbol of priceless mountain wildness, "looking like a little clod of mud" with "the oddest daintiest mincing manners" but miraculously adapted to its life around and within mountain streams and a brilliant singer the year round. It is possible to follow the evolution of how he described the ouzel from the first journal entries made in the mountains to several eloquent pages in *My First Summer in the Sierra* and on to its life history in *The Mountains of California* and to the gracious summary in *Our National Parks*. The extended essay in *The Mountains of California,* which recalls Wilson and Audubon but outdoes them in precision and especially in warmth, shows Muir's ability to give life to one small actor in the outdoor drama. In *Our National Parks* Muir characteristically saw the bird as integrally blended with its environment: "No wonder he sings well since all the air about him is music; every breath he draws is part of a song, and he gets his first music lessons before he is born; for the eggs vibrate in time with the tones of the waterfalls. Bird and stream are inseparable, songful and wild, gentle and strong."

The perspicacity of Muir's bird observations show him the intellectual equal of any ornithologist, but he had no interest in the empirical views of the specialist. Instead he preferred to think that "a bird is not feathers of certain colors, or members of a certain length—toes, claws, bill, gape, culmen—and of a group so and so. This is not the bird that at heaven's gate sings. . . ."

Like Audubon and Wilson, John Burroughs and John Muir knew each other, shared some fundamental ideas, but went their own ways in personal outlook. Burroughs met Muir in New York in 1893, and Muir visited Burroughs at Slabsides three years later. They both went on the Harriman Alaska expedition in 1899, occupying adjacent ship cabins; for the voyage John O'Birds was designated historian and John O'Mountains, glaciological adviser. By the end of this magic journey they had become friendly rivals who traded teasing jibes, and once they entertained the other travelers with country dances. Later they traveled together to view the Petrified Forest, the Grand Canyon, and Yosemite Valley. Muir wondered if Burroughs could appreciate these vast specta-

A detail of Audubon's portrait of dippers, Muir's favorite mountain bird.

cles of nature, but Burroughs, if well fed and rested, responded to them with quiet warmth.

Before becoming popular spokesmen for the out-of-doors at either end of a continent, the two naturalists shared some formative experiences: both spent their childhoods on farms and always had a love of the outdoors; each had to find his own education and each adopted ideas stemming from transcendentalism. Burroughs's family worked a well cleared farm settled by his grandfather in the gentle rolling hills below the Catskills. Burroughs's father held to a Christian ethic that kept him at work for the family's good. Muir's father let religion literally carry him away from home, leaving John to labor at wresting a frontier farm from the wilderness.

Burroughs, coming from more benign origins, became a simple gentle man who loved to stay home and mull the footprints around his doorstep, whereas Muir traveled everywhere in quest of the grand gestures and epic changes of nature. Modest and calm, Burroughs was a recluse, who in late middle life built a woodland retreat. Muir after years of searching out the lessons of the mountains came down from them to farm and have a family. In later life he devoted his many talents to conserving the nature that had nourished him.

Guided by the New England school of transcendentalism, the basis of contemporary natural history, both Burroughs and Muir learned the catechism of nineteenth-century nature worship: that the outdoors had its own continuous, generative forces, constant only in change, linking part to part in an unbreakable chain and not beholden to man. Perhaps both naturalists' religious fathers should be thanked for driving their sons to rebel and look to nature for what God created. Burroughs and Muir were both men of deep religious feeling, based on a theism that found God in all living things.

Each of these practical men, when called upon to serve their families, operated successful farms. Along with their lyrical feelings for nature they could make room for more concrete, even analytic aspects of its appreciation. A more reasoned approach blended with subjective litany so that each reinforced the other. Burroughs, for example, was a teacher, both in the wooded classroom around Slabsides and in the messages of his essays. Muir owed his revelation of the Sierra's glacial origins to scientific deduction aided by dogged independent observation. John Burroughs and John Muir as thinkers on nature played prophetic roles in different ways; each found a way to advance natural history in his own time and to point toward its future course.

Chapter Six

╱╱ ╱╱

The First Fifty Years of the Audubon Movement

*T*oward the end of the nineteenth century bird lovers, both amateur and professional, became passionately concerned about the widespread killing of birds for plumes on women's hats. Several scientists from the newly formed American Ornithologists' Union, writing in a February 1886 supplement of the journal *Science,* issued pleas for the protection of birds based on recent brutal facts of their destruction. Joel A. Allen, curator of birds at the American Museum of Natural History, who had already condemned the shooting of birds for their feathers ten years earlier, made the lead statement. He called for controls on egg collecting and the killing of plume birds, sacrificed at an estimated rate of five million a year for milliners' profit and women's vanity. He offered devastating statistics on the murder of wildlife and urged the public to speak out against the harmful style of wearing plumes. Forty thousand terns met death in one year on Cape Cod, he reported. A village on Long Island supplied 70,000 skins for the hat trade in just four months. One plume dealer prepared 11,000 dead birds in three months for shipment to New York, where a single millinery firm could transform 30,000 birds into adornment annually. It was this threat to birds in the gilded age of high Victorian fashion that first brought wide support for

HAND TAILORED SUIT HATS

PARTICULARLY DESIGNED FOR SPRING OR SUMMER WEA

VERY LATE STYLES BEAUTIFULLY MADE AT PRICES WHICH WILL INTEREST ALL CAREFUL BUYERS.

No. 18K16000 Ladies' or misses' stylish Street or Suit Hat. Is made of fine quality satin finished Jap braid in short front mushroom shape. Hat is trimmed in front with a large natural wing in large twist of fine quality Jap silk, this silk extending in folds around the base of crown. Hat is finished with a half round bandeau of silk velvet and is silk lined. Colors, white, brown, navy or champagne, all with trimming to match. Be sure to state color wanted.
Price ....(If by mail, postage extra, 24 cents.) **$1.19**

No. 18K16010. Ladies' or misses' handsome tailored Suit Hat. Is hand made, on a wire frame, with short front and long, drooping back. Hat is made entirely of all silk pyroxylin braid with large Tam o' Shanter crown. Trimming of this hat is decidedly simple but very swell. It is composed of folds of fine quality chiffon drawn around the crown and finished on left side with four full rosettes of the same material. This is one of the neatest styles shown in our line. Colors, black, brown, navy or champagne, with trimmings to match. Be sure to state color wanted.
Price...... **$2.45**
If by mail, postage extra, 19 cents.

No. 18K16018 The New French Sailor. Wide brim slightly shortened in front. Is entirely made of fine quality taffeta silk with tucks running two ways. This hat is trimmed in front with a large butterfly bow of best taffeta silk to match the hat. A band of folded silk around the crown completes the trimming. The large silk bow is very well wired and will hold its shape. Comes in black, brown, navy or champagne. Be sure to state color wanted.
Price...... **$2.98**
If by mail, postage extra, 20 cents.

No. 18K16002 This stunning Suit Hat at a popular price is made of combination very fine split Jap braid with crown of fine natural Milan braid in white. The edge of braid is draped into a very pleasing mushroom style and caught up very high on the left side with a large crush rosette of silk velvet. Three long quills finish the side trimming. Hat is bound with velvet to match trimming, as is the round bandeau. Comes in natural and brown, natural and navy, natural and dark green, or natural and black. Be sure to state color.
Price.. **$1.49**
If by mail, postage extra, 20 cents.

No. 18K16012 Ladies' small modified mushroom style in a beautiful tailored Suit Hat. Is hand made on a wire frame of best quality imported pull braid. The edge of the brim and crown are prettily trimmed with rows of fluted braid. Very stylish combination in the trimming effect is obtained by the use of three quills artistically pierced through front of hat. These quills are intertwined with long loops of fine quality satin taffeta ribbon held in place with two large trimming pins. The ribbon extends in a fold around the entire crown, adding a pretty finishing touch. Colors, black, brown, or navy. Be sure to state color wanted. Regular $3.50 value.
Our price..... **$2.48**
If by mail, postage extra, 20 cents.

No. 18K16020 Striking ne style in rolli front mus room shap Made on a buc ram frame of fi quality shade taffeta silk. T simple trimmi consistsof one ve large French bo all wired, which e tends entirel across the fro and over the sid of crown. A sple did value at an e ceedingly lo price. Color brown, navy champagne black. Be sure state colo wanted.
Price.. **$3.**
If by mail, postage extra, 25 cents.

No. 18K16006 A beautiful mushroom turban effect in a very clever style. Made of a combination of very fine quality split Jap and imported tuscan straw braid, sewed row and row. The brim is caught up all around in a graceful manner, and the trimming consists of a large rosette of silk velvet centered with a fancy effect of very narrow tuscan braid, the rosette being edged with same material. Two handsome quills are brought through the hat to the left side front. A silk velvet drape extends around the crown to the back and ends in a pretty loop effect. Colors, natural tuscan with brown, navy, black, cardinal or green trimmings. $3.00 value. Be sure to state color wanted.
Our price.. **$1.88**
If by mail, postage extra, 20 cents.

No. 18K16014 One of the most stylish tailor made Suit Turbans shown this year; hand made on a wire frame. Crown and sides are made of finest quality allsilk pyroxylin braid draped artistically in folds. Under brim is made of the finest quality closely tucked chiffon. Hat is trimmed on left side with two large quills, held in place with three cut ostrich pompons. A band of velvet ribbon brought around right side of the hat and finished with jet buckle completes the trimming of this swell walking hat. Comes in black only.
Price **$2.95**
If by mail, postage extra, 20 cents.

No. 18K16022 Ladies' or misses' hand made Suit Hat in very stylish toque effect. Our illustration does not begin to show the beauty of this hat. Frame is entirely covered with silk and hair combination braid in pretty pattern, edge of brim and crown being finished with a wide fluted ruffle of braid. Trimming consists of a very large rosette effect made of rows of best taffeta silk and fluted braid laid in alternating folds. Double wing effect protruding from the rosette gives a finishing touch. The rosette is centered with a large ball pin. Wide folds of taffeta silk extend around the entire crown. Comes in black, brown or navy. Be sure to state color wanted. Real $5.00 value.
Our price...(If by mail, postage extra, 21 cents.).. **$3.4**

No. 18K16016 Elegantly tailored Suit Hat for misses or ladies. This handsome style is hand made on a wire frame with under brim facing of all silk pyroxylin braid, upper brim and crown being made of closely sewed rows of narrow imported hair braid. The simple but effective trimming consists of a wide drape of fine quality black taffeta ribbon laid in folds around the crown and gathered into a twisted drape effect in combination with the braid. On the left side three beautiful quills pierce this rosette. Plain but very stylish model, particularly easy to wear. Comes in black, brown, navy or garnet. Be sure to state color wanted.
Price **$2.98**
If by mail, postage extra, 22 cents.

No. 18K16008 A close fitting pointed front Turban. A stylish suit hat for ladies or misses. Is made of best quality imported hair braid, the upper crown and under brim being in a pattern effect while the sides are done in perfectly plain narrow braid. A drape of good quality taffeta silk fills the space between the upper edge of crown and brim. This silk is brought over the left side and twisted into a pretty knot effect. Three loops of braid complete the trimming of this very stylish hat. Comes in black, brown or navy.
Price **$1.99**
If by mail, postage extra, 16 cents.

The values offered in our lace and embroidery sections on pages 1014 to 1026 deserve your particular attention.

No. 18K1602 Our ver finest an most stylish ha made Suit Hat. Sho front, rolling slightly o the left side with sligh ly drooping brim. Ma of fine quality narro silk and hair brai sewed row and ro Left side is caught u with a wide band fancy crimped ha braid with double ruffle folded and plaited si Long quill is drawn throug this side trimming. Wi drape crown trimming crimped hair braid gives finishing touch to th very handsome hat. Colo black, brown, navy leather. Be sure state color wanted.
Price....... **$3.6**
If by mail, postag extra, 16 cents.

LEFT. Women could order hats with wings and feathers by mail. The Audubon association responded by promoting the birdless hat, above.

bird protection and led to the founding and growth of the Audubon society movement.*

The early Audubon movement started with a rush of popular support, taking inspiration from people everywhere who saw the need to protect birds. George Bird Grinnell, sportsman, editor of *Forest and Stream,* and founder of the first national Audubon society, as early as 1883 was inundated with letters decrying the decline of field birds and those used for millinery, especially gulls and terns. In February 1886 in a *Forest and Stream* editorial Grinnell pleaded for the formation of an Audubon society devoted to bird protection. He had no hesitation in giving it the name of John James Audubon, for Grinnell was a kind of adopted Audubon grandson. He had grown up in the neighborhood of Minnie's Land, the Audubon family compound in upper west Manhattan, and had attended Lucy Audubon's school after her husband's death.

The response to Grinnell's proposal for an Audubon society was overwhelming and went beyond anything he was prepared for. Membership was free and open to all, and within a year and a half 30,000 were enrolled. Letters of support came from such figures as Oliver Wendell Holmes, John Greenleaf Whittier, and Henry Ward Beecher. Grinnell spelled out three objectives for the society: to prevent the killing of wild birds except for food; to halt collecting of nests and eggs; and to stop the wearing of feathers as ornaments. The society's aim was to educate the public, especially women and the coming generation, rather than to gather scientific information. Since a publication was essential to these goals, Grinnell launched the *Audubon Magazine* at the end of the society's first year. He was its editor, and *Forest and Stream,* its financial backer. The magazine was consciously addressed to families and regularly printed children's stories. An appended "Audubon Note Book" gave news of the society, administrative notices, and bird sightings.

Sadly, Grinnell's Audubon society could not sustain its initial momentum and the enthusiasm of a fast start led to just as rapid a collapse. The *Field and Stream* office could not manage the increased paperwork and could not finance *Audubon Magazine,* which folded at the end of 1888. The first Audubon society failed for these reasons: too much centralization with dependence on a single leader and lack of broad

---

*Since the National Audubon Society has had several names during its history and the many state and local societies are variously named, the expression "Audubon movement" will be used here to refer collectively to these organizations and their work.

financial backing from local groups or a dues-paying membership. But within ten years on the state level and fifteen nationally the Audubon movement returned with new leaders astute enough to avoid the errors of the 1880s.

Another organization for bird study and protection, the American Ornithologists' Union, was formed in 1883 also in New York City. The AOU is the long-standing professional group of American ornithologists and, though a full discussion is not a part of this book, its origins are tied to those of the Audubon movement and so must be touched on. The AOU was formed just when Grinnell began to hear rising protests about the decimation of birds. The organization of scientists grew directly out of the Nuttall Ornithological Club in Cambridge, Massachusetts, with which it shared both aims and leaders. The Nuttall Club's bulletin in that year became *The Auk,* the venerable journal of scientific ornithology. The AOU set up a structure of committees covering bird nomenclature and classification, anatomy, migration, that problem immigrant the English sparrow and, at the urging of William Brewster of Harvard's Museum of Comparative Zoology, bird protection.

Brewster's appointment as chairman of the AOU's Committee on the Protection of North American Birds marked the formal entry of professional ornithologists into the field of conservation. Brewster went on to serve for forty years as the union's president and assumed the same role in the Massachusetts Audubon Society. In the late 1880s Brewster's committee was on hand to guide the formation of a bird protection movement when Grinnell's national Audubon society folded.

In another article in the *Science* supplement William Dutcher, a successful Manhattan insurance executive and an effective member of Brewster's committee, provided more evidence of the destruction of bird life. Dutcher noted the disappearance of terns from New Jersey in violation of local protective laws for birds, and he documented the complacent acceptance of the faddish feathered hats with a quote from the New York *Sun:* "Miss Brady looked extremely well in white, with a whole nest of sparkling scintillating birds in her hair, which it would have puzzled an ornithologist to classify." The remaining essays in the *Science* supplement bore down on the viciousness of egg collecting, discussed current misconceptions of which birds were harmful and which of use in agriculture, defined effective state bird protection laws, and ended with "An Appeal to the Women of the Country in Behalf of the Birds."

The committee included in the supplement an ideal state law for bird protection, the AOU Model Law, which soon gained renown as the union's most telling contribution to the conservation movement. Devoid of legal verbiage and concisely worded, the Model Law was simple and clear. It first defined the game birds subject to controlled hunting as swans, ducks, and geese; rails, coots, and gallinules; all shore birds (plovers, surf-birds, snipes and woodcocks, curlews, and sandpipers); and turkeys, grouse, partridges, pheasants, and quail. All other birds except the English sparrow were to be fully protected. The Model Law endorsed an ancient distinction between game and non-game birds, traditional categories only recently modified by modern ecology and environmental laws. The AOU protectionists did not explicitly prohibit plume hunting, but they knew that most of the birds killed for plumes came under the protected non-game umbrella. The law also prohibited the destruction of eggs or nests except those of the English sparrow and

William Brewster taking a break in the field.
Massachusetts Audubon Society.

granted scientific collectors license to take specimens if certified—a crucial clause for the ornithologists.

The AOU did little to advocate the Model Law in the state legislatures. Because of its political nature this task fell to the National Association of Audubon Societies. Thanks to the persuasive powers of William Dutcher, then of his successor T. Gilbert Pearson, most state legislatures gradually adopted the AOU Model Law in some form. This early campaign was one of the most effective in bird conservation.

The American Ornithologists' Union spawned another institution devoted to bird study and conservation when in 1885 it proposed an office of the federal government for ornithology. Such was the union's prestige that this was set up forthwith and headed at the outset and for over twenty years by Dr. C. Hart Merriam, an eminent naturalist in a number of fields. The agency, at first a section of the Department of Agriculture called the Division of Economic Ornithology and Mammalogy, conducted research on the value of wild animals, their relation to agriculture, and their use as food when hunted.

Hart Merriam was deeply committed to developing a scheme of zonal distribution for wildlife. His office prepared zonal maps which underwent constant study and revision as biological statistics accumulated. So it became appropriate to give the office a new name as the Division and, in 1906, the Bureau of Biological Survey. The ornithologists under Merriam such as A. K. Fisher, T. S. Palmer, Henry Oberholser, and Alexander Wetmore turned out fine technical studies of bird life on such matters as predation, migration, and eating patterns, usually published as departmental bulletins. Eventually the bureau expanded its program to include supervision of bird-banding and federal sanctuaries, an area which required working closely with the Audubonists. It evolved into the Bureau of Fish and Wildlife and in 1939 in a political maneuver moved to the Department of the Interior where, following bureaucratic titular progress, it is now called the Fish and Wildlife Service.

Unfortunately the American Ornithologists' Union experienced the same birth pangs that fatally weakened the first Audubon society. After half a decade of enthusiastic endeavor the initial momentum lapsed and interest fell off. By 1890 only two states, New York and Pennsylvania, had passed any sort of Model Law, which they soon weakened with amendments. In 1888 Brewster had to resign as chairman of the bird protection committee due to ill health. The AOU wisely felt that they could not effectively agitate for popular understanding of bird protection through public education, nor could they lobby for supporting laws. A broad-based institution of wide appeal was needed to spread the gospel of bird appreciation and protection.

Sentiment was again moving toward support for an Audubon society, this time spurred on by the specialized advances made by the AOU and by Merriam's office. In 1894 William Dutcher and Frank Chapman, a young curator of birds at the American Museum of Natural History, revived the bird protection committee, but recognized that without popular backing they could not fight the war against plume hunting. In 1901 Dutcher devoted himself to founding the National Committee of Audubon Societies, and by serving both it and the AOU he provided useful liaison between amateur birding and ornithology. Chapman, realizing that *The Auk* was not the appropriate journal to handle the flood of minor birding reports that poured in, in 1899 founded his own magazine, *Bird-Lore,* which the Audubon movement was to use as its organ.

The vital impulses of the Audubon movement, as Grinnell's intervention had already made clear, arose spontaneously from the bird-loving public. The birth of the state Audubon societies occurred in response to the indignation of one bird lover whose efforts led to the founding of the first state Audubon society for Massachusetts in 1896. Mrs. Augustus Hemenway, sitting in her parlor in the Back Bay district of Boston one winter morning, came upon an account of a desecrated heronry written by T. Gilbert Pearson, who was then a young bird explorer and later the Audubon association's secretary and president. He spared his reader no gruesome details:

> I had expected to see some of the beautiful herons about their nests, or standing on the trees nearby, but not a living one could be found, while here and there in the mud lay the lifeless forms of eight of the birds. They had been shot down and the skins bearing their plumes stripped from their backs. Flies were busily at work. . . . This was not the worst; in four of the nests young orphan birds could be seen who were clamoring piteously for food which their dead parents could never again bring them. A little one was discovered with its head and neck hanging out of the nest.

Mrs. Hemenway did not hesitate. That day she called in several friends and they went through the social directory ticking off the names of ladies in the plume-wearing set, who were then urged to join in forming a society for the protection of birds. This group, including several men interested in hunting or ornithology, met at Mrs. Hemenway's home on February 10, 1896, and formed the Massachusetts Audubon Society.

Its stated purpose was "to discourage the buying and wearing, for ornamental purposes, of the feathers of any wild birds, except ducks and gamebirds, and to otherwise further the protection of native birds." Within months the phrase "except ducks and gamebirds" was deleted from this statement, giving the Massachusetts society a more comprehensive program of protection than the AOU Model Law, which allowed the hunting of game birds. The Massachusetts society elected William Brewster its president and soon had a membership rich in New England talent. Its officers included the historian Charles Francis Adams, the nature writer Bradford Torrey, Henry L. Higginson, Maine author Sarah Orne Jewett, and Elizabeth Cary Agassiz, founder and first president of Radcliffe College and wife of the great Harvard naturalist. Before a year had passed the society had nearly 1300 members, including 384 schoolchildren.

From its inception the Massachusetts Audubon Society has been an enduring leader among the state groups. The bird study it has sponsored, starting with George Mackay's work on the gulls and terns of the local coasts, has contributed to both science and conservation. The number and quality of its sanctuaries are outstanding, and it has trained leaders like Carl Buchheister, later president of the national society.

Evidently by the mid- and later 1890s popular sentiment was prepared to encourage the founding of other state Audubon societies. In the same year Pennsylvania followed Massachusetts, and in 1897 nine more societies were formed in Connecticut, the District of Columbia, Illinois, Maine, New Hampshire, New Jersey, New York, Rhode Island, and Wisconsin. The strongest response at first was in the East, as was true of the national association. But within another year the movement was spreading west as societies were formed in California, Indiana, Minnesota, Ohio, Tennessee, and Texas. The decline in promoting bird protection due to the failure of Grinnell's organization and of the AOU's early efforts was reversed by this surge of popular enthusiasm. The AOU bird protection committee, now thriving under William Dutcher's leadership, also benefited from the spread of the state societies. By 1905 twenty-eight states, one territory, and the Northwest Territories of Canada had accepted the Model Law. Dutcher accomplished this marvel of legislative persuasion with the support of the state Audubon societies, which sometimes joined him on the lobbying circuit. He and others now felt a need for a national coordinating agency to guide birding activities.

Consequently representatives of the state societies and of the AOU met in November 1901 in New York, thereafter always the seat of the Audubon movement, and formed a loose umbrella organization of state societies, calling it the National Committee of Audubon Societies. William Dutcher chaired the organizational meeting and the resulting committee. Part of the program of the new organization was to provide liaison between the professional ornithologists and the Audubon movement. Dutcher first coordinated the work of both groups, and cooperation between them endured through men like Frank Chapman and his popular successor at the American Museum, Robert Cushman Murphy, president of the Audubon association in the late 1930s. The professionals considered themselves the certified leaders in the field but, just as the AOU promoted the Biological Survey to oversee government work in bird study and protection, it came to rely on the Audubon movement as its link to the general public. For decades the two groups shared a number of leaders, and not until thirty years later was there any question of conflict of interest due to dual office-holding.

A crucial factor in directing the national movement was the relation in function between the state societies and the central organization in New York. It was decided, because of the earlier development of the state groups and their instant success, that state societies would maintain their individual identity, while the national committee would constitute no more than a loose federation, in the manner of a holding company with independent subsidiaries. To some extent this arrangement persists today, though it has sometimes caused problems of shared membership and financing between state and national organizations. Year by year the national association has gained power through its publications, growing endowment and membership, and the resulting more ambitious programs. Progressively as they gained more centralization and power, the national leaders were able to dominate the state societies by providing increasing financial and other less tangible support. In many states, for example, joining national Audubon results in a bonus membership in a state society. But some state societies, especially in New England, still adhere to the 1901 agreement and insist on autonomy, and a few other states lack Audubon organizations altogether. Undoubtedly this irregularity in organizational patterns has somewhat weakened the Audubon effort over the years.

By 1905 the central Audubon committee had attracted enough gifts and bequests, including some real property, to require defined legal status. It therefore incorporated and took a new name, the National Association of Audubon Societies for the Protection of Wild Birds and Animals, Inc. Dutcher became president, and the organization's office moved from his home to a room on Broadway. At that time a statement of aims appeared in *Bird-Lore:* to hold meetings, lectures, and exhibitions about wildlife and its protection; to publish books and maintain a library on this subject; to work in cooperation with the federal and state governments, and with natural history and state Audubon societies, to disseminate knowledge of birds; to seek a permanent endowment of $1 million; to assist and organize local societies; to maintain and enlarge a program of wardens in sanctuaries; and to circulate books on nature in remote rural areas. The association achieved all these goals and more, except the last.

William Dutcher put the Audubon agenda more succinctly and even with some bite: it aimed to reach the unthinking class through education and to control the selfish through law and by creating refuges protected by a warden system. It seems curious that the summary of policy in *Bird-Lore* stressed education, Dutcher's first point, but said little about bird protection, the organization's other and most urgent goal at the time. With its heritage of AOU ideals passed along by Dutcher, the Audubon association from the start directed its energies to bird preservation. Born in the crisis brought on by the massacre of shore birds—egrets, gulls, terns, spoonbills and pelicans, cormorants, cranes, and every kind of heron—and also field and wood dwellers, the Audubon movement's imperative was to fight the plume wars, as they are called, on the broadest front. Nothing can fuse a new organization's sense of purpose like a call to battle. The Audubon association might not have started with such promise without the pluming massacres. Some fifteen years after its founding through its campaign of legislation, courting public opinion, and sanctuaries, the association had largely won the plume wars and so justified its ideals through action. The Audubon movement, a little taken aback by its own success, had now to scratch about for other issues. None was ever found that was quite so pressing and dramatic.

Women first showed off bird roosts on heads and hats in the 1870s when designers concocted this vulgar fashion as a manifestation of the Gilded

Age. Little did these fashionably dressed ladies of the late Victorian decades know that their decorative dead birds would provide motivation for a popular coalition to preserve living birds. After the turn of the century the counterattacks of the Audubon movement, Congress, the state legislatures, and other allies slowly stopped the killing, though illicit pockets of plume commerce turned up as late as 1940.

In 1886 when the fashion was raging, a young birdwatcher took two famous walks to judge its impact. His choice of habitat was unusual, New York's busiest shopping district along Fourteenth Street, and the birds he observed were dead, perched whole or in parts on women's hats. The birder was Frank Chapman, later assistant and successor to J. A. Allen, but at the time a commuter to a bank. "It is probable," he wrote in his autobiography, "that few if any of the women knew that they were wearing the plumage of the birds of our gardens, orchards and forests." Yet the number and variety were astounding: of the forty species in all, the cedar waxwing numbered twenty-three, there were twenty-one flickers and common terns, followed by sixteen bobwhites, fifteen snow buntings, and nine Baltimore orioles. More of the birds came from woods and field than from the shore, represented by eight species. Some of the more surprising victims were the brown thrasher, blackburnian and blackpoll warblers, a northern shrike, a pileated woodpecker, and a saw-whet owl.

Plumes from snowy egrets were in greatest demand for hats. *Samuel Grimes.*

The popularity of field birds for hat roosts diminished as demand grew, because they made fleeting targets and were difficult to bag. Some time after Chapman's listing the focus of slaughter shifted to larger shorebirds which nested in colonies vulnerable to mass destruction. The two egrets especially, because of their exotic breeding plumes ("aigrettes"), the ibises, all kinds of sandpipers, and even ordinary herring gulls were favorite targets, and within a few years their populations plunged toward extinction. W. E. D. Scott, an ornithologist at Princeton University, made a heartrending tour of the Florida coast in 1887 and reported to *The Auk* that the plume hunters not only murdered the more common species but also cormorants, pelicans, frigate birds, and spoonbills. It is hard to conceive that this fad once decimated such familiar birds as the herring gull, lesser yellowlegs, egrets, and ibises, reducing their numbers to the danger point. Other less common birds like the roseate spoonbill and the curlews may not have fully recovered today from the mass murders of a hundred years ago, and they may never.

The Audubon movement responded to this critical situation with campaigns on several fronts: in the political sphere its officers lobbied for legal protection; in the field, wardens patrolled sanctuaries; and in the classroom the educational program offered teachers and future generations the joys of bird appreciation. The battles in the plume wars that directly concern conservation, such as those related to laws and government sanctuaries, will appear in the next chapter. What the New York Audubon association undertook to do about the plume and other issues is most authentically told in *Bird-Lore.*

Frank Chapman, founder of this monthly journal in February 1899, personally remained the sole owner, publisher, and editor of *Bird-Lore,* America's most popular birding magazine, for thirty-five years. It was a role he much suited. Born in 1864, early enough to know and admire older all-around naturalists like John Burroughs and Theodore Roosevelt, Chapman could still join the coming generation of ornithologists during training at the American Museum of Natural History under J. A. Allen and George Sennett, whom he later succeeded. Although without academic training in ornithology, he became a regular field researcher, and a pioneer in bird photography who was also committed to educating the public through his magazine. At the museum one of his principal interests was the production of habitat groups, or dioramas.

Before issuing the first number of *Bird-Lore,* Chapman contacted the state Audubon societies. He sought their support and in return offered to publish their news. While it remained a private venture, *Bird-Lore* from the beginning had links of mutual benefit to the Audubon movement. When the national association was formalized in 1905, its relation to the magazine was guided by an unwritten understanding that endured with little strain for thirty years. Audubon members received the magazine at production cost, and the association paid for the sections it produced in its own cause: the educational department addressed to its school clubs, the executive department recording the central office's political and conservationist work, and an annual report, covering both national and state organizations and published since 1905. In this way *Bird-Lore* gained many automatic subscribers and thus a larger press run with a smaller unit price, and the Audubon association had an outlet which drew together its membership.

Frank M. Chapman, bird curator, conservationist, and editor of *Bird-Lore*. *Department of Manuscripts and University Archives, Cornell University Libraries.*

In 1917, however, wartime shortages drove up production costs and threatened the low subscription rate. Then, with the common touch which was one of his virtues as editor, Chapman polled his readers to ask whether a higher price or reduced size was more acceptable. Loyally the readers chose the increase in price.

Bird-Lore in its first three decades under Chapman was a modest publication, but it had a broad, even sometimes folksy appeal, and its staff was talented. Dutcher considered it "scientifically correct and correctly popular." Chapman avidly believed that the camera was an invaluable birding tool, and his magazine was strewn with bird photographs, some brilliant, others barely distinct. In the early issues the birds depicted were often stuffed. In 1900–1901 the nature writer Edwin Way Teale counted eighty-eight photographs of mounted specimens versus seventy-six of living birds, some in zoos, on the pages of *Bird-Lore*.

Chapman struck a consistent and appropriate tone in his editorials and in the articles he elicited, somewhere between the voice of an informed teacher, who could simplify without talking down, and that of a committed salesman, with an occasional touch of the boy scout leader or country preacher. Readers submitted brief reports of bird sightings or of experiences which kept them involved in the sport. The editor patiently accepted and printed these, appending corrective comments with restraint. He never seemed to mind reporting another albino robin or a flock of evening grosbeaks at the winter feeder. This policy of popular response was an outgrowth of Grinnell's journalistic touch in his *Audubon Magazine.*

Once the national Audubon association was formed, talent soon came forward to manage its sections in the magazine. Mabel Osgood Wright, a native New Yorker and Chapman's close friend, a trenchant and successful writer, later president of the Connecticut Audubon Society and founder of Birdcraft Sanctuary (which is still extant in downtown Fairfield) took over the executive department. Her reports of administrative work were not just factual but eloquent with a crusading zeal that kept the daily work rolling.

For the schools department President Dutcher summoned T. Gilbert Pearson from North Carolina. Pearson, raised a Quaker in rural Florida, attended Guilford College in North Carolina, earning his way by supplying bird specimens to the college museum. While traveling to learn more about American natural history, he met Dutcher, who urged him to organize an Audubon society in North Carolina. Pearson did this so effectively that the state society gained the right to recruit North Carolina game wardens. His society earned a unique status by serving as a direct arm of state conservation.

Dutcher then persuaded Pearson to come to New York and work part-time for *Bird-Lore*. Pearson was a graceful public speaker, conservative but attuned to the give-and-take of state politics, and a tireless

In the 1930s, *Bird-Lore*'s old cover was enlivened by Roger Tory Peterson.

traveler and worker. In a few years he became the secretary of the Audubon association. When a stroke paralyzed Dutcher in 1910, Pearson served as its acting head until Dutcher's death ten years later, and then succeeded to the top post for the next fourteen years.

Bird-Lore, like any lively organism, evolved over time. In 1914 the Audubon association added a Department of Applied Ornithology, concerned with questions of economics and feeding, under Herbert K. Job, a professional field researcher. Job submitted frequent reports of his work to *Bird-Lore,* replacing an earlier listing of related information from the Biological Survey. Three years later *Bird-Lore* added a regular department called "The Season," which gathered regional reports from various contributors and sought to treat patterns of bird movements. This feature was first edited by Charles H. Rogers of the American Museum of Natural History, and later by J. T. Nichols and then William Vogt. In 1937 an association employee, Joseph Hickey, instituted a breeding bird count, and *Bird-Lore* regularly published the tabulations he gathered from a network of agents.

The association was notably successful in keeping up a fine level of talent in departmental writers. Pearson moved on from the education department to administrative responsibilities about 1910 and therefore took over the executive reports. Arthur A. Allen was an inspired choice to replace him. Allen, a professional ornithologist and professor at Cornell University, had a finely tuned light touch in addressing the school clubs. He was also one of the most talented bird photographers of his generation, another benefit to *Bird-Lore.* Later in the 1930s the polymath birder Roger Tory Peterson held the post of schools editor. The emphasis on this department in *Bird-Lore* and the quality of its successive editors bear witness to the Audubon association's commitment to education for the young.

During the long stable tenures of president Pearson and editor Chapman *Bird-Lore* changed little except for modest expansion to add several new features. In each issue the articles led off; they concerned topics like birding expeditions, the life history of a species, and new techniques in bird photography (other optical aids like binoculars and telescopes were less often discussed), birders themselves with profiles of founding fathers like Burroughs, Grinnell, J. A. Allen, and Elliott Coues, and historical sketches of birding groups such as the Nuttall Club, the AOU, and the Audubon societies.

Bird-Lore was always alert to the latest crisis in conservation and included discussion of issues ranging from aggression by cats and house wrens and the killing of hawks and owls to high bridges and lighthouses, automobiles and oil spills. Sanctuaries under state, local, Audubon society, or private auspices were the subjects of articles that gave particular attention to the private sector, especially William Watson Woollen's refuge near Indianapolis, Bird Haven in Olney, Illinois, created by Robert Ridgway, Mabel Wright's Birdcraft in Fairfield, Connecticut, and E. A. McIlhenny's controversial hunting preserve and egret refuge at Avery Island on the Louisiana gulf coast.

Following the articles came the field notes, short reports of sightings and every kind of personal adventure in the bird world submitted by readers. Book reviews, terse and bland, were mostly written by the editor, and Chapman's editorial might air several issues of the day in succinct paragraphs.

In the Audubon association's pages the school material led off, usually centering on a simplified life history of one species or family or perhaps the mechanics of some portion of bird anatomy such as the bill or claws. Every aspect of the lesson was amply illustrated, and it was designed to be distributed to the school clubs as reprints. The association's executive department came next, reporting the concerns of the central office. Once a year the annual report of the Audubon association appeared, and early in the year there was a tabulation of the nationwide census of birds during Christmas week (see Chapter Fifteen).

The stability and slow, confident growth of *Bird-Lore* over thirty successful years also charted the effective progress of its affiliates, the local Audubon societies. Where all went well with both partners, there seemed little need to change. But when *Bird-Lore* reached the age of thirty, and the Audubon movement approached fifty, events forced change on them both.

Chapter Seven

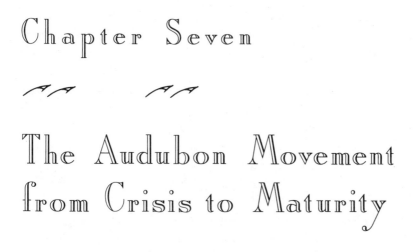

The Audubon Movement from Crisis to Maturity

In the 1930s the Audubon movement, stable in leadership and purpose until then, made the turning to modernity. The crises of the Depression years forced both the association and *Bird-Lore* to rethink their policies. Their history falls into two periods before and after the crises of the Hoover and Roosevelt years. Money of course became more of a problem. By 1933 *Bird-Lore* had to cut back, and the national Audubon association found fund raising more difficult. Its membership was defecting due to the general financial picture but also to crises within the association.

In central birding circles it seemed a time for new blood, and in any case the moment had come for the old warriors, Pearson and Chapman, to retire. Pearson, in some degree forced out by critical attacks the association was then trying to parry, withdrew in 1934. Kermit Roosevelt, Teddy's son, briefly replaced him, followed within three years by Robert Cushman Murphy, and John H. Baker, an investment banker and chairman of the Audubon board, moved into the new post of executive director. At the same time Chapman retired from the editorship of *Bird-Lore* and sold his magazine to the national Audubon association.

Once again in a time of change, the central Audubon movement was able to locate some fine talent. William Vogt had taken charge of "The Season" as associate editor of *Bird-Lore* under Chapman, and he was now ready to step into the editorship. Vogt's career had some sharp turning points, brought about by his passionate and vociferous concern with conservation. One of his best services to birders was to encourage Roger Tory Peterson to publish his innovative *Field Guide to the Birds,* which came out in 1934, dedicated in part to Vogt. Vogt and Peterson together revamped *Bird-Lore.* The editor wrote hard hitting editorials, and the bird artist designed striking covers that were partly in color. Peterson pumped new life into the schools department, while other young talent in the association fanned out toward all corners of bird study and protection, sending in occasional reports to *Bird-Lore.* These scouts included A. H. Hadley, lecturer and Pearson's friend and assistant; Richard Pough, a field guide author in charge of Audubon's campaign for predators; Allan Cruickshank, the virtuoso photographer then serving as the association's agent for Long Island; and the ebullient Robert Porter Allen, supervisor of sanctuaries and field investigator for threatened species.

The clublike informality of Audubon administration could not survive in this difficult period. Director Baker and editor Vogt were both characters of strong mind. When, inevitably, they clashed and Vogt agitated to line up the office staff behind him, the trustees naturally sided with the executive director and the editor had to go. In 1939 Vogt removed himself far from the scene, taking a post with the Peruvian government to do research on cormorants and their guano. He later published his brilliant book *Road to Survival,* as seminal to the conservation movement as Rachel Carson's *Silent Spring.* His concern with conservation, especially in South America, led him to espouse one of its most fundamental methods, birth control—ironically a cause the Audubon society has recently come to support. Vogt ended his career as president of Planned Parenthood, a cause not so remote from bird conservation, since both movements seek to aid the interdependent ecologies of today's world.

After the crises of the early 1930s and the resulting changes, *Bird-Lore,* as an exclusively Audubon publication, more closely reflected association policies. Chapman had pointed out in a *Bird-Lore* editorial of December 1925 that the entire nature of birding had changed, and its spokesmen like him could only follow along. The numbers of birders had increased, and ornithologists were more specialized; the collecting of specimens had all but ceased, and students watched live birds, identifying them by behavior as well as by appearance; museums replaced personal collections as centers of research; and bird-banding and photography became new tools of both scientists and laymen. All these changes led ornithologists and birders alike to a broader outlook, to interests beyond taxonomy and anatomy in areas like color determination, migration patterns, the derivation of species, and sex and nesting rituals.

The chief officers of the national Audubon association were no longer birdwatchers like Dutcher and Pearson but a shipping executive and occasional explorer, Kermit Roosevelt, and a banker, John Baker, men who looked first to national political issues rather than to the needs of birds. In early 1941 Chapman's charming name *Bird-Lore* was dropped in favor of *Audubon Magazine,* a title which stressed the proprietary organization and its history going back to Grinnell's days. This change coincided with the upgrading of the association's name to National Audubon Society in 1940.

A junior Audubon club with the fruits of their labor. *Department of Manuscripts and University Archives, Cornell University Libraries.*

Another Audubon tradition slid into history in the 1930s: the school club section of *Bird-Lore,* which once reached almost four million children at a time, disappeared. Instead the association organized a summer camp for science teachers on a Maine island, headed by Carl Buchheister, later Audubon president, and enlivened by the energy of Allan Cruickshank. Audubon's educational efforts, apparently reduced, were focused more diffusely on the teachers of bird students and no longer directly on children. Just after the war the society developed the vastly popular Screen Tours of slides and films, also aimed mainly at adult audiences. The bird notices from everywhere and executive news prominent in *Bird-Lore* now appeared in a supplement called *Audubon Field Notes,* the predecessor of today's *American Birds.*

After William Vogt's departure the editorship of *Bird-Lore,* soon to be *Audubon Magazine,* passed to Peggy Brooks, the association's librarian. This choice seemed to indicate that the magazine was becoming more professional and more allied to the organization. When Brooks married her colleague Joseph Hickey and moved away, her successor was another capable woman, Eleanor Anthony King. In 1956 a learned bird man and sensitive all-around naturalist, John Terres, began the longest tenure as editor since Chapman. Terres, a former government scientist, brought a serious tone to the magazine, encouraging scientifically sound articles with footnotes and for the first time paying the contributors.

After World War II color printing of reproductions became feasible, and the first full-color cover of *Audubon Magazine* appeared in 1952. Since 1961 these have become standard, and the present editor, Les Line, a skilled photographer of wildlife in the Chapman tradition, has let color flow throughout the magazine. Its illustrations now are eye-opening but more artistically appealing than scientifically informative, and the articles are by professional nature writers. *Audubon* today is a glossy production that bears little resemblance to its homey predecessor, *Bird-Lore.*

One of the most successful undertakings of the National Association of Audubon Societies, begun as soon as it was formed, was to provide wardens for bird sanctuaries and coastal breeding areas. Congress, sensing the popular appeal of bird protection, had passed the Lacey Law in 1900 to halt foreign and interstate commerce in birds if state law protected them first. But there was a glaring flaw in efforts to help the

Audubon warden on the
lookout for plumers at
Bird Island sanctuary
near Gainesville, Florida.
From *Bird-Lore*.

birds by law or by creating refuges. Enforcement in the field was vital. Lawmakers seemed to assume that local police would provide the expected constraint, but this was not feasible for bird colonies on remote breeding islands, where plumers went unhindered to do their mayhem.

The suggestion that the Audubon association dispatch wardens to police bird areas came from an unexpected quarter. Abbott Thayer, a New Hampshire artist and bird student, first broached the need to William Dutcher about 1901. Dutcher was enthusiastic; if Thayer could find the money, the association would run the program. Thayer was successful in raising funds for this specialized patrol force, money thereafter called the Thayer Fund. The states cooperated by naming the guards deputy game wardens and giving them authority to arrest. One purpose of the national Audubon committee when it formed was to coordinate the warden program. As early as 1904 thirty-four wardens were on patrol in ten states, including ten in Maine, eight in Virginia, and four each in North Carolina and Florida.

The Audubon association initially emphasized protecting the New England coast, Maine above all, since the AOU had first detected plume hunting in the northeastern gull and tern colonies. Herring gulls at the time bred only in downeast Maine beyond Penobscot Bay. Though the state had an older law protecting terns, enforcement had never been feasible until the Audubon wardens went to work. To back up efforts for the gulls in Maine, Dutcher persuaded New York, seat of the millinery industry, to change its bird law to block the commercial importation of that species. The association allocated $500 of the Thayer Fund to patrol the Maine coast, and Dutcher was astute in recruiting experienced outdoor men as wardens, often drawn from the ranks of lighthouse keepers or fishermen. The program used part-time personnel, since the greatest threat to the birds was during the breeding season. Dutcher took the trouble to visit and get to know the wardens and wrote them frequently. The early focus of warden protection soon shifted from New England to the South and especially Florida, as the plumes of egrets, herons, pelicans, and other southern species became the rage.

The term "plume wars" has been applied to the battle first against the milliners and also to the front line where Audubon wardens confronted the feather robbers. The expression may seem too strong but the issue in time exploded into violence. 1905 was a year of triumph. President Roosevelt at William Dutcher's suggestion created the first national sanctuary at Pelican Island in the Indian River of Florida, guarded by Audubon wardens. Fifty-two more government refuges soon followed, decreed by T.R. and his successor, President Taft. But 1905 was also a year of tragedy for the Audubon association. Its warden for the Cape Sable area of south Florida, Guy Bradley, was murdered in the line of duty by a plume hunter.

Bradley from the porch of his house at Flamingo had observed the schooner of a well-known plumer, Walter Smith, anchoring off Oyster Key. As the warden rowed over to speak to Smith, he heard shots nearby. When close to the ship he saw Smith's son and another man going aboard with two dead egrets; he had caught them red-handed. Smith asked him what he wanted, and Bradley replied he had to arrest his son. Smith said come and get him if you want him, and Bradley, seeing that the plumer was armed, asked Smith to put down his rifle. As Bradley moved his skiff closer, Smith fired a single bullet into Bradley's chest, killing him instantly. His floating body was found the next day by two boys.

Smith was never indicted because witnesses refused to say they had seen the actual shooting, but his house was fired by his own neighbors. The grisly death of Guy Bradley may have driven the Audubonists to greater effort, since that was all they could do about it, and it may have heightened the awareness of a few plumed-hat wearers. More tragic reminders followed: within a short time plume hunters killed two more wardens in Florida and South Carolina, and as late as 1929 a third was shot point blank in the face by an Italo-American small-bird hunter at Jamaica Bay, New York.

The Audubon warden program in its heroic early phase turned out to lead on to more far-reaching solutions. The effort endured and even expanded through the first two decades of this century but then conditions changed. The effort to protect the egrets gained increasing priority. In 1914 sixteen wardens patrolled egret colonies exclusively, while the corps of guards protected around 550,000 birds in all, according to association estimates. A survey of Florida nesting colonies in 1922 concluded that the egret population was still declining, no longer so much from pluming as from casual shooting by tourists and from the theft of eggs by fish crows. Whatever setbacks the campaign for egrets suffered, the results today appear fully to justify the effort to encourage these now plentiful birds.

By about 1920 the Audubon association began to phase out the program of wardens. By then plume hunting was much diminished under new prohibitive laws and women's fashions changed. In addition, the federal government was gradually moving to take over some of the functions of private conservation as these became too overwhelming for smaller organizations to manage. A precedent for centralization had occurred when the U.S. Biological Survey took over the migration studies that an AOU committee had begun.

In 1913 Congress passed a major bird law, the Migratory Bird Act, known at the time as the Weeks–McLean Bill (see Chapter Eight). This legislation undertook to resolve an old troublesome question: who owns wildlife? Common law held that the states did, but in a modern society, informed about migration and looking to wildlife conservation, it only made sense to place control in the hands of the central government. So Congress gave the Biological Survey supervision of all creatures in national forests, parks, and sanctuaries and indirectly elsewhere.

Still moving toward concentrating authority, Congress in 1919 passed a law prohibiting an employee from working at the same time for the government and a private organization. Some of the Audubon wardens were lighthouse keepers, park rangers, and other federal employees, and they now reverted to full government employ. These changes did not mean that the private force of Audubon wardens ceased to exist. They were now assigned, as they still are today, to the association's own sanctuaries, which were beginning to increase. By 1934 Audubon was maintaining wardens in 130 areas under its own supervision.

Creating refuges, a stated aim at the founding of the Audubon association, was more complex than deploying wardens or lobbying for wildlife laws. The establishment of a sanctuary sometimes required research into the ecological needs of breeding and migratory birds before finding suitable land with money to buy or rent it. The legal and budgetary powers of the federal and state governments enabled them to create protected areas, but the National Audubon Society's present chain of about sixty sanctuaries offers a solid contribution to the whole refuge effort. The older ones stretch mostly along the Atlantic and Gulf coasts from Maine islands to lagoons near the mouth of the Rio Grande. The smaller sanctuaries overseen by the state societies bring the number of Audubon refuges close to the federal total of over 400. The national Audubon sanctuary program tended first to concentrate on eastern and coastal regions, perhaps because the movement began a century ago with concern for New England gulls and terns and because wildlife preservation in the west has centered on the huge tracts of federal land there.

At the outset the Audubon sanctuary project had a few setbacks. In its early days of struggling finances its best hope of launching this endeavor was through donation of already established private refuges. Two such hoped-for sites were William Watson Woollen's sanctuary near Indianapolis and Robert Ridgway's farm, which became a bird sanctuary when he retired from the Biological Survey in 1914. But these two good sites slipped through the association's fingers when financing to help Ridgway fell through, forcing him to sell his place, and Woollen decided to bequeath his property to the city as a park. Yet the first two Audubon sanctuaries did result from completed private gifts, and the striking difference between them indicates a willingness to think flexibly. The association did not bring off these projects in refuge creation until its third decade in the 1920s.

These first sanctuaries were in honor of two naturalist-hunters, Theodore Roosevelt and Paul Rainey. When the ex-president died in 1919, sentiment at Audubon headquarters, fostered in particular by Frank Chapman, strongly favored a memorial honoring this leader who had created the first federal refuges. At the association's suggestion the Roosevelt family donated eleven acres of land at the president's home, Sagamore Hill in Oyster Bay, Long Island, adjacent to his grave. Dr. Eugene Swope, appointed to oversee the sanctuary, had the site landscaped to attract songbirds. Bessie Potter Vonnoh received a commission for a sculptured fountain by the gate, supported by a public subscription organized by the Audubon association. By 1927 this work was ready for dedication. In this sentimental sculpture the Audubonists may have strayed from their field; two lightly clothed children—a prepubescent nymphet and a distracted boy—hardly seem appropriate symbolism for Roosevelt's vigorous ideals.

The Rainey sanctuary, the second Audubon holding, has a different scope. Located in marshland on the gulf coast of Louisiana at the strategic base of the Mississippi flyway, it is still Audubon's largest refuge, covering forty square miles of habitat for waterfowl. The story of the Rainey Sanctuary had a few stormy moments, kindled by two picturesque villains, E. A. McIlhenny, an obstreperous local land baron, and Rosalie Edge of New York, an aggressive moralistic conservationist. Audubon President Gilbert Pearson, who liked to dream of a chain of refuges for waterfowl along every flyway, approached McIlhenny about purchasing some of his vast Louisiana tidewater holdings used for shorebird hunting. The owner came back with an offer that was outlandishly overpriced and demanded settlement in a week.

Turning his back on that, Pearson discovered that a large tract next to the McIlhenny hunting preserve belonged to Paul J. Rainey, an avid hunter recently deceased. Pearson persuaded Rainey's sister, Grace Rainey Rogers, a gracious New York philanthropist, to donate a gift of land to the Audubon association in memory of her brother. She not only created the huge Paul J. Rainey Wildlife Sanctuary, but contributed almost $157,000 as an endowment for its upkeep. McIlhenny, meanwhile, was not quiescent. Before Audubon took possession he tore down every structure on the Rainey land, claiming he had built them, and for some years he pummelled the Audubon association for hunting rights in the Rainey sanctuary and the nearby Rockefeller and Russell Sage State Refuges—a license he was never granted. McIlhenny redeemed himself somewhat by establishing a breeding colony for the beleaguered egrets, still active today, in a pond next to his mansion.

In pursuing its sanctuary program the Audubon association had overall success based on the expert knowledge available to it. The Audubonists could tap into the best ornithological advice, and as a private organization, though without the financial resources of the government, could act decisively to acquire land when opportunity came. Two choice examples of the Audubon refuge program must exemplify the whole: the sanctuary on Plum Island near Newburyport, Massachusetts, now nationalized as the Parker River National Wildlife Refuge, and Corkscrew Swamp Refuge in southwestern Florida, inland from Naples. An Audubon affiliate acquired the Plum Island property through the bequest of Annie Brown of Shoreham, Massachusetts, along with a generous provision of cash for the central association, its second largest gift so far. Plum Island, a barrier beach, consists of dunes, salt and artificial freshwater ponds, thickets, and some woods. The island strip, seaward beyond vast marshes, is a stopping or breeding place for every kind of shore bird and some bush dwellers such as the Ipswich sparrow. While not a dramatic landscape at first sight, it is a coastal idyll with a broad ecological mix and a list of more visiting and resident birds than most eastern sanctuaries.

The National Audubon Society bought Corkscrew Swamp in 1954 with the help of multiple gifts. It is a strategically located refuge because it serves two purposes simultaneously. This swampy area of almost

11,000 acres, traversed on a mile of boardwalks, contains the largest extant virgin stand of towering bald cypresses with their semitropical undergrowth offering a romantic evocation of Florida as William Bartram knew it. The picture is enhanced by the nesting wood storks that swarm through the cypresses where this uncommon bird, America's only stork, has its principal breeding colony. In one stroke the Audubon society put its mantle of protection over two unusual species, a rare tree and a rare bird, and it went a welcome extra step by allowing foot access to this precious ecology.

Along with lobbying for protective laws and mapping out sanctuaries and bird education in the schools, the National Association of Audubon Societies found a number of lesser issues falling in its lap. These were of disconcerting variety and turned up in surprising corners. In some cases there was no way to fight back except with repeated sermons, while others were subject to personal or political pressures. A lasting problem was the shooting of predatory birds in the countryside. Long after legal protection had been gained for song and shorebirds, farmers still followed the primitive right to gun down any animal that moved and continued to kill hawks well into the twentieth century. They believed, with no basis but country lore, that these predators were a threat to poultry, even though studies of hawks' eating habits proved that their diets consist largely of small rodents and insects, the farmer's enemies. Even when the scientific facts were known, a cease-fire could be attained only through a slow process of persuasion. The states which offered bounties for dead hawks as late as the 1930s eventually reconsidered and protected them by law, but they made exceptions for the bird-eating Cooper's and sharp-shinned hawks, which conservationists could never bring themselves to tolerate.

Eagles and ospreys posed similar problems, especially in Alaska and wherever fish hatcheries and weirs were vulnerable to raiding. Alaska had long had a bounty of fifty cents for each dead bald eagle, a bird so common there that thousands of claims were made each year. Strong political support for the law came from fishermen, who felt the eagle was cutting into the salmon catch. There was little information available to the Audubon association about the bird's local eating habits with which to build a case in defense. So T. Gilbert Pearson, after inconclusive correspondence with the Alaska governor, went there himself to initiate a study of the eagle's diet. Unfortunately the resulting report was not altogether favorable, concluding that eagles did take some salmon, young deer and small animals though without seriously reducing these populations. Though unable to advance the strongest arguments, the Audubonists continued to fight for the Alaskan eagles, and the bounty was eventually lifted when their population began to decline.

Fishermen also tried to mount a war in the continental states against those birds believed to feed at hatcheries and fish traps, particularly ospreys, herons, cormorants, and pelicans. The association was able to provide exonerating information about what the birds in fact were eating, which generally was not fish caught for commerce. For example, in 1927 a study of 65,000 brown pelicans found that they were eating mainly menhaden, a fish not useful for human consumption.

Other problems in bird preservation were tractable enough so that the Audubon association could close in on them at once. E. I. DuPont de Nemours Company perpetrated one of these when it misguidedly organized a crow-shooting contest at the end of World War I. This ploy had no apparent purpose but to encourage people to buy shells containing powder made by DuPont. So it was not hard for the Audubonists to undercut such destructive recreation with a little publicity. It is a sign of advancing times that Crawford Greenewalt, a later president and chairman of DuPont, is an ornithologist of professional standing and an authority on bird photography and hummingbirds.

Some problems of bird preservation resisted any solution within the Audubon association's scope. There were collisions, for example—literally and symbolically—between bird life and modern technological society, with birds killing themselves by smashing into lighthouses, high bridges, or automobiles. The automobile, indispensable to birdwatchers, does kill birds, but the association could devise little to alleviate the problem beyond an editorial in *Bird-Lore* urging drivers to slow down when passing a flock. Birds flying into broadcasting towers and high bridges, especially night migrators, are another case that resists solution. Complaints arose when the Cooper River Bridge at Charleston, South Carolina, was completed in 1930, since its dense girders span a bird-filled estuary and arch right over an island where white ibises roost. One suggestion was to raise the red aircraft warning lights on the bridge fifty feet higher in hopes that the birds would give it more clearance, but the idea was never tried.

The poet and nature writer Celia Thaxter, whose father was a lighthouse keeper on the Isles of Shoals, recognized all too well the hazard that lighthouses pose for birds:

> Beneath the tall white lighthouse strayed the children
>   In the May morning sweet;
> About the steep and rough gray rocks they wandered
>   With hesitating feet;
> For scattered far and wide the birds were lying
>   Quiet and cold and dead;
> That met while they were swiftly winging southward
>   The fierce light overhead.

The Audubon association once proposed to buy up decommissioned lighthouses from the federal government and tear them down, but this undertaking never came off. *Bird-Lore* noted that a Dutch engineer, Dr. Jacopus Thijsse, had invented a bird-saving device for lighthouses, tiered metal racks below the light where birds could land and perch while they reoriented. Though tried in Great Britain and Holland, this invention remained an unattained refinement in America, costly to erect and objectionable to the Coast Guard because it might block their beams.

Lighthouse equipped with perches to prevent collisions at night. From *Bird-Lore*.

Current problematic issues for the Audubon association are oil spills and the length of hunting seasons for game birds. Oil spills began to pose a problem only when petroleum became widely used after 1920. A 1926 conference among industrial nations produced model legislation on spills, but only England and the United States passed any kind of controlling law, which was limited to oil ships in nearby coastal waters. In 1930 Audubon lobbyists and other conservationists, fiercely opposed by Standard Oil spokesmen, persuaded Congress to extend existing prohibitions to all American waters. No law can prevent shipwreck, and oil spills today occur with growing frequency, whether caused by act of God, errors of command, or military attack. When birds are the victims of spills, the only known solution is to clean them by hand, a painfully laborious task which may not even then save the birds' lives.

In the 1930s the Audubon association was obliged to pressure the Biological Survey and the state legislatures for shorter duck-hunting seasons because drought was diminishing the duck populations. The issue became political and pitted the preservationists against a vociferous corps of hunters. Since the middle position is the likely result of political maneuver, the association won some points and lost others. The final tally went against it when at the end of the decade a dictatorial Secretary of the Interior, Harold Ickes, gave way to popular pressure and expanded the duck season from forty-five to sixty days. But by then the water shortage had eased. The Fish and Wildlife Service is still responsible for adjusting hunting seasons, with the states obliged to follow along. By now the procedure is so established that the authorities make adjustments automatically, according to statistical and demonstrated needs, and so circumvent political wrangling.

*T*he intramural activities of the National Association of Audubon Societies—work that was once reported in the executive department of *Bird-Lore*—regained momentum following the Depression and expanded after World War II to national, sometimes even international dimensions. The growing scope of the National Audubon Society is indicated by the appointment of a president following Carl Buchheister who was not from the bird world but a national figure, Elvis Stahr, former Rhodes scholar, university president, and Secretary of the Army. In the 1960s the society, increasingly concerned for its influence with the lawmakers, retained a full-time lobbyist in Washington. The warden program, cut back by lack of funds in the Depression, came slowly to life again but took on new emphases. The wardens were no longer expected just to guard the birds but now serve as educational officers who conduct tours and supervise sanctuary nature centers. A field agent like Alexander Sprunt, a trained ornithologist who covered South Carolina and Florida for the society, divided his career between spreading the word to visiting audiences and research on southern species.

Other educational endeavors flourished as well. Gone were the days when an Audubon lecturer, arriving at a country church doubling as an auditorium, jacked up the rear of his tin lizzie, ran a belt around a wheel to a generator, and lit up his stereopticon projector, to the delight of an audience who had never seen such a thing. Audubon lectures that were more easily staged continued to be popular after the war, and Audubon Screen Tours became popular across the nation. The summer teachers' camp in Maine has pursued its work in nature education for teachers, and educational centers for both adults and children are active in six locations across the country, two in Connecticut at Greenwich and Sharon, and one each at Dayton, Ohio, in Milwaukee, and in Tiburon, California.

Audubon leaders have always endorsed ornithological research, particularly on declining species. The ivory-billed woodpecker was long in danger of extinction, but, unlike the passenger pigeon and the heath hen which died off under full public scrutiny, reports trickled in that the secretive ivory-bill still lurked in the southern woods. In 1932 Audubon sanctuary director Ernest G. Holt and President Pearson were convinced they saw ivory-billed woodpeckers in Louisiana. Subsequently the association gave an intern, James Tanner, a research fellowship to determine the bird's status. He diligently studied all the sporadic reports and spent much of three strenuous years in the woods. He did find the bird but fewer than two dozen individuals, and it is now accepted that none is left in the southern states. Recently, however, a surviving remnant turned up in Cuba.

Robert Porter Allen, the spirited sanctuary director of the later 1930s and postwar years, specialized in studies of threatened species. His search for the whooping crane's nesting grounds through the vast wetlands of northwest Canada was no less heroic a saga of bird study for its failure to spot the breeding couples. The plight of this delicate and striking American species caught the attention of the Audubon authorities only after the war and, since the whoopers' wintering ground centers on the

Aransas National Refuge along the Texas gulf coast, research on them came under federal authority.

In the late 1930s Audubon investigators including Alexander Sprunt studied the great white heron, then thought to be a species but now classified as a color morph of the great blue heron. Its numbers in the Florida Keys, its only home, were once dangerously low, but they have improved satisfactorily, thanks to a refuge the association set up in 1938. After the war the Audubon society took up the cause of the bald eagle and the California condor. The condor research project was halted for evaluation when Audubon researchers were left with a dead condor chick on their hands as the one worker who had been able to reach its nest was attempting to weigh it.

Over the years the National Audubon Society steadily gained prestige and support as a leading force in the growth of the conservation movement. Through aggressive drives its membership and finances have increased vigorously; among conservation organizations in America it is second only to the National Wildlife Federation. Membership declined only once during the Depression, when it dropped to 3,500, but soon began to swing upward stimulated, some say, by the publication of Peterson's field guide in 1934. At first the number of national members was small, 2,558 in 1915 but 11,000 by 1931. Membership support today totals more than half a million, and there are 540 affiliated state and other societies.

Correspondingly the Audubon financial picture continues to enjoy a rising curve. The early years were financially precarious. William Dutcher had a bold vision for the association and was willing to spend every penny and more to launch its programs, even risking deficit financing. In 1905, the first incorporated year, its income was $12,500. Gilbert Pearson, Dutcher's successor, was a conservative administrator who insisted on putting an annual surplus aside for endowment. With an income of $172,150 in 1924 the endowment had grown to $744,000, and just seven years later these figures were $300,000 in income and nearly $1.5 million permanently invested. In 1929 Pearson reported that the Audubon education program, then near the height of its accomplishment, comprised 123,900 school clubs reaching 3,984,000 children at an annual cost of some $820,000. Yet Pearson uttered a standing complaint that the national association had been unable to reach donors capable of making major gifts. Its support historically had a broad base of modest contributions from the bird-loving everyman, but little help from major philanthropists.

As noted earlier, the Depression years were crucial to the story of the National Association of Audubon Societies, bringing first crisis, then change as the personable clubroom mode of the association's early decades matured into hard-hitting zeal. Contributing factors included not only the financial strictures suffered universally after 1930, but criticisms which seared the association's ethical dignity and cut into its membership support. A *dea ex machina* named Rosalie Edge, Audubon life member and intense conservationist, dealt these blows with relish, without mercy and, it seems, justly.

In 1932 Edge routinely received an envelope of reports from the Audubon association including the annual financial statement. What most members would drop in the wastebasket after a glance she typically scrutinized and found under rentals a curious entry of income for $100,000. Rosalie Edge was well known in Audubon circles as a complainer, and no doubt its administration viewed her as a pest. She alone dared to stand up in annual meetings and put sensitive questions to the officers. These at first concerned how the association intended to respond to a pamphlet critical of its activities written by Willard Van Name, a disenchanted and eccentric curator at the American Museum of Natural History. Her other cohort was Irving Brant, a journalist who supported her views and had brashly attacked the Audubon association for crawling under the wing of the gun manufacturers. Twenty years earlier Winchester Arms had offered financial help to the Audubon board in return for expertise in game management. Some members objected, but Pearson was interested, and the board closed the deal after Grinnell, a former hunter, changed his mind to favor it.

Rosalie Edge sensed she might have a cause of her own against the Audubon powers in the unexplained $100,000. Doggedly she fired rounds of questions at the association offices, and finally the small matter was explained in a way that she did not find small and soon made larger. The income item was from the sale of 289,940 pelts of muskrats, raccoons, and other animals trapped over three years in Audubon's Rainey Sanctuary in Louisiana. Rosalie Edge was shocked at this destruction of animals for commercial purposes by a conservation agency, and she lost no time in demanding that the board put a stop to this anomaly. She also objected to the misleading reference to this activity in the financial statement. She pointed out that the association had concealed its dirty laundry behind a facade of virtue before. In refuting Van Name's attack, it had issued a statement whitewashing itself and President Pearson while discussing his enforced retirement behind closed doors. So the Audubon authorities surprised no one by remaining complacent after Edge's plea for the muskrats. Trapping such animals was a sacred privilege in Louisiana, and the Biological Survey recommended controlling them since the muskrats consumed grasses eaten by the geese that were the refuge's major visitors. These easy rationalizations may have fed on Gilbert Pearson's axiom, insistently repeated, that the Audubon association did not oppose hunting but only wanted to have it reasonably regulated.

When Edge lost the first skirmish in the muskrat war, she revised her tactics and, with Brant, wrote a vivid pamphlet on muskrat trapping, illustrated with photographs of the animals bleeding in steel leg traps. To distribute this exposé she requested the Audubon mailing list and was of course refused. Promptly she took the matter to court and in due time won. Her muskrat pamphlet went out to the membership, and within a year sixty percent of them failed to renew, dropping their total to the level of just before 1910. The society did not recover the pre-muskrat membership figure until 1947. In her second clash with the Audubon powers Edge gained leverage with pressure on the sore point of membership.

Rosalie Edge fretted over other Audubon sins besides the trapping at Rainey refuge. She felt the organization had made itself too comfortable for its commitment to service and demanded that it dissolve its building fund and transfer it to the sanctuaries. Here too she had a point; the association soon bought a patrician Fifth Avenue mansion across from the Metropolitan Museum, and after the war pursued its rise in real estate with a landmark Georgian house farther up Fifth Avenue. (Today it has quarters in a Third Avenue office building.) Edge had gathered her little rebel band into a group called the Emergency Conservation Committee, which operated out of a one-room office and never had a budget over five figures. She directed her puritanical strictures most pointedly at President Pearson, because she felt he kept the association too much in his own pocket. Evidently the Audubon board of directors, deliberating secretly, agreed with her, for it moved to trim Pearson's power dramatically.

Rosalie Edge's next sally was tactically predictable: a campaign to penetrate the board of directors with her own nominees. She collected 1,659 votes to this end but the house nominees won by nearly two-to-one. This setback did not halt her battle since draining the membership by exposing muskrat terror was a message the directors heard clearly.

While her war against the Audubon association did not win every skirmish, it forced the issue of reform. In 1934 Pearson resigned under pressure, and the presidency, occupied by Kermit Roosevelt, became a figurehead post. The operating power came together in the hands of John Baker, an upright and vigorous leader given the title of executive director. One of Baker's first acts was to stop all trapping in the Rainey sanctuary. At this time, as noted, a fresh wave of young talent revived the Audubon headquarters, including men like William Vogt, Richard

Rosalie Edge, with binoculars, and friends at
Hawk Mountain Sanctuary, her creation.
Hawk Mountain Sanctuary Association, Maurice Broun.

Pough, Roger Tory Peterson, Robert Porter Allen, and Allan Cruick-shank. This new blood helped the Audubon association recover some of its momentum.

Once Rosalie Edge saw the national Audubon association in hands she trusted, she directed her watchdog energy and the Emergency Conservation Committee to other causes. Aping an Audubon theme, she published a series of educational materials on nature and directed it to the schools. She took up a cause of her ally Van Name, agitating to save a sugar pine grove near Yosemite National Park, and preserved the trees but lost the volatile Van Name in an argument over how to deal with the park superintendent. She joined others in campaigning to establish the controversial Olympic National Park.

But her crowning coup was in the cause of a rocky hill called Hawk Mountain in the Kittatinny Ridge along the southern rim of the Poconos in northeastern Pennsylvania. Here, she discovered, men came during fall migration to massacre hundreds of hawks that passed overhead, shooting from lust for blood and leaving the corpses and the wounded where they fell. She reported this horror to the Audubon association and suggested it buy up the whole area, but got no response. So she arranged to rent the crucial outcroppings and slopes of the ridge, later bought them, and in 1938 turned the site over to the Hawk Mountain Sanctuary Association. The curator she recruited, Maurice Broun, and his wife, Irma, made Hawk Mountain the protective and research center for hawks it still is. The appeal of Rosalie Edge's Hawk Mountain has grown with the general birding explosion to become, it is likely, the most popular of any independently run refuge.

The events which preoccupied the National Association of Audubon Societies in the early 1930s seem petty, diffuse, and even verging on the comic. But when revolution is due the first shots are not likely to be aimed decisively. After three decades of stability under men like Dutcher, Pearson, and Chapman, the association was ripe for change. The need to revise it was internal, as Rosalie Edge perceived and its own officers slowly and defensively accepted. But more considerations lay on the table than turmoil in the Audubon office. As Chapman appreciated as early as 1925, birding had changed, beginning to leap ahead in popular appreciation, even though ornithologists still shot specimens for study.

The founding leaders of the Audubon association, in tune with their time, were old-style birders. Dutcher was a former hunter who once on

Long Island shot a plover he did not recognize; in seeking its identity the joys of bird study dawned on him. Pearson collected and sold specimens while in college and worked in a traditional natural history museum. Like Dutcher and Pearson the scientific ornithologists were still dissecting and classifying when the Audubon association began. The Audubon movement also went along with the times in focusing on species as defined biological units, first selecting those pressured by plume-hunters, arguing to protect this predator but not that, and helping precarious species like the roseate spoonbill, the great white heron, and the bald eagle.

When Pearson retired in 1934 and leadership passed to John Baker, change began. Baker, though an amateur birder all his life, had been an administrator in the more mundane field of banking. The various interests of the men on his staff indicated the divergent paths now open to the association: Vogt, editor of *Bird-Lore,* was an adamant conservationist; Cruickshank photographed birds with modern esthetic insight; Peterson drew them in a current style and published an experimental field guide, as did Pough; and Robert Allen was a field investigator who studied bird behavior by living intimately with birds. Carl Buchheister, Baker's successor, took decisive steps toward the organization's present philosophy. Buchheister was earlier a teacher, but his later life was given over to the Audubon movement as director of the Maine summer camp, as executive director of the Massachusetts society, and as a ranking aide who was summoned to the president's office in New York.

Carl Buchheister while president of the National Audubon Society. *United States Coast Guard.*

Carl Buchheister was able to take a broad view of the conservation movement as it became a national concern. Baker announced, somewhat after the fact, at the fiftieth annual Audubon convention in 1954 that the society had moved beyond a program of protecting birds toward understanding and conserving whole ecologies with their interlocking life forces. The era of protection, he said, had given way to one of conservation. It was Buchheister who was prepared to turn this change of policy into action. The association leadership bowed to the dictates of history, and that explains why their publications now contain not just bird notes but discussions of soil erosion, polluted water, and acid rain. Today the society is purely a conservation agency and, as noted, has even taken up the cause of birth control, which the exiled William Vogt perceived forty-five years ago as the ultimate solution to the world's ecological ills.

Rosalie Edge, after driving Gilbert Pearson from the temple, seemed content to lay off the beleaguered association and to let John Baker go his way. Not that she found him an ideal leader or hardly an adequate one; she viewed him as an old-time headmaster who could assert some dictatorial authority in the classroom but was merely ineffectual outside. He declined to lobby on conservation issues in Washington because he worried that the association might lose its tax-exempt status, as had the Sierra Club, and this withdrawal from such a major front further piqued Edge's ready anger. But, occupied with other matters, she did not speak out again on Audubon failings.

To her Buchheister arrived like a knight on horseback. He was the first Audubon officer she could respect without reserve, and his immediate plunge into conservation campaigns brought her joy. "I feel myself personally blessed to have lived to see my hopes fulfilled," she said of his succession. At the 1962 annual meeting President Buchheister presented her to his colleagues, who rose as they applauded. Rosalie Edge had rounded a circle from raucous agitation at Audubon complacency to a hero's greeting as the savior of Hawk Mountain. At the time of this redemption she was eighty-five years old and she died three weeks later.

Chapter Eight

Saving the Birds

*B*ird conservation was by no means a new idea when Congress enacted the first major protective law in 1900. Game birds had been of course a valued source of food since the settling of America. Earlier laws had regulated only the killing of game birds, which took precedence because they served man's appetite. Excessive shooting of edible birds was a concern as early as the seventeenth century. The traveler John Josselyn, surveying new England in the late 1600s, complained of the settlers' voraciousness in netting too many pigeons and decried the diminishing population of wild turkeys. The state lawmakers first mapped the path to game bird protection, and later to saving other species. Beginning in the eighteenth century but more often in the early nineteenth, legislators met the need to protect edible game birds by limiting the seasons and types of arms used in hunting. But these laws varied chaotically from one state and county to another and were mostly limited to the East and North. Only in the 1850s did the mid-Atlantic and New England state legislatures begin to broaden their laws to cover non-game species such as songbirds and various others. And it was only in the last two decades of the nineteenth century that bird conservation abruptly caught the attention of both ornithologists and the bird-loving public, when many came to believe then that the situation of the birds was going from bad to desperate.

After the 1890 census the Census Bureau quietly made an announcement that astounded many Americans: the frontier was closed. There was no more unclaimed land between the Atlantic marshes and the cliffs of the Pacific. The migration to the frontier had offered Americans a gift of land that was rich and theirs to use, along with the right to live both off the land and on it. The closing of the frontier signaled the end of an era when the wild woods covered more land than the cornfields. But many Americans refused to give up the frontier vision and continued to pursue its dream of unregulated rights, including access to free game. In the late nineteenth century hunting as a sport, sometimes as a business, was increasing as never before, and its techniques of destruction were becoming more murderous. Even after the passing of the frontier Americans cherished a longing to reenact an earlier age of heroic freedom. Each hunting season offered a way to relive something of the frontiersmen's skill and self-reliance.

Technology and political clout further emboldened the hunters. Game seasons, especially for ducks and waterbirds, the least protected by law, were generous, often stretching from the breeding months to the end of the year. Spring hunting was always controversial, with many states wavering between prohibition and the pressure for more hunting rights. Bag limits were almost farcical and had no effect on sport hunters, who could seldom reach the limit, while professionals and members of some hunting clubs, knowing they could never fill the bag, voluntarily accepted lower limits.

Gun manufacturers offered every device for quickly slaughtering as many birds as possible. Some of these were so vicious that lawmakers banned them within a few years of their invention. But hunters in remote areas where patrols by game wardens were infrequent knew that they could continue to operate outside the law. Large-bore guns, capable of wiping out half a flight of ducks in one shot, were one abomination. These were either swivel guns mounted on the bow of a boat, like a man o'war's raking cannon, or punt guns fired on the shoulders of two men. Around the turn of the century every major gunmaker started to market pump and automatic shotguns. The pump gun could fire six shots in as many seconds when reloaded and cocked by pulling a cylindrical handle under the barrel, while the fully automatic gun fired five shots in four seconds with a mechanism powered by its recoil.

Hunting clubs often had their own networks of stands and blinds. In addition, a well-outfitted hunter after waterfowl could use a sink-box, a small float with its deck at water level and a sunken cockpit in which the gunman could crouch for a lower silhouette. Or alternatively the hunter could take to the water in a small sailboat called a sneakbox, popular in the New Jersey and Maryland bays, with hull and decks tapered to the gunwale in the shape of a pumpkin seed, allowing it to slither silently through the marshes. With such ingenious devices, vicious and uncontrolled hunting was likely to follow.

The most vivid chronicler of the crimes of hunters was William T. Hornaday, director of the New York Zoological Society, a radical and passionate conservationist who attacked not only opponents of animal protection but supporters of it unwilling to go as far as he did. Hornaday's books recorded countless incidents of animal massacre. To mention just two of his horror tales, in 1911 in South Dakota two hunters proudly reported to *Outdoor Life* that they had attacked a flock of geese scared up by a companion as they flew just thirty feet overhead. In seconds they downed twenty-one cripples or corpses with their pump guns. And in Louisiana in 1928 game wardens uncovered what Hornaday called "the champion game-hog record" of the year when they caught eight hunters with 656 illegally killed geese, packed in nine barrels and weighing almost two tons.

Gunners frequently used artificial decoys to lure water birds to their stands and sometimes also baited the nearby water with grain. Much worse was the use of live decoys around the shooting post, kept in range by clipping their wings or blinding them; or of caged birds released on signal to fly upwards a few yards toward an incoming flock until jerked down by leg tethers. Except for the use of wooden decoys, laws eventually curbed most of these unsportsmanly tactics, but usually not until hunters' clubs and magazines had called attention to them.

The founding of the American Ornithologists' Union in 1883 was the first organized response to these transgressions. However, the chief concern of the AOU and its bird protection committee was the decimation of birds by plume hunters, and the prime motivation of the ornithologists, working with the early Audubon movement, was to halt this destruction. Once the educational and political strategies of these organizations gained momentum, state and federal governments responded by initiating better bird protection laws. These laws were immensely helpful as long as enforcement was feasible, but even with legal backing, surprising problems in avian protection kept turning up. One involved ingenious hunters who began to shoot birds from airplanes, a method that might have had a precedent in the Sacramento Valley, where rice farmers hired pilots to fly through flocks supposedly raiding their crops.

The conservation of birds depends directly on knowledge of their habits. For example, both the Biological Survey in Washington and the Audubon association based their campaign to save the raptors on sound ornithological studies of their life histories. This investigation resulted in dividing the hawks into those that were beneficial to the countryside like the red-tailed hawk and destructive predators like the bird-eating sharp-shinned and Cooper's hawks. The public had every opportunity to grasp this distinction through the Audubon and other educational programs, but it was soon found that gunners could not tell one hawk species from another. For want of more widespread education the program to assist the raptors threatened to come apart. But the campaign at least underlined the value of bird education in the schools as promoted by the Audubon association.

So ingrained was the bias against raptors that many states retained bounties on them after other species came under some sort of protection.

Human predator poses with the innocent victims of his hunt.
From *Bird-Lore*.

The bounty on Alaska's bald eagles survived years of Audubon agitation and was finally lifted only when the eagle population dropped. Bird conservationists disapprove of the bounty system because it leads to indiscriminate gunning of misidentified species and ends in more killing than intended. Bounties on predators are today a relic of the past, thanks to widespread appreciation of the ecological axiom that every species has some place in nature, regardless of men's opinions about its habits. Even so, ignorant shooting of large birds in the name of sport continues sporadically in unpatrolled remote country. Gunners may have gone so far as to shoot down a few whooping cranes as they migrated over upper midwestern farmland, possibly because of suspicion of any large birds feeding in fields. In the east two sites once favored by hawk marksmen, the migratory funnels at Cape May Point, New Jersey, and at Hawk Mountain west of Allentown, Pennsylvania, are now peaceful sanctuaries for raptor watching.

The changing circumstances of nature itself can also deflect the intended goals of bird conservation. Inadequate understanding of nature's processes becomes all too clear when efforts to manipulate the ecology backfire and leave the manipulators looking foolish. One such paradox emerged when the founders of the AOU, initially concerned with plume hunting, looked to the northern New England shore and the fate of its gulls. Massachusetts and Maine had already established legal protection for both gulls and terns. But as the gulls thrived, the tern population declined, because where both species shared breeding islands the more predatory gulls ate the terns' eggs. This problem, pinpointed ninety years ago, is still a cause for concern today. The gulls therefore lost their legal benefits—but before long they were endangered again. The Audubon association reported in 1907 that Maine fishermen in Lubec, among other places, were shooting gulls because they raided fish drying racks, wharves, and weirs. The seesaw relation of men to gulls in this instance is just one of the frequent anomalies that nature inscrutably invents to confound the best plans of conservationists.

Other paradoxes in conservation were outgrowths of man's misguided efforts to manage nature. In 1929 the Audubon association discovered that the Game Conservation Institute in Clinton, New Jersey, engaged in training gamekeepers, allowed its apprentices to practice shooting any creature classified as vermin. They had just killed 296 hawks and 179 owls. Even the U.S. Biological Survey was often ambiguous in its policies toward wildlife. For years it carried out a program of poisoning wolves, coyotes, and rodents such as pocket gophers, and thus gained the support of politically vociferous western ranchers. The government expanded this campaign when it was taken over in the 1930s by the CCC, the outdoor national make-work force of the depression years. But as early as 1920 wildlife experts found that birds were also eating the poisoned bait and dying. Such an unwanted outcome shows again that man cannot safely poke his finger into the delicately tuned polyphony of nature at just one point without disrupting its inviolable wholeness.

Another tragicomic drama of man's meddling with nature occurred at Lower Klamath Lake on the California-Oregon border. This lake was a major waterfowl stopover on the Pacific flyway, for which the Audubon association once provided a warden and a patrol boat. But the water level went down and the ducks went away, suggesting to federal authorities that draining the lake would create new farmland, a plan applauded by local farmers, who trusted the wisdom of their public officials. When the lake was empty an infertile alkaline plain emerged, as useless to farmers as to ducks. Thanks to a later government effort in favor of waterfowl sanctuaries, water now fills Lower Klamath Lake again, and the upper lake is the site of a national refuge where waterfowl are welcome.

*I*t is now time to look at some positive results of bird conservation. From the beginning the conservation movement had adopted a primary method, as the most effective thrust of its strategy: legal restraint. The campaign for bird laws started in earnest when ornithologists and amateur birders banded together in the 1880s, but before then, as noted, the states had passed a patchwork of regulations, mostly concerning game birds. As early as 1708, for example, New York enforced a closed season on some hunting grounds for upland game birds—heath hens, ruffed grouse, bobwhites, and turkeys—and later added the woodcock. In 1818 Massachusetts legislated limited seasons for all these birds, and also included the snipe and two songbirds, the meadowlark and robin. This state gave protection to the endangered, now extinct heath hen as early as 1831. Laws like these spread slowly across the eastern and northern states through the first half of the nineteenth century. Some jurisdictions also outlawed such hunting techniques as night shooting and the use of large-bore guns, but most of the statutes were only local and often lacked provision for enforcement.

It was not until the mid-nineteenth century that some eastern states gave broader protection to song and field birds. In 1850 Connecticut and New Jersey, followed by Vermont and Massachusetts, legislated against the killing of selected non-game birds. Other state lawmakers soon concurred until by 1864 laws in favor of songbirds had been passed in thirteen states. This early legislation was far from watertight, however, because of various loopholes. The New Jersey statute permitted hunting on a proprietor's own land, and in New Hampshire and Massachusetts towns could change the bird laws by local vote. Many state laws were concerned with only selected birds, and vague terms such as references to "harmless" or "insectivorous" species made problems in enforcing these conservation laws.

By the 1880s no laws had yet addressed the crime of plume hunting by granting protection among any of the large shorebirds which were the plumers' most frequent victims. Nor had any legislature moved to protect other species under attack including hawks, owls or pigeons. When the AOU was formed in 1883, it was these non-game species unprotected by any law that inspired the scientific conservationists to devise the influential AOU Model Law. Much of the history of legal bird conservation evolved in the slow step-by-step adoption of the Model Law by the state legislatures. But, as the dissemination of the Model Law advanced, the venue of bird protection began to shift to the federal level and to Congress. In line with an emerging tendency to centralize efforts to save the country's natural resources, Congress now began to take up some of the increasingly popular issues of conservation, and from this time on the principal lawmaking in this field was national.

Representative John F. Lacey of Iowa took the initial but tentative step toward national bird protection when he presented a bill in 1897 founded on the interstate commerce concept. It sought to consolidate prior state legislation by outlawing interstate markets in birds, as well as to encourage their propagation, to prohibit all importation and to limit the ornamental use of feathers. Lacey's act provided federal aid for the breeding of threatened species, control over the importation of any foreign birds dead or alive, and fines for interstate shipment of bird skins if illegally killed under a state law. This last clause was a weakness in the bill, since bird laws were not standard and only two legislatures had passed the Model Law that provided the required backup protection. Nevertheless, by offering federal funds and power based on the doctrine of interstate commerce to control trade in birds, the act took a prophetic step toward establishing a rationale for later federal conservation laws.

For a while Congress balked at the Lacey law, feeling that such a shift of power from the states to the federal government might be too radical, and so the bill did not get enough support at first reading. Congressman Lacey reintroduced it in 1900, when it passed and was signed by President McKinley. John Fletcher Lacey's genuine concern for the cause of conservation to which he had devoted so much inventive legislative talent was reflected during deliberations on his bill when he said: "There is a compensation in the distribution of plants, birds and animals by the God of nature. Man's attempt to change and interfere often leads to serious results. We have given an awful exhibition of slaughter and destruction, which may serve as a warning to all mankind."

Congressman George Shiras III of Pittsburgh, another prominent defender of wildlife, took the next step to broader bird protection. Like a number of other conservationists, Shiras was a reformed hunter. Having given up his gun for a camera, he perfected ingenious devices to make his subjects trip the shutter themselves and take their own portraits. George Shiras planned to serve only one term in Congress from 1903 to 1905 and then to return to his field researches, which were centered on a family camp in the upper peninsula of Michigan.

Like some earlier nature students, William Bartram first of all, Shiras saw the needs and numbers of birds as ever changing with shifting migratory patterns. He believed that as the birds came and went they seemed more numerous than they were, so that the state legislatures tended to favor "an open season on migrant game birds when they are within the state and a closed season during their absence." By the time Shiras reached Congress he felt strongly that the next step was to bring migrating birds under legal shelter. He submitted a comprehensive bill which covered all migratory game birds that bred wherever they were not hunted. The Shiras Law listed all the species it intended to shield and empowered the Department of Agriculture, as host to the Biological Survey, to impose closed seasons as needed. Shiras proposed this legislation as a draft that was theoretical and educational in aim, for he realized that his short time in Congress would not enable him to sponsor the law through the required committees and floor votes. The bill never went beyond intramural circulation, but, relying on the precedent of Shiras's work, Congress soon returned to the preservation of migratory birds and within nine years passed a bill more sweeping than the Shiras draft.

Dubbed the Weeks–McLean bill after its sponsors in the two chambers of Congress, the new bill took the Shiras draft as a close model and focused initially on migratory game birds. Since it called for much expansion in federal commitment to wildlife, this new act met with opposition from groups that had earlier sided with Lacey, including sportsmen, commercial hunters and, on the constitutional issue of state vs. federal rights, legislators from the South and West. William T. Hornaday, who fought a lifelong battle to cut back game limits, along with Dutcher and Pearson, lobbied diligently for the migratory bird law, and some help came from an unexpected source. Henry Ford was a bird enthusiast who installed bird houses throughout the grounds of his Michigan estate. Hearing of the debate over the Weeks–McLean bill, he instructed 600 Ford dealers to pressure their congressmen on how needed it was, and dispatched one of his company's public relations men to Washington with instructions not to come back until the bill had passed.

During the usual prolonged congressional deliberations Dutcher and Pearson, backed by Hornaday, took a broader view of this opportunity for a breakthrough in conservation and proposed expanding the bill to cover all migratory birds, game and non-game alike. But Congress, responding to the hunters' lobby, typically became embroiled in the politics of bird hunting. How to force this issue, dear to bird protectionists but of no advantage to the more numerous hunting fraternity? Eventually in the fall of 1912 Hornaday, a master of the *coup de main*, arranged a dinner in New York for about fifteen leading conservationists and easily guided the table talk to the Weeks–McLean bill. Enthusiasm for broadening the act to cover all migratory species built up around the room, a copy of the bill happened to appear, and the expert guests forthwith rewrote it at table to include the perching birds. This grand change was dubbed "the dickey-bird amendment"; inserted in the rewritten bill, it went to Congress in March 1913 and was accepted with little objection. Still the act could not survive without further maneuver, and so it was attached as a rider to the Department of Agriculture appropriations bill. It reached President Taft's desk in the last hectic hours of his administration, and he later admitted that he signed it without noticing what it was, though on more considered subsequent review he judged it unconstitutional and said he should have vetoed it.

Following the passage of the migratory act the prior Secretary of

State, Senator Elihu Root, suggested that the State Department, with the technical help of the Biological Survey, negotiate a treaty with Canada containing the same provisions to protect migratory birds as the American law. T. S. Palmer of the Biological Survey, an expert on wildlife law, drafted the treaty and negotiated some changes sought by the Canadians, and John Burnham, head of the American Game Protection Association and a loyal campaigner for the bill, went to Ottawa to speak for the treaty. With little delay the United States, Canada, and Britain agreed on the treaty, which was signed in the summer of 1916 and promptly ratified by President Wilson. Within two years Congress, consistent with its prior vote, passed an enabling bill, the United States Migratory Bird Treaty Act. Eight years after the proposal of this major bird law, which was presaged by George Shiras's trial balloon, it was formally espoused by Congressman Weeks and Senator McLean, liberally enlarged by conservationists Pearson, Palmer, Hornaday, and Burnham, among others including Henry Ford, and only granted legal status to shield its migrating clients by means of international diplomacy and the final approval of the U.S. Supreme Court. In the intentionally staged test case of the Migratory Bird Treaty Act heard before the Supreme Court in 1920, entitled *Missouri vs. Holland,* Justice Oliver Wendell Holmes wrote for the court: "Here a national interest of very nearly the first magnitude is involved. . . . Wild birds are not in the possession of anyone. . . . But for the treaty and the statute there soon will be no birds for any powers to deal with."

A new law required appropriate enforcement. Congress, better attuned to the needs of wildlife regulation than in Lacey's time, provided $50,000 to administer the migratory bird law, a modest sum later raised to $190,000, enough for the Biological Survey to start disseminating the new measure in the field. It put together an advisory board of experts, including bird defenders like Pearson, Grinnell, Hornaday, and Lacey, to counsel the survey in its broader responsibilities. John Burnham, a protégé of Grinnell, was appointed chairman, even though the American Game Protection Association which he headed was a known front for the gunmakers. (Congress only heard about this connection half a dozen years later from a young New York representative, Fiorello H. La-Guardia, just before Burnham resigned from the board.) The members did not agree easily among themselves nor with the government scientists, who favored less bird protection than the advisory board. Hornaday complained that "all our recommendations were hilariously dumped in the wastebasket" by the experts in Washington. But the survey cut all spring hunting seasons, stopped commerce in wild game, and set the fall season at no more than three and a half months with a bag limit of twenty-five ducks and ten geese a day—still a generous limit. These regulations took enough pressure off the game birds so that they enjoyed a partial recovery during the 1920s until populations slumped again in the depression decade.

Constitutional doctrine on interstate activity limited the scope of national wildlife laws in the Lacey Act, the Migratory Bird Treaty, and in all successive related legislation. A curious result was that the migratory bird law could cover only birds traveling between states but not those who stayed at home. As the federal bills could not reach every local area of avian life, bird advocates had to find other measures for more complete coverage. The Audubon association officers were in the forefront of this effort to augment statutory protection. Even the milliners showed early interest in bird preservation by legal means, the remedy that had proved most effective so far. In 1900 their association proposed a legal agreement with the Audubon committee to cease using the plumes of North American birds, with exceptions for the feathers of foreign, barnyard, edible, or game birds. While the offer seemed to have merit, the Audubon board rejected it because categories like "barnyard" and "edible" were unclear, and because it seemed wrong to qualify the prohibition when so many kinds of birds beyond those specified remained in danger.

After the milliners' proposed concession failed to impress the Audubon officers, Dutcher and Pearson directed their persuasive skills to another arena, the New York legislature, and launched a sustained effort to regulate plume use in the hat factories centered in New York City. After a five-year debate against the milliners' dubious claims (for example, that many plumes were already shed and picked up off the ground), the preservationists won a sweet victory in the 1910 Audubon Plumage Bill. This outlawed the sale of aigrettes in New York, as well as parts of any birds protected by the state and of birds from outside it, as long as they were in a bird family legally protected within the state. (The unusual clause about families was designed to stretch coverage to the egrets, which were not native to New York but members of the local heron family.) The exceptions to the bill were game birds, hawks, crows, and grackles, snowy and great horned owls, and of course the unpopular English sparrow.

* Audubon political activity led in 1913 to another step forward when Congress inserted a prohibition in a tariff bill against importing plumes from abroad except those of ostriches and domestic fowl. This placed enforcement of the Lacey Bill in the hands of the Customs Service, and within days stylish ladies returning from Europe with plumes for their hatmakers were shocked to find them plucked from their luggage. The anti-plume campaigners were later rewarded for their efforts when customs sent them a bale of confiscated plumes, which the Audubon staff rearranged in thirty-nine educational exhibits designed to demonstrate criminal hat decoration.

Once the Migratory Bird Treaty Act was in place, buttressed by the state and federal laws directed at plume hunting, the bird protection movement could take new directions. Reduced to the bluntest form, the question was, now that we've saved all these birds, where are they to live? When the question is so simply put, the answer is apparent: the birds needed more sanctuaries. This new direction in protecting birds led to two more historic efforts in federal conservationist legislation, the last described in this narrative, the Migratory Bird Conservation Act or Norbeck-Andresen Bill of 1928 and its sequel the Pittman-Robertson Bill of 1937.

The chief sponsor of the Migratory Bird Conservation Act to foster sanctuaries was Senator Peter Norbeck of South Dakota, an advocate of wildlife farsighted enough to serve not just a constituency of voters alone but one of outdoor creatures. As early as 1923 Norbeck introduced in Congress a law tentatively called the "game refuge bill" which proposed to work with the states in setting up shorebird sanctuaries financed by a one-dollar federal hunting license. A clause in this draft bill gave conservationists pause: a provision that certain of these new refuges were to be "public shooting grounds," available for legal hunting of the birds innocently attracted there by government hospitality.

The game refuge bill, some said, amounted to little more than the latest self-serving tactic of the hunters. Hornaday, absorbed in his endless campaign to lower bag limits, became alarmed that the bill would upstage his own cause. He wrote Senator Norbeck, emphatically as usual, that it will "put the federal government into the business of *founding and maintaining duck-shooting resorts,* and generally promoting the *killing* of waterfowl." Norbeck replied that the bill under his sponsorship would be revised from top to bottom and would close at least sixty and up to ninety percent of the refuges to hunting.

The senator, as good as his word and better, deleted the whole provision for shooting grounds and, in a bold move against the hunting block, struck a blow for conservation by rewriting the bill to support sanctuaries exclusively. The federal hunting license, long a bone of contention, died ungrieved, but a more unprecedented provision replaced it, the budgeting of funds directly appropriated from the Treasury to finance the new refuges. While some senators suggested $1 million annually for five years for this purpose, Norbeck found the Senate open to more, and ended with funding of $10 million over ten years, plus $50,000 seed money. The sanctuary program depended on joint work between state and federal governments, with the states consulting the Biological Survey in laying out the reserved acreage, and with the local share of the guarding duties covered by federal funds. The Senate unanimously passed this surprisingly liberal act in April 1928, and the House, less easily persuaded, fell in line ten months later.

The actual appropriation to fund Norbeck's Migratory Bird Refuge Act was $7.8 million, less than the bill requested. After the demise of the federal hunting license proposal some legislators still felt that the large gunning brotherhood should support sanctuaries. So a Migratory Bird Hunting Stamp Act was passed to supplement the refuge act, requiring hunters to attach special federal stamps to their licenses to provide additional income for refuges. This device in effect revived the purpose of the federal hunting license and is still widely used on the state level today.

But many of the conservationists favored an excise tax on guns and shells as a surer, fairer way to exact funds from sportsmen to benefit wildlife, a method later used in the Pittman-Robertson bill of 1937. There the proceeds went not only for sanctuaries but for wildlife study and propagation programs run by the states and overseen by the Fish and Wildlife Service. This act, formally known as the Federal Aid in Wildlife Restoration Program, reversed the trend of keeping control of conservation in Washington by granting the states three federal dollars of the hunting excise tax to one of state funds.

Since its passage Congress has occasionally amended the Pittman-Robertson Act in minor ways to increase its revenues, now set at an average level of an eleven percent excise tax, or $114 million annually, funds used by the states to maintain ongoing wildlife projects and initiate new ones. Under this program the government logically applied its revenues, because they stemmed from a hunters' tax, mostly to game birds and animals. But in 1980 Congress passed the Fish and Wildlife Conservation Act, formulated along related lines but for non-game species. This further step, a reasonable expansion of the whole program, is to draw on direct financing from Treasury funds, but these have not at this time been appropriated.

The Pittman–Robertson Act was the last major legislation in a coordinated campaign over forty years that brought a national program of legal protection for birds and other creatures. In the late nineteenth century all the cards were in the hunters' hands and they could play them almost as they wished, but forty years later they were obliged to pay an automatic tax on each shot aimed at wildlife. The creatures of nature could still provide sport for them but also now offered an available source of visual pleasure for all who cared. It was a radical change but one which the nation sought and came to enjoy. The politicians and wildlife advocates who spilled so many words to bring about this new approach had the force of the American public on their side.

Duck stamp sales help support wildlife refuges.

*A*s the sequence of major congressional bills indicated, the refuge movement emerged more slowly than legal methods of conservation. But
support for sanctuaries gained momentum in the early twentieth century
and reached an astounding pace in the 1930s, perhaps never to be
surpassed. The first bird sanctuary in America, a local one, started the
movement almost seven decades before this culmination, in the time
when Burroughs and Muir were perceiving nature for its own sake and
when Joel Allen first warned of the pluming crisis. In 1870 the city of
Oakland, California, set aside the small downtown Lake Merritt as a
sanctuary, which has been profitably shared ever since by migrating
ducks and office workers on lunch hour. States and municipalities were
slow to follow Oakland's example. Indiana, always exemplary in conservation work, was the second state to have its own refuge, but not
until 1903. In the same year President Roosevelt decreed the first federal
sanctuary on four-acre Pelican Island in Florida's Indian River, which
housed a breeding colony of 2,000 to 3,000 brown pelicans and was once
a plumer's Golgotha. The AOU and the Biological Survey, following
up efforts by the state of Florida, requested the administration to set aside
the island as a reservation, and in March 1903 T. R. so declared it by
executive order after thinking for no more than a few seconds and
questioning his counsel briefly about the legality of this unprecedented
intervention. From this small beginning the vast federal refuge program
grew to its present scope of about 425 units. Roosevelt himself, a
devoted conservationist, did not stop at guarding an islet of pelicans but
obtained approval from Congress in 1905 for the eventual designation
of sanctuaries by executive order. By the end of his administration in
1909 he had established as many as fifty-two.

In the first eager days of refuge making nobody paused to ask how
the birds would react to these sheltered environments. Over time they
have responded to protection with satisfying enthusiasm, but the pelicans of Pelican Island did not at first take easily to federal patronage.
For the new refuge the Audubon association assigned a warden, who
erected a large sign, legible from the river, declaring the island a
sanctuary closed to trespassers. The following spring the warden returned to check on the breeding birds, but no pelican was in sight. He
mounted a search along the river, and found the colony on an unguarded
island fifty miles downstream. The warden guessed that the trouble
might be the sign, the only physical change on the island, which he
removed. The next spring the pelican colony returned to its unmarked

island as before. Man may not understand the limits set by the behavioral norms of wild creatures nor is he always aware that meddling with their lifestyles can prove risky.

These limits when applied to bird preservation in the field led to dividing federal refuges into two types, general and special. The special refuge benefits one species with clear environmental needs which determine the locale of the refuge. The great white heron sanctuary in the Florida Keys, an Audubon association undertaking later nationalized, corresponds to this morph's range, and the Red Rock Lakes Refuge in Montana offers a year-round home to rare trumpeter swans. Other species than the intended protégés may use these special sanctuaries; Pelican Island is also home to white ibises, both kinds of egrets, and four species of herons. Breton Island near the Mississippi's mouth is protected as a breeding territory for terns and skimmers in summer, but numerous kinds of ducks and shorebirds stop there in winter.

General sanctuaries do not answer to the needs of one or a few species but serve any birds that find their ecology adaptable. The topography, botany, and other environmental components of any site suit some species and not others. The Aleutian Islands contain a huge refuge strung out through 1200 miles, which is visited at one time and place or another by every Pacific seabird, while an example of an upland general refuge is Desert National in Nevada, comprising Lake Meade, created by the Hoover Dam, with almost 660,000 acres that shelter many kinds of mountain and desert birds plus big horn sheep.

In the most primitive sense, as explained by Ira Gabrielson, director of the Biological Survey in the late 1930s and overseer of an outburst of new refuges, a sanctuary may come into being simply by barring hunters, marking its borders, and dispatching a sporadic patrol. In practice, though, much more is involved. Siting must take into account the behavior and populations of birds, topography, and edible plant life, even facilities and attitudes in nearby human communities. Once a locale is designated a refuge, it is seldom left in a wild state, since its managers try to regulate nature to enhance its usefulness to birds. For waterfowl refuges, engineers may design elaborate water control systems with dams and gates to control levels and salinity. Refuges often include farms, worked by their own personnel or on a sharecropping basis by neighboring farmers, to provide grass and grains, especially corn, for geese and ducks, or perhaps millet for small birds.

Most federal refuges allow fishing, and just over half of them are open to hunting, since game management is a traditional concern of the Fish and Wildlife Service, which views animal overpopulation as a threat to any well-run sanctuary. Wildlife experts consider it ideal if a state game management area is adjacent to a refuge, as happens at Bombay Hook on Delaware Bay, since the two reserves reinforce each others' purposes and the animals can seek shelter in the refuge during hunting season but submit to population control on the state shooting ground. The Edwin B. Forsyth (formerly Brigantine) National Wildlife Refuge near Atlantic City, New Jersey, and the sanctuary at Chincoteague, Virginia, are famous for their graceful natural appearance, but in fact their ponds and dikes have been designed by man to augment the ecology for shorebirds.

Secondary advantages of such management are control of seaside soil erosion and flooding. With the water under man's rule, fresh or brackish pools can serve dabbling ducks next to salt coves for bay and ocean ducks. Even a slight alteration in water level can eliminate or encourage certain reeds and grasses, which can determine whether a species of waterfowl moves in or goes elsewhere. These adjustments of the ecology may backfire, however, and force a refuge director to make uneasy choices. The ubiquitous bulrush crowds out other marsh grasses needed by ducks and geese. Muskrats, abundant in most waterfowl refuges, undermine and kill the bulrushes but also eat the birds' eggs and tunnel through dikes. The managers of most marshland refuges prefer to skirt this conflict by trapping the muskrats for their valuable pelts while suppressing the bulrushes and encouraging the grasses by planned burning.

This description of refuge management stresses the program for assisting migratory waterfowl, and so does the entire federal sanctuary system, which tends to cluster along the flyways used by ducks and geese. In the late 1920s and early 1930s, while the annual slaughter of waterfowl went on during the traditional hunting seasons, ducks, geese, and other shorebirds had to face new threats from both man and nature. Canada and the United States had a vast program to drain marshland for agriculture, which absorbed nearly 100 million acres of wetlands. By unhappy coincidence severe drought worsened the effect of this campaign to remove natural water from the environment. These adverse conditions alerted government conservationists to the need for replacing waterfowl habitat. The advent of the New Deal presented political and practical opportunities to expand the refuge system for birds needing water. Succoring the ducks and geese had a more intangible advantage:

their large size, flocking behavior, and life in open watery spaces gave them visibility and a familiarity to most people, who could better understand a program of protection for such well-known birds. It was unlikely that Fish and Wildlife could find much popular support to make refuges for tiny, nearly invisible birds like sparrows or warblers.

The largest number of national refuges in the special category, over one-third of the system, are for migratory waterfowl. These in turn serve three needs: resting and feeding on migratory flyways, breeding, and wintering. Flyway refuges provide a protected stopping place and food, often in the form of cultivated grasses, for migrants in transit. A map of national refuges shows the greater portion of them grouped along the four principal migratory routes, the Atlantic, the Mississippi, the central, and the Pacific.

While local tactics contribute to siting a single refuge, a larger strategy applies to interrelating them. Ducks migrating down the Atlantic Coast can find stopovers conveniently spaced much as a human traveler might hop from one motel to another of a chain for which he has a charge card. Ducks coming from the eastern Canadian coast can pause first at the Rachel Carson Refuge near Kennebunk, Maine, and then make an easy flight to Parker River at Plum Island on the Massachusetts north shore near Newburyport, or all the way to Block Island off the Rhode Island shore. The passage over the metropolitan New York area might present a problem, but the Gateway Recreation Area sanctuary at Jamaica Bay under the landing paths of Kennedy Airport is well suited for ducks.

On the next stop southward the pools of Brigantine Refuge offer every comfort, and it is not a long jump on to Bombay Hook or Prime Hook on Delaware Bay, or even to the Virginia barrier beaches and ponds at Chincoteague. The next stop might be the bays enclosed by the national seashore at Cape Hatteras or, just inland from there, huge Lake Mattamuskeet, if water space could be found among the 15,000 wintering swans. The island refuge at Cape Romain, South Carolina, is the next resting place of choice. The lower Carolina and Georgia coasts present several opportunities for federal hospitality, and the journey might end, or have its last American stopover, at Merritt Island Refuge on Cape Canaveral, a shared project with NASA, which conceded it would prefer a bird sanctuary as a neighbor to any other use of the nearby land.

The functions of breeding and wintering waterfowl refuges have bases that are evident and crucial. Breeding grounds for ducks and some for geese tend to be far north in Canada, but the upper Midwest provides a great cluster of them, mainly in North Dakota and Minnesota. Refuges for wintering are in more southerly locations for evident reasons. The greatest wintering flocks crowd the Louisiana and Texas gulf coast refuges, vast seaside marshes too watery for automobile access.

The most ambitious scope in expanding wildlife conservation had to await the Alaska National Interest Lands Conservation Act of 1980. No description can convey the sweep of the Alaskan refuges; a few dry statistics must serve. Eighty-one percent of the largest state's land is federally owned, and one-third of that is protected for wildlife. As a comparison, refuges occupy twelve percent of all national land in the forty-eight states, an area the size of Arkansas. Alaska's sanctuaries comprise 78 million acres, a figure almost beyond comprehension, over eighty percent of the total area in all the continental federal refuges. Yukon Basin is Alaska's largest protected area covering just under 20 million acres. Brigantine, in comparison, is one of the largest U.S. east coast refuges and comprises about 19,000 acres. One wonders, if bird conservation had come of age sooner, what some of the older states would have for refuges had a wildlife policy as generous as that in Alaska touched them in time.

In contrast to the massive federal intervention in Alaska are the state sanctuaries, mostly small, often the result of a gift or bequest of an already protected area, more rarely a purchase with solicited funds. State sanctuaries are confusing in variety of function and legal status, they fluctuate in number, and no one has undertaken a survey to reveal their extent. The quick growth and success of the federal system inspired the widespread making of sanctuaries on every level, and earlier in this century they tended to spring up in surprising corners. In 1917 Northern Illinois State Normal School declared its campus a bird refuge, and all its students gave a nickel or a dime toward hiring a warden. In 1924 the city of Dallas made itself a sanctuary in its entirety by ordinance. Ingeniously the Audubon association campaigned to persuade golf courses to enforce protection for birds within their bounds, and some clubs responded with effective rules. Military colleges and even some bases declared their status as refuges, an early one being the Aberdeen Proving Ground in Maryland.

The strained but innovative years of the Depression during Franklin Delano Roosevelt's first two terms brought a creative surge to the refuge movement. Sanctuary making in the 1930s acquired renewed momentum inspired by a wildlife crisis, some strong personalities and that ubiquitous but shadowy eminence in conservation, politics. This heroic period of wildlife support had a designated hero at stage center: Jay Norwood Darling, called "Ding." He was a cartoonist from Des Moines, Iowa, whose work was syndicated nationally to some 300 newspaper outlets. Along the way Darling was a dairy farmer who made Roquefort cheese, a gardener and avid fisherman, a birder and duck hunter; he was also a bubbling extrovert, a social man widely known and liked. His cartoons often commented trenchantly on issues of conservation, particularly on the misdemeanors of hunters.

In the early 1930s a decline in waterfowl added another disaster to the economic collapse. In the first four years of the decade the duck population fell to twenty percent of its 1930 level due to the combined effects of land drainage and drought. President Roosevelt wished to empower a small elite group to study the wildlife problem, the President's Committee on Wildlife Restoration. For the purpose he recruited brilliant talent that went beyond the predictable: Aldo Leopold, the respected father of game management; Thomas Beck, head of the Crowell-Collier Publishing Company and a sportsman in the Boone and Crockett spirit; and, more surprising, Ding Darling. Darling, although a Republican, was a hometown friend of FDR's Secretary of the Interior, Henry Wallace, and like the other two committeemen was a knowledgeable duck hunter, whose ethical vision of conservation made his drawings more than amusing cartoons. The cartoonist sat comfortably on the president's committee, which quickly issued a report that called for buying about 17 million acres of little used land for $50 to $75 million and adding it to the refuge program.

For months Wallace sat on the Leopold-Beck-Darling report. When he eventually circulated it, its recommendations hardly made a dent on the preoccupied New Deal leaders. Apparently Wallace undercut it with the president as too costly and politically risky with rural landowners. Darling, disappointed, went back to Des Moines and his drawing board, and his cartoons grew more bitterly critical of inroads on nature. Content with his role as a critic from afar, he nevertheless soon heard again from Secretary Wallace, who urged him to take the directorship of the Biological Survey. Though suspicious of bureaucracy, Darling gave in to the secretary's persuasive point that only six months' or a year's work of reorganization could turn the bureau around. Darling's most zealous friend among conservationists, Rosalie Edge, was shocked at what she saw as his surrender to the forces of hold-back and do-nothing. It took all of Darling's cheerful charm to win her reluctantly back.

The cartoonist was a New Dealer now, and like his colleagues he felt the conflict between the demands of his constituents, in his case the wild creatures, and the needs of men in hard times. He endorsed the survey's vermin poisoning program, and Rosalie Edge pounced on him like a sharp-shinned hawk. The gun companies, true to form, offered a hefty endowment for wildlife based on ten percent of their sales if the government would drop its excise tax on ammunition. Darling, crying for new funds, was amenable on grounds of need, but the administration vetoed the plan as politically and ethically hazardous.

But in another area he succeeded brilliantly, for he found money for sanctuaries right and left, attracting it chiefly with his vibrant personality or, as he confessed, with a straw that "sucked funds for wildlife out of the other fellow's barrel." While he never reached the extreme figures of the presidential committee's report, he pursued its policy of using unwanted land for wildlife on a sweeping scale. From emergency funds of various sorts he captured more than $8 million for refuge construction and another $6 million from land reclamation, drought relief appropriations, and from WPA engineering money. Darling learned how to exploit a quirk in the New Deal mode of government when he found that other agencies, often too generously funded, were willing to justify their swollen budgets by transferring money to the wildlife program. The CCC sent squads to sanctuaries like Brigantine and Blackwater, which today still show the good effects of these extra hands. The Reclamation Service often rescued marginal wasteland which it was willing to convert to refuge use, and the Resettlement Administration turned over land from failing farms or sometimes located land-poor farmers on sanctuaries where they paid their rent with labor.

By the spring of 1934 Darling's program also began to benefit from the Migratory Bird Hunting Stamp Act, which brought in from $.5 million to $1.2 million annually. The refuge movement's activities under Darling were so manifold that it is difficult to survey them justly. Through 1935 thirty-two new refuges were in construction and 653,000 acres of land were under contract for the program, valued at nearly a million dollars. In the summer of 1935 Congress, respectful of a show of political virtuosity, gave Darling another $6 million. Always the optimist, yet always pushing for more, Darling went to the president and asked for a further $4 million. Roosevelt was never sure about

Darling and may even have been a little jealous of a personality as buoyant and persuasive as his own. Though the president was once a birder, circumstances now made him consider people more needful than ducks. He called Darling the first man in history to hold up the U.S. Treasury and get away with it, and for once the Biological Survey director went away empty-handed. He had done his part and more and had stayed twenty months, much longer than Henry Wallace had asked. His career as cartoonist was always waiting, and two months after FDR bested him he went back home to Des Moines.

In later years Ding Darling, along with flocks of waterfowl, wintered at Captiva Island next to Sanibel, the two barrier beaches off Fort Myers, Florida. Most of the mainland side of Sanibel Island is now a national refuge for herons, egrets and smaller waders, ducks, geese, and some spoonbills, and it is named after Darling. The passages through it by car and foot give a more intimate view of bird life than in almost any sanctuary. Ding Darling would hardly be taken aback to know that at twilight the vacationers on Sanibel come out to view the bird scene and find it just the place for a few tailgate cocktails.

*A*n arm recently added to bird conservation, and now reinforced by research and national law, is the endangered species program. It is centrally managed by the Fish and Wildlife Service, with advice on botanical concerns from the Smithsonian Institution. The beginning of systematic consideration of endangered species occurred in 1964 when nine government biologists came together as the Committee on Rare and Endangered Wildlife Species.

That year the committee published the first edition of the Redbook, the official list of endangered species, which included sixty-three vertebrates. The scientists admitted that this first attempt was tentative and to some degree based on intuitive decisions, but they set a good precedent for future lists by excluding economic considerations such as a creature's utility to man, or lack of it. The new program's needs were many: more research to evaluate the status of species, congressional authorization to release appropriations for personnel and for specialized sanctuaries, and when possible a campaign of positive restoration to salvage those species with some hope of survival. The Redbook listing was a first signal for action, but to turn its warnings into full-blooded resuscitation was a long-term challenge.

Several endangered species of birds—the whooping crane, bald eagle, bobwhite, and the colorful roseate spoonbill—are well known to the public. Their ups and downs rate newspaper headlines, and any government aid to them has broad-based appeal. So legislative backing for the new Fish and Wildlife program was not slow in gaining attention on Capitol Hill. Over the seven years from 1966 to 1973 three Endangered Species Bills passed Congress, all unanimously. Each act replaced a more limited prior one, and a bill considered forceful and comprehensive enough did not pass until the most recent one in 1973. The point of all the laws was to halt man's destruction of the habitats of these vulnerable creatures and the exploitation of the birds through hunting.

The final Endangered Species Act of 1973, still in force today, contains strong wording that promises to make it endure. The prohibited "taking" of any endangered or threatened species covers every conceivable harm including harrassing, pursuing, hunting, shooting, wounding, killing, trapping, capturing, collecting organisms, or attempting any of these aggressions. The bill also made provision to buy land inhabited by endangered creatures. Congress had no quarrel with this forceful measure, seeing it as low in cost and widely popular.

The programs of action under the Endangered Species Act are only getting underway. Some endangered species have nevertheless lived under restorative protection for decades before the 1973 act (for example, whooping cranes since about 1945), while others await the research that is necessary before intervention, since a misstep from lack of understanding could mean a demise for all time. As the 1973 bill anticipates, a reconstruction of habitat may be enough to pull a species back from decline. The Red Rock Lakes National Refuge in southwestern Montana was designed in the mid-1930s intentionally to serve as a home to the fading trumpeter swan, which has been stabilized there as a full-time resident and become capable of modest increase.

The ultimate technique of last resort for an ailing species is to transfer part of a population to a new environment, carefully selected for compatibility, or to relocate adults or eggs to a controlled artificial setting. If breeding succeeds there, return of selected birds to the wild may follow. The wild turkey is spreading through the intervention of man, with flocks now being moved from Vermont to the New Jersey hills. The whooping crane, the condor, and some raptors harmed by DDT—the peregrine falcon, osprey, and bald eagle—have all been subject to transfers of eggs for incubation under man's eye, with results varying from one species to another. Some whooper chicks have emerged, but results for the condor have been minimal. Survival programs for condors and for northeastern bald eagles have resorted to double-clutching. In this tactic biologists take the eggs from the nest and place them for incubation with a captive female of the same or a related species or in an incubator, knowing that the wild bird will then replace the missing clutch and so double the chance for offspring.

A technique which has had much success among birds deprived by DDT of the ability to lay durable eggs, such as ospreys and the peregrine falcon, is the restocking of their nests with normal eggs from elsewhere. Ospreys on the New Jersey coast declined from 500 to fifty breeding pairs between 1950 and 1973, when DDT was outlawed, but a state program of importing chicks and eggs from the Chesapeake Bay region has made a solid start toward recovery, and the local breeding population has reached 108 couples. The most rewarding restoration may be that for peregrine falcons owed to the program at Cornell's Laboratory of Ornithology. In a recent year 127 peregrines hatched there and will soon be ready for training as hunters ("hacking"), which is done by inducing them to attack domestic pigeons, and then for release into the wild.

Man's intervention in the workings of nature is ambiguous in outcome: foolhardy when it fails, a triumph of science when it helps. An obligation to aid creatures made vulnerable by man's vandalism or by changes in nature is now widely recognized and must be undertaken, even if doing so means taking chances with natural mysteries sometimes too obscure for man to comprehend.

Audubon humanized the California condor.
The species is no longer found in the wild.

Chapter Nine

Women and Bird Conservation

When the Audubon society movement began its difficult campaign against the destruction of bird life, women bird enthusiasts started to contribute to the organization's aims. Their participation was particularly welcome since the slaughter of birds to decorate women's hats was directly responsible for the alarming decline of American bird populations. Concerned women began to encourage birdwatching as a way of instructing their sisters about the beauties of avifauna. Women were encouraged to study birds by women writers who frequently published informal essays about birds and flowers even though they were prevented by convention from undertaking serious ornithological research.

The emergence of women nature writers and birdwatchers coincided also with the growth of a class of women who had sufficient leisure and education to take up an avocation like birding. The pioneer woman homesteading with husband and children before the Civil War had no time for nature study. But with the greater prosperity of post–Civil War agriculture, many farm wives found themselves and their children transformed into prosperous country families with gardens, orchards, and a staff to maintain them.

The outline of Althea Sherman's life illustrates this rising curve. Sherman's parents, of yeoman English stock, journeyed to northeastern

Iowa where they established a homestead in the wilderness. Her father's involvement in local land speculation allowed him sufficient wealth to build a substantial farmhouse with orchard and to educate his two daughters. Althea graduated from Oberlin College in 1875 and, after studying art in Chicago, taught school for several years. Returning home to care for her aging parents, Sherman began her serious study of birds; she published dozens of articles on the behavior of local species and developed into an accomplished nature artist. Her career as amateur ornithologist was possible because of her father's financial success.

At about this time, membership lists of local Audubon societies began to swell with women bird enthusiasts. In 1905, when the several dozen local Audubon societies formed a National Association of Audubon Societies, women were quick to join this new parent organization. In the first year, 229 of the 621 national members were women. But women rarely served as officers of the movement. The conventions of late Victorian society dictated that they play a modest, behind-the-scenes role. On the local level, women were more visible. Some acted as presidents of their home chapters and twenty-three out of twenty-eight recorded organizations had women officers. At the third annual conference of the National Association several women delivered addresses on characteristic activities: for example, Olive Thorne Miller spoke about ornithology in the public schools, and Hilda Justice chose the topic of traveling libraries and lectures.

The contributions of women were conspicuous in the pages of *Bird-Lore* from its inception in 1899. They often presented short notes on field observations, reported on the activities of their local Audubon chapters, and participated in the annual Christmas bird census. Photographs of local Audubon societies occasionally published in *Bird-Lore* revealed a preponderance of women in their ranks.

This enthusiasm is connected with more leisure time for women and with women's growing commitment to politics. The temperance movement, a grass-roots, decentralized campaign centered in small-town America, fostered the political emergence of women after the Civil War, and through it middle-class women gained experience as political organizers. Women came to realize that birds were defenseless creatures, and bird slaughter constituted a poor example for youth that was contrary to Christian values. So widespread was women's participation in the bird conservation movement that in 1907 the General Federation of Women's Clubs, in response to the pleas of national Audubon association secretary T. Gilbert Pearson, passed a resolution binding all members of local chapters:

Whereas: the beautiful white herons are rapidly diminishing, with a
            likelihood of their becoming extinct, and,
Whereas: the demand for aigrettes for millinery purposes is
            responsible for the slaughter of these feathered innocents
            and the consequent death of the nestlings, therefore
Resolved: I pledge myself not to wear any such badge of cruelty as
            the aigrette, or the plumage of any wild bird, and that I
            will use all possible influence to restrain others from doing
            so.

The wording of the resolution indicates that bird conservation, like temperance, was welcome as part of the effort to preserve enduring Christian virtues. Egrets were viewed as morally innocent and requiring protection from women whose thoughtless adherence to fashion was causing their decimation.

Another factor fostering women's interest in birdwatching and nature study was the emergence in the last years of the nineteenth century of higher education for women. Nature study was considered a suitable undergraduate field. Several prominent women nature writers majored in zoology in college, even though they found their way blocked to graduate training and turned perforce to home bird study.

Smith College educated two distinguished graduates who made significant contributions to birdwatching. Fannie Hardy Eckstorm, Maine anthropologist and bird student, was sent to Smith in 1885 by her father, Manly Hardy, a fur trader who was an amateur ornithologist and expert on the local fauna. At college Eckstorm founded an Audubon society and gave informal instruction to her fellow students during nature walks in the countryside. Her brief marriage to the Norwegian-American cleric Jacob Eckstorm ended in early widowhood, and she returned to her home at Brewer, Maine, with her two children. There, supported by her father's considerable wealth, she took up serious nature writing as well as research on the Penobscot Indians. Her two earliest books, *The Woodpeckers* and *The Bird Book,* were designed for amateur bird students, especially young readers, and offer an ingenious mixture of information, folklore, and wit. Although Eckstorm later concentrated her formidable intellectual powers on investigating Maine's cultures,

Indian and European, she continued to contribute occasional short essays on birds to *Bird-Lore*. Smith College had given Eckstorm the fundamentals of zoology and anthropology, a background she used effectively for the remainder of her fruitful life. Like many other brilliant collegians of her day, Eckstorm's career unfolded exclusively from the stronghold of her private home, but it was still richly productive.

Florence Merriam Bailey, the first woman elected a fellow of the American Ornithologists' Union, also began her career at Smith College. Bailey, a few years younger than Eckstorm, participated in the college's Audubon society. Her brother, C. Hart Merriam, was a professional zoologist and served as the first director of the Biological Survey, parent organization of today's Fish and Wildlife Service. Florence Merriam Bailey had already published birdwatching essays while an undergraduate. After attempting a career in social work, a field newly opened to collegiate women, Bailey contracted tuberculosis and went for a rest cure to California, passing her days of enforced leisure watching birds. She returned to Washington, D.C., and devoted the remainder

Florence Merriam Bailey. From *Bird-Lore*.

of her life to bird study. In 1898 she published *Birds of Village and Field,* one of the most successful early bird guides for beginners. George M. Sutton, ornithologist and bird illustrator, recalled that another of her guides, *The Handbook of Birds of the Western United States,* given him on his fifteenth birthday in 1913, altered his life: "On . . . May 16 . . . came a present from my parents that replaced conflict with peace, sorrow with gladness, loneliness with companionship—a copy of the third edition of Mrs. Bailey's *Handbook of the Birds of the Western United States.* I unwrapped the package with fingers that would not behave. If words did not express my gratitude, the look on my face must have done so."

Florence Merriam married Vernon Bailey, a mammalogist with the Biological Survey. Together they undertook several arduous field trips to New Mexico, culminating in Florence Bailey's monumental work, *The Birds of New Mexico,* for which she was awarded an honorary LL.D. from the University of New Mexico. Bailey's career took two different directions, a common occurrence for women at the time. *The Birds of New Mexico* was a scientific work intended for the professional, but her other writings and activities were directed toward the encouragement of amateur bird appreciation. In 1897 she founded the Audubon Society of the District of Columbia, and for many years gave lessons on bird-watching techniques to public school teachers. She intended her enjoyable bird essays such as those in *Birds Through an Opera Glass* of 1889 and even her field guides for leisure use by hobbyists.

Margaret Morse Nice, distinguished ornithologist, also began her career at one of the prestigious women's colleges. After majoring in zoology at Mount Holyoke College, Nice attended graduate school at the Clark Institute in Worcester, Massachusetts. She held two master's degrees (one in zoology and the other in psychology) but never sought a Ph.D. In 1909 she married fellow graduate student Leonard Nice, a physiologist who held his first position at the University of Oklahoma. Margaret Nice had four daughters to raise but as time permitted undertook the study of birds. At first she aspired only to write educational bird essays in the manner of John Burroughs and, in an effort to popularize birding in Oklahoma, she and her husband compiled *The Birds of Oklahoma,* a task involving exploration of wilderness areas in the state to locate bird habitats.

Nice's original dedication to serious ornithology returned after her family moved to Columbus, Ohio. In the forty acres of scrubland behind their new home, she discovered an ideal outdoor laboratory. Intrigued with the new field of animal psychology based on the direct observation of subjects in the field, Nice began her monumental study of song sparrows, color-banding individual birds in order to observe their life cycle. Her resultant data and the conclusions she drew once they were accepted revolutionized the practice of American ornithology. The principle of territoriality in nesting which Nice demonstrated in her study is still one of the basic behavioral tenets of modern bird study. She established this principle, suggested by other scientists but never proved, through thousands of hours of observations.

In large measure self-taught and isolated from academic colleagues, Nice learned to read German in order to study the behavioral literature emerging from European universities. Her lengthy manuscript on the song sparrow was rejected for publication in America, but while attending an ornithological conference in Germany, Nice made contact with such scientists as Erwin Stresemann and Ernst Mayr who understood the significance of her work. Her two-volume study was first published in German and only later appeared in English, not as a publication of the American Ornithologists' Union, which thought it too long, but of the Linnaean Society of New York.

Nice gained considerable renown in her lifetime but worked to the end without institutional support. She relieved her professional isolation with organizational work, serving as the first woman president of the Wilson Ornithological Club. She continued to cherish her international contacts, such as her stimulating friendship with Konrad Lorenz with whom she had studied briefly. Toward the end of her life, Nice was granted an honorary Ph.D. from her alma mater, Mount Holyoke College, and eventually was chosen for membership in the AOU but serious ornithology for her was a frustrating endeavor, characterized by rejection, isolation, and discouragement. Nice's career also reflected the values of nature education which had initially motivated her bird studies. To share her work with amateur bird students she wrote a popularized account of the song sparrow study. *A Watcher at the Nest,* the first book to be illustrated by Roger Tory Peterson, failed to attract many readers.

Both Nice's and Bailey's accomplishments were ahead of their time but several aspects of their careers serve to reflect more traditional female concerns. Attracted to the goals of nature education, and also to the pursuit of serious scientific inquiry fostered at Mount Holyoke and

Smith colleges, both Margaret Nice and Florence Bailey found a way to balance between the two concerns. But nature education was by far the most attainable and realistic endeavor for women naturalists. Most of the women described here can be termed educationists rather than scientists. Nature education involved fewer conflicts with roles considered appropriate for women and could be undertaken in voluntary, noninstitutional contexts.

The nature education movement had its origins in the struggle to save American birds from extirpation by the millinery trade. The National Association of Audubon Societies launched a massive schools campaign leading to the establishment of Junior Audubon societies in public schools throughout the country. This program was so successful that in 1904 the Illinois Audubon Society, for example, reported a membership of 1,035 adults and 16,094 children.

It was thought that teaching the nation's children to appreciate native birds would then logically discourage destructive activities—untrammeled gunning, nest-robbing, and the wearing of feathers. This commitment to childhood education was unwavering. *Bird-Lore* published educational pamphlets and bird cards for classroom use and sponsored birdhouse building and poetry-writing contests. Children were encouraged to submit short essays on their observations of birds, and the best appeared in the magazine. Most school teachers at that time were women and to them the Audubon society directed its pleas for bird instruction in the curriculum. Summer nature institutes for these teachers were popular, providing recreational outlets for single women.

Mabel Osgood Wright and Anna Botsford Comstock, two of the most prominent figures in the nature education movement, came from different social backgrounds and developed contrasting public styles. Mabel Osgood Wright was born in 1859, the daughter of a scholarly Episcopal minister with a prosperous congregation in New York City. Her father had ties to the intellectual circle surrounding the early romantic poet William Cullen Bryant and was an active participant in contemporary theological debates. Although Mabel Osgood Wright was sent to a fashionable girl's school in Greenwich Village, she never attended college. But as she indicated in her autobiography, *My New York,* she was educated thoroughly in literature and the arts by her father and her childhood was filled with the spirit of intellectual inquiry.

After her marriage in 1884 to James Wright, an English antiquarian bookseller, Wright settled with her husband in Fairfield, Connecticut, on her father's farm. For the next twenty years she published over thirty books. Many were entertaining social novels but the most enduring were about birdwatching and nature appreciation.

In 1898 Mabel Wright helped found the Connecticut Audubon Society and later was a director of the National Association of Audubon Societies. Almost from its earliest issues, she served as Audubon societies editor of *Bird-Lore,* working with editor Frank Chapman to produce a bimonthly journal with a lively personality. In her column, which appeared in every issue, Wright assiduously reported on the progress of the bird conservation movement, often amusingly chastising her sisters for wearing feathers. When Wright retired in 1907, Chapman wondered whether he could continue without her.

Mabel Wright's most lasting contribution to birdwatching remains

LEFT. Mabel Osgood Wright with her book *The Friendship of Nature.* From *Bird-Lore.*

OPPOSITE. Museum at Wright's Birdcraft Sanctuary near her home in Fairfield, Connecticut. *Connecticut Audubon Society.*

her nature books. *Birdcraft, A Field Book of 200 Song, Game and Water Birds* of 1895, illustrated with eighty plates by Louis Agassiz Fuertes, was one of the most popular field guides of its era and was reprinted nine times, the last in 1936, after which it was eclipsed by Peterson's new guide. In 1896 Wright published *Citizen Bird*, a fanciful didactic entertainment intended for children and co-authored by Elliott Coues. Wright pursued a rich and varied career but, typical of her time, she undertook her work entirely from her home. Under this umbrella of domesticity, Wright labored incessantly for the causes of bird conservation and nature education, devoting her final years to establishing a bird sanctuary and nature center near her home. Called Birdcraft Museum and Sanctuary, it is still active as a facility of the Connecticut Audubon Society.

Anna Botsford Comstock, a leading advocate of nature education, was untroubled by the restrictions of gentility which Mabel Osgood

Wright imposed on herself. Comstock came from a prosperous Quaker family in upstate New York. After attending a Methodist female college for two years, she transferred to Cornell University in 1874. In her first year she enrolled in a zoology course taught by her future husband, John Henry Comstock. After two years at Cornell, Anna Botsford married and gave up her studies to become her husband's assistant. Later, having taught herself the technique of wood engraving, she illustrated her husband's entomology handbooks.

Comstock was drawn into the nature study movement in 1895 when she was appointed to the New York State Committee for the Promotion of Agriculture, sponsored by philanthropic financiers seeking to halt the agricultural depression and the exodus from country to city. Nature study, the committee concluded, would encourage children to value country life. Anna Comstock was commissioned to design a pilot program in the Westchester County schools, and in 1896 the state government funded an expansion of the project to be based at Cornell. Anna Comstock devoted the next decade to the implementation of her educational program, lecturing, writing leaflets, and teaching. The culmination of this experience was her publication of the monumental *Handbook*

Anna Botsford Comstock, leader of the nature education movement. *Department of Manuscripts and University Archives, Cornell University Libraries.*

of Nature Study in 1911, a lesson manual for school teachers, translated into eight languages and kept in print until 1939. In her section on bird study Comstock suggested that the teacher keep a brooding hen in the classroom so that the children could observe first-hand the details of bird anatomy and reproduction.

Comstock frequently taught the methods of nature study in Cornell's extension and summer schools. In 1920 she became the first woman at Cornell to be appointed a full professor. Her influence spread well beyond her college circle, thanks to the *Handbook*'s popularity and her organizational talents. She served as contributing editor and then editor of *The Nature Study Review,* the organ of the American Nature Study Society, later incorporated into *Nature Magazine.* She also helped found *Country Life in America,* a magazine intended to encourage interest in rural pursuits. Her activities were so admired that in a 1923 poll conducted by the League of Women Voters Comstock was named one of America's twelve greatest living women.

Almost singlehandedly Comstock provided the materials for natural history instruction in the public schools. Her lesson plans were witty, creative, and sure to appeal to children. They often involved outdoor activities like bird walks and cultivating a school vegetable plot. As a professional academic, Comstock pursued her career with the enthusiastic support of her husband, and through her efforts and those the Audubon society, school children learned to appreciate birds.

*A*mong the many women who joined Wright and Comstock in the nature education movement, none was more famous than Gene Stratton Porter, the foremost woman nature writer of her time, a paragon of the freelance nature educator and birdwatcher at the turn of the century. Like Althea Sherman's parents, Porter's family had homesteaded in the wilderness regions of northeastern Indiana. Her father had already achieved a measure of prosperity that freed him from farming to resume practice as a Methodist minister. With education at home and in local schools, Porter's childhood was comfortable, and she had ample freedom to wander in the countryside around her home, an experience that was to enrich her nature writing.

In 1896 the twenty-three-year-old Gene Stratton married Charles Darwin Porter, a druggist from Decatur, Indiana. The couple immediately prospered; lands that Gene Porter owned were rich in natural gas.

They moved to the edge of a swampy wilderness called the Limberlost, where Gene Porter designed a rustic cabin in which they lived with their only child, Jeannette, until the swamp was drained for agriculture. During this time at the Limberlost Porter began to focus on nature study. In 1895 Charles Porter gave her camera equipment, and she began, without professional instruction, to photograph birds on their nests in the swamp. She submitted some of these photographs to magazines such as *Field and Stream.* Soon an invitation to accompany these superb photographs with text led Porter to her first literary efforts. A somewhat hackneyed and anthropomorphizing early book, *The Song of the Cardinal,* was not particularly successful but in 1904 she hit upon a formula which gained her fame and wealth.

The novel *Freckles,* a romantic tale about a humble Scottish orphan set in the Limberlost Swamp, was intended both for juvenile and adult readers. *Freckles* and its sequel, *The Girl of the Limberlost* of 1909, sold over 9 million copies, making Porter one of the most popular writers of all time.

Both novels are structured around old-fashioned rags-to-riches plots but the protagonists achieve success through the redemptive qualities of nature study. Freckles, the lonely hero of the first novel, befriends the birds in the swamp which nurture his soul and stimulate his spirit of inquiry. A bird guide he purchases early in the story opens new and exciting vistas for him. Instead of birds, moths figure prominently in *The Girl of the Limberlost.* The heroine finances her high school education by selling rare specimens of moths she collects in the swamp after school hours. The message in the two novels is the same: nature study uplifts the spirit and nourishes the mind. Porter was an unrivaled master of old-fashioned yarn spinning. The combination of this talent with nature study distinguishes her work from that of other late Victorian novelists.

Porter was seldom associated with the popular causes of nature study or bird conservation movements. Yet no other nature writer except John Burroughs could claim such a large following, nor could anyone so consistently hold the public's interest. Porter was always accurate in her description of birds, revealing familiarity with geology, entomology, and botany as well. Her success may not have come from her memorable plot inventions alone, but also from her moral posture. For Porter, a quintessential Victorian, viewed the preordained habits of the animals she studied as analogs for human family life. In nature study she found the keys to defining wholesome Christian values. She offended no one and pleased everyone—educators, religious leaders, and her young readers.

It is not possible to overestimate the effect of this copious literary effort on behalf of bird conservation and nature appreciation. Mabel Wright, Fannie Eckstorm, Florence Bailey, and others popularized birdwatching as an educational hobby for American women. They urged readers not just to learn identification of common backyard birds but to observe their habits and keep detailed records. They defined birdwatching as a valuable avocation for women with leisure time who had received some knowledge of scientific method in college.

Bird-Lore and the magazines published by local Audubon societies printed short essays by amateur observers, often women. Women authors were apt to illustrate their articles with amateurish photographs, but sometimes untrained photographers advanced to excellence.

Cordelia Stanwood of Ellsworth, Maine, became a superb bird photographer. She was the daughter of a prosperous sea captain who early recognized Cordelia's intellectual promise and sent her to relatives in Providence in search of broader education. She trained as an art teacher and for two decades held various teaching positions in New England industrial towns. But the isolation of an itinerant teacher's life in strange cities overwhelmed Stanwood, and she collapsed. She returned to the family home in Ellsworth and, confused and restless, rambled daily in the woods and pastures, beginning an obsession with birds she spent hours observing. Stimulated by the guidelines for amateur bird students proposed in *Bird-Lore,* Stanwood kept meticulous notes.

She tried to publish some of her findings in *Bird-Lore,* but Frank Chapman suggested she take up photography, and even advised what equipment to buy. Stanwood became one of the best photographers of birds, producing portraits of gentle subtlety. Her images of the species nesting in central Maine are intimate and revealing. She used some of them to illustrate the handful of small articles she subsequently published. Stanwood's writing style was awkward, even inarticulate, and a projected handbook of Maine birds failed to find a publisher. Yet her reputation as an expert on nesting woodland species such as warblers, nuthatches, and thrushes was so great that the ornithologist Arthur Bent consulted her when writing his *Life History of North American Birds* and incorporated several of her photographs in the volume on thrushes.

Stanwood's accomplishments were not typical of amateur birdwatch-

Cordelia Stanwood specialized in photographing
young birds like this helpless broad-winged hawk.
Cordelia Stanwood Wildlife Foundation.

ers. Her natural aptitude for observation led her to an unusual intimacy with birds. Lacking other occupation, Stanwood became obsessed with bird study. Her correspondence with several famous ornithologists whom she never met was her single link with the world outside Ellsworth.

Other women bird observers took up amateur ornithology. A survey of the bibliographies in Bent's *Life History of North American Birds* reveals numerous articles by women observers. Over forty women supplied information on nuthatches, wrens, and thrashers; over twenty-six appear in the volume on larks, swallows, and their allies; twenty-five contributed to the thrushes volume; and remarkably over 150 wrote on cardinals, buntings, sparrows, and finches. Most of the items by women Bent cited were short notes on the habits of a single species observed in back yards, orchards, and fields. Professional ornithologists like Bent relied on these reports supplied by untrained amateurs, and Bent recognized the composite value of these minute observations. Darwin had used just this kind of data in formulating his evolutionary model.

Women observers, significantly, rarely contributed to the study of birds beyond the yard, park, or orchard. Bent cites only three women birdwatchers in the volume on ducks and geese, even fewer on herons and waders, and none at all on sea birds. Apparently few women made birdwatching expeditions to remote areas. Trekking seems to have been the province of intrepid male observers who found in the hunting tradition a ready-made model for ornithological exploration. But as backyard observers, women formed a hearty corps of reporters, their careful notes the fruits of nature education and the Audubon movement.

Chapter Ten

Nature Fakery and Concealing Coloration

*I*n 1903 John Burroughs, America's most distinguished writer on the outdoors, wrote an intense attack in the *Atlantic Monthly* against the misrepresentation of nature in popular animal stories. He accused two writers in particular, Ernest Thompson Seton and William Long, of deliberately fabricating unusual and scintillating events which they claimed to have witnessed in the wilderness. The reason for Burroughs's attack, which was unusually acerbic for a man of such saintly forbearance, can be found in his system of values. Seton and Long were challenging the established superiority of human society over the life of wild creatures. It was not the strict truthfulness of Seton's and Long's stories which was at issue—although that was the main thrust of attacks by Burroughs and others—but the *intent* of actions attributed to wildlife. Their heresy against accepted thinking drove the American community of natural historians, and birdwatchers in particular, to angry action. At the center of this storm was none other than President Theodore Roosevelt, committed patron of bird conservation and distinguished zoologist.

Today the nature faker controversy seems inconsequential; we take for granted the behavioral points of view held by Seton, and we no longer feel uneasy with the similarities of behavior between human and animal societies drawn by Seton and Long. But before the revolutionary work of Sigmund Freud and Konrad Lorenz, to name but two giants of our present consciousness, animal behavior was explained largely as blind instinct. The teachings of early Darwinism, coupled with absolute faith that man's ability to learn separated him from the lower animals, led naturalists to reject the concepts of animal behavior acknowledged today. The nature faker controversy, inevitable at the beginning of the century, is unthinkable today.

Ernest Thompson Seton was the most famous author accused of nature fakery. Not exclusively a bird student, Seton in his stories painted a revolutionary portrait of animal life that was applicable to birds as

Ernest Thompson Seton drawn by E. A. Burbank. *Dee Seton Barber.*

well. His point of view changed forever our perceptions of birds as slaves to their instincts, reminding us that birds grieve, play, and love. Seton was born in northern England in 1860. His family emigrated to Canada, where the family assumed a certain social superiority based upon a (probably spurious) link to a Scottish noble house. Seton early showed a talent for drawing and after completing public school in Canada, went to London in 1879 to study at the Royal Academy, but he returned to Canada in 1881 desolated by poverty.

Seton then passed four years in the wilderness of Manitoba, expanding his childhood passion for nature study and hunting. In 1885 he moved to New York and began to sell his first animal stories to magazines. But his emotional and intellectual apprenticeship was not yet over, and between 1890 and 1896 he either studied painting sporadically in Paris or returned to Canada, where he struggled to establish his reputation as a nature painter. Finally in 1896 Seton acknowledged that he was not a great painter in oils and would never be one. He was a superb illustrator, however, and for the next thirty years he settled in the suburbs of New York, and wrote and illustrated the colorful nature stories which were to bring him fame. Among his friends he counted Frank Chapman and other naturalists, and with Theodore Roosevelt he shared a passion for hunting and the out-of-doors life.

Seton wrote over thirty books, mostly collections of animal stories. *Wild Animals I Have Known* of 1898 and its several sequels appeared at regular intervals to critical and popular acclaim and were considered essential reading for young boys. His monumental four-volume *Lives of North American Game Mammals,* ten years in the making and completely illustrated by his own drawings, stands as Seton's serious contribution to American natural history and won him the Burroughs Award in 1926. The nature faker critics did not take issue with this more serious side of Seton's writing, but only with his stories of heroic animals, a type of fiction that he invented.

In the typical Seton story the animal itself is the protagonist and humans are kept to a minor role. Seton always wrote about animals with recognizable personalities and gave each a specific identity and personal name. The reader is drawn into the drama of the animal's life. The mysteries of life among the wild creatures are effortlessly and beguilingly unlocked.

"Redruff, the Story of the Don Valley Partridge," is the final chapter in Seton's most famous book, *Wild Animals I Have Known.* In it Seton endowed his hero, a male ruffed grouse of unusual size and beauty, with a recognizable personality. Seton did not bluntly anthropomorphize Redruff, but he did individualize him, giving him a strongly delineated character and emotional range. In his description of Redruff's encounter with his new mate, Seton pulled out all the emotional stops: "He turned to a statue and watched; he knew he had been watched. Could it be possible? Yes! There it was—a form—another—a shy little lady grouse; now bashfully seeking to hide. In a moment he was by her side. His whole nature swamped by a new feeling—burnt up with thirst—a cooling spring in sight. And how he spread and flashed his proud array! How came he to know that that would please?"

But Redruff's season of joy turns, as in all Seton stories, quickly to autumn. And at the center of this darkness is man, the predator. Redruff's mate is shot at the height of the breeding season, leaving him to raise his brood alone. Seton vividly describes Redruff's emotions in response to his mate's death:

> Who can tell what his horror and his mourning were? The outward signs were few, some minutes dumbly gazing at the place with downcast, draggled look, and then a change at the thought of their helpless brood. Back to the hiding-place he went, and called the well-known "Kreet, kreet." Did every grave give up its little inmate at the magic word? No, barely more than half; six little balls of down unveiled their lustrous eyes, and, rising, ran to meet him, but four feathered little bodies had found their graves.

Redruff's tragedy repeats itself as, one by one, his chicks die, victims of predators and of winter storms. In the heartbreaking conclusion Redruff, who had outwitted the gunners numerous times, is finally snared in a leg trap set for him by the unscrupulous hunter who had taken his mate. In an extraordinary condemnation of man's cruelty to wild creatures and in an equally daring commitment to animal psychology, Seton concluded his story with a description of Redruff's last hours:

> Have the wild things no moral or legal rights? What right has man to inflict such long and fearful agony on a fellow creature, simply because that creature does not speak his language? All that day, with growing, racking pains, poor Redruff hung and beat his great, strong wings in helpless struggles to be free. All day, all night, with growing torture, until he only longed for death. But no one came. The morning broke, the day wore on, and still he hung there, slowly dying; his very strength a curse. The second

night crawled slowly down, and when, in the dawdling hours of darkness, a great Horned Owl, drawn by the feeble flutter of a dying wing, cut short the pain, the deed was wholly kind.

To Seton's critics, the implication that Redruff had such powerful emotions was impossible to accept. Seton was not just spinning a good yarn. He was preaching a radically new approach to animal behavior, one which ran counter to echoes of transcendentalism that still prevailed in Burroughs's ideology.

The kind of animal story acceptable to Burroughs was invented by Henry Thoreau, transcendentalist nature student. Thoreau, mainly in his journals and subsequently in his formal writings, described his experiences of a particular animal or bird. The point of view in Thoreau's nature sketches is always the narrator's, never the animal's. And even if Thoreau muses lightly on the behavioral traits of the creatures he observes, usually he expected no concrete answers to his queries. He might perceive some of the mysteries around him but for both him and later Burroughs, nature remained aloof from interpretation. Outdoor study for the transcendentalists was a way to sense God's presence in nature, a mystical perception leading to an ecstatic glimpse of the impenetrable complexities of the natural world.

For Seton this was all so much nonsense. Self-educated in the infant science of ethology or animal psychology, fascinated with the multiple implications of Darwinian theory as it reformulated the natural world, Seton invented a new kind of animal story with the creature itself at its center. He abandoned without question the leisurely and for the most part uneventful—even boring—nature rambles of the post-Thoreau transcendentalists like Burroughs and Bradford Torrey. He replaced the Sunday afternoon walk with the drama of man's predation upon the beasts and the stark realities of animal psychology.

Burroughs in his famous attack on Seton and Long declared that man cannot understand the language of the wild creatures. Seton denied that statement in his stories by claiming to differentiate perfectly well among an animal's various sounds. And of course he was correct; animal communication is comprehensible to the field biologist if he takes the time to crack the code. But for Burroughs the incomprehensibility of animal language was a major tenet of his unshakable transcendental creed, and he could not let Seton's and Long's threat to open up nature's mysteries go unchallenged.

Burroughs was sufficiently sophisticated to recognize that animals might feel emotions, but he refused to acknowledge that animals can reason: "Of course it is mainly guesswork how far our psychology applies to the lower animals. That they experience many of our emotions there can be no doubt, but that they have intellectual and reasoning processes like our own, except in very rudimentary form, admits of grave doubt." Burroughs was horrified because Seton's animals could reason. Seton granted the animals a level of behavioral complexity which Burroughs refused to acknowledge.

An ethologist today would assert that an animal's process of reasoning is complex, made up of his instinctual responses interacting with his environment and modified by cerebral capacity. This same ethologist would say that animal society is complex and contains elements of behavior related to our own society. He would suggest that the only way to test the truthfulness of Seton's stories would be to spend at least five years in the field as well as in the laboratory discovering what grouse, for example, do and why they do it. Seton always claimed that his stories were based upon personal experience and there seems to be no reason to doubt his word even though he was called a liar by the anti-nature faker contingent. Theodore Roosevelt, however, repeatedly defended Seton's integrity, as did Frank Chapman. Seton erred in his interpretation of events he had witnessed in the wilderness. The field of animal psychology was in its infancy and little was understood about the relationship of instincts and learned behavior to motivation. This relationship was only discovered and elucidated several decades later by such scientists as Konrad Lorenz.

For Burroughs, however, nature was unfathomable. He had understood enough Darwin to recognize the pattern of evolution but refused to admit that this pattern was due to chance. Burroughs had manipulated Darwin's theory to reaffirm his own transcendental faith. Each organism had developed in perfect harmony with its ecological niche. For him the behavior of each species was fixed by inherited instincts. Animals could not reason or think, and they did not learn. Since emotions are instinctual, he allowed animals to feel. But teach their young? Lead their packs? Figure out a trap? NEVER! And Burroughs's attitude was the prevailing one among American naturalists, birdwatchers included. Burroughs and his circle placed man at the center of the universe.

Seton actively debunked this position and he paid dearly for it. The normally mild, even benign Burroughs lit into him mercilessly and

Seton was unable to defend himself. By synthesizing social Darwinian ideology concerning shared qualities of man and the animals with the radical new theories of animal psychology, Seton articulated a personal view of nature intended to shock and instruct. Obviously it shocked, but too much to teach anything. Seton along the way told an entrancing story and this readability made him too influential for his critics. Because Seton's animals were drawn so articulately they were more fascinating than Burroughs' and Thoreau's subjects. Although Seton's stories may seem emotionally florid to us today, they retain more conviction than Burroughs's delicately colored descriptions of the birds in his backyard. Seton declared in his animal stories that there was a complex world out there charged with emotion, a world in which man was perceived as predator and where instincts, emotions, and reason combined in an animal psychology which man could and should understand. Nonsense, said Burroughs, Theodore Roosevelt, and the pundits at the American Museum of Natural History. Quite true, says the history of science today.

As a result of Burroughs's attack, Seton decided to turn his hand to more orthodox scientific writing. Chapman even brought Seton and Burroughs together, and after an uncomfortable two hours they became friends. But Seton never regained confidence in his scientific ability. His *Life History of the North American Game Mammals* is a classic, but the drama of Redruff is gone from its pages and with it the excitement of the new scientific era. Redruff was dead in more than one way.

*S*eton was largely left alone in the subsequent vituperation against nature fakery which filled the pages of popular journals for several years after Burroughs's first broadside in 1903. For the pundits found a far more successful and thus more hateful shammer in the figure of the Reverend William J. Long, author of numerous books of nature stories with coy titles such as *Ways of the Wild* and *School of the Woods.* Long was much more popular than Seton and much more dangerous. His books, like Burroughs's, had become part of the nature education curriculum of many public school systems and it was this access to young minds which prompted the campaign against him. The battle raged on because Long would not back down and defended himself persuasively in print. This irritated his critics even more. He cared little for their acceptance of his work, and fought all the harder every time he was attacked.

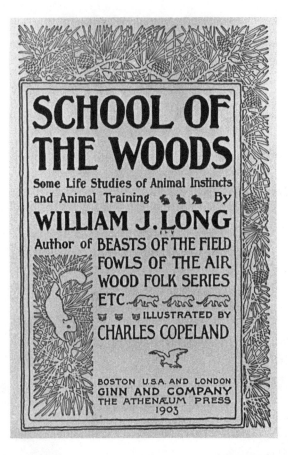

SCHOOL OF
THE WOODS

Some Life Studies of Animal Instincts
and Animal Training ♦ ♦ ♦ By
WILLIAM J. LONG
Author of BEASTS OF THE FIELD
FOWLS OF THE AIR
WOOD FOLK SERIES
ETC
ILLUSTRATED BY
CHARLES COPELAND

BOSTON U.S.A. AND LONDON
GINN AND COMPANY
THE ATHENÆUM PRESS
1903

Title page of William J.
Long's most controversial
and popular book.

William J. Long was born in 1866 and in 1892 received an A.B. from Harvard. Three years later he graduated from the Andover Newton Theological Seminary. For the next three years he studied philosophy and theology at Heidelberg, Berlin, and Paris, obtaining the Ph.D. from Heidelberg in 1898. He was called to the Congregational Church in Cambridge, Massachusetts, but lost his job because of his radical ideas. In 1899 he transferred to the First Congregational Church in Stamford, Connecticut. After 1904 his books had begun to pay and he resigned his pulpit.

Long's radical tendencies and his fascination with philosophical questions of identity and morality lay behind his interest in natural history and animal psychology. He considered himself a pioneering intellectual in philosophy and in science, and his arrogance fanned the flames of the nature faker controversy. Four of his didactic nature books appeared before 1905 and they continued to come out up to his death in 1952.

The one book which brought the birdwatching contingent down upon Long's capacious head was his *School of the Woods* published in 1903. In a lengthy introduction Long boldly raised his colors. The sole purpose of these stories was to demonstrate that animals are taught most of what they know by their parents much in the way human children are taught. Long claimed to have observed a mother otter teaching her cubs to swim and drew broad implications from the incident:

> That interesting little comedy by the quiet river . . . opened my eyes to the fact that all wild creatures must learn most of what they know as we do; and to learn they must be taught. . . .
>
> That animal education is like our own, and so depends chiefly upon teaching, may possibly be a new suggestion in the field of natural history. Most people think that the life of a wild animal is governed wholly by instinct. They are of the same class who hold that the character of a child is largely predetermined by heredity.
>
> Personally, after many years of watching animals in their native haunts, I am convinced that instinct plays a much smaller part than we have supposed; that an animal's success or failure in the ceaseless struggle for life depends, not upon instinct, but upon the kind of training which the animal receives from its mother.

With this one declaration Long sealed his fate with Burroughs, Chapman, and Roosevelt. They despised his childish didacticism and his manipulation of appearances. Ironically this point of view endeared him to teachers and parents who saw him as an educator who demonstrated to their children with charming, nonviolent stories the importance of attention to their elders.

Long's stories differed from Seton's in many ways, but they shared a preoccupation with issues of animal psychology. In Long's typical story the narrator remained at the center, describing disarmingly benign little incidents of animal behavior. But Long carefully constructed these vignettes to make a point about animal behavior. The events Long chose to describe were improbable and his interpretation of them arrogant. He produced violent reactions among the naturalists. One of his assertions particularly irked his critics. In *School of the Woods* Long claimed to have witnessed an osprey teaching its young to fish. It had stocked, according to Long, a small pond with fish it had previously maimed, making them easier for his fledglings to catch. These stories were hopelessly unlikely but Long repeatedly contended that he had personally observed or confirmed all the events in his stories; he had spent weeks in the wilderness compiling the data for them, and he defied anyone to prove otherwise. His faithful readers believed him and his stories.

Burroughs devoted over half of his attack on nature fakery to refuting Long's approach to animal learning. He dismissed as preposterous all of Long's examples of animal education:

> There is nothing in the dealings of animals with their young that in the remotest way suggests human instruction and discipline. The young of all wild creatures do instinctively what their parents do and did. They do not have to be taught. They are taught by nature from the start. . . . Mr. Long would have us believe that the crows teach their young to fly. Does the rooster teach its young to crow, or the cock grouse teach the young males to drum? No bird teaches its young to fly. They fly instinctively when their wings are strong enough.

The modern ethologist would see the problem in a more complex way, saying that animals learn through parental instruction but that each species has to be studied for years to discover which behavior is learned. Neither Long nor Burroughs had any scientific bases for their points of view. Roosevelt privately took Burroughs to task for rejecting the concept of learning in the animal world. Even in 1904 natural historians recognized that certain animal behavior is learned.

Long discredited his arguments with far-fetched interpretations of activities he claimed to have observed. An excerpt from his famous story "Animal Surgery" illustrates this tendency.

> Twenty years ago while sitting quietly by a brook at the edge of the woods in Bridgewater, Mass., a woodcock fluttered out into the open and made his way to a spot on the bank where a light streak of clay showed clearly from where I was watching . . . and my first impression was that this was a wounded bird that had made a long flight after being shot at, and had now come out to the stream to drink or to bathe his wound, as birds often do . . . but the bird was acting strangely in broad daylight. . . .
>
> At first he took soft clay in his bill from the edge of the water and seemed to be smearing it on one leg near the knee. Then he fluttered away on one foot for a distance and seemed to be pulling tiny roots and fibers of grass, which he worked into the clay that he had already smeared on his leg. Again he took more clay and plastered it over the fibers, putting on more and more till I could plainly see the enlargement. . . . Then he stood perfectly still for a full hour under an overhanging sod where the eye could with

difficulty find him, his only motion meanwhile being an occasional rubbing and smoothing of the clay bandage with his bill, until it hardened enough to suit him, whereupon he fluttered away from the brook and disappeared in the thick woods.

I had my own explanation of the incredible action—namely, that the woodcock had a broken leg, and had deliberately put it into a clay cast to hold the broken bones in place until they should knit together again. . . . For years I questioned gunners closely, and found two who said that they had killed woodcock whose legs had at one time been broken and had healed again. . . . I examined hundreds of woodcock in markets in different localities and found one whose leg had at one time been broken by a shot and then had healed perfectly.

All this proved nothing to an outsider. . . . until last winter, twenty years afterwards, when the confirmation came unexpectedly. . . . A gentleman . . . came to me and told me eagerly of a curious find he had made the previous autumn. He was gunning one day with a friend, when they shot a woodcock, which on being brought in by the dog was found to have a lump of hard clay on one of its legs. Curious to know what it meant, he chipped the clay off with his penknife and found a broken bone, which was then almost healed and as straight as ever.

Not surprisingly, Long's critics had a field day. In the year after the story was published, *Science Magazine* carried refutations of Long's woodcock story without even giving him the opportunity to defend himself. The attacks were vicious and *ad hominem.* Long frequently published defenses of his own work in other journals but these only angered his critics all the more. Unlike Seton, Long could be attacked on the grounds of sheer nature fakery. But it is easy to see why readers were seduced by Long's stories. He constantly reassured them that he had difficulty in believing his own eyes and that he only wrote about an incident when he had corroboration. Long skirted the truth without recognizing the danger to himself.

Frank Chapman, in a measured letter to *Science* in 1904, expressed the official position of the scientific and educational inner circle. In a voice that bore little resemblance to his invariably genial book reviews, he said: "Are we to believe the accusation that the author in question . . . is a liar or have we in Mr. Long a naturalist whose powers of observation, discrimination, and interpretation are so far beyond those of any other student of nature, living or dead, that he is in effect a Galileo among animal psychologists?"

Chapman had hit the nail right on the head. He was savvy enough not to attack the scientific principles Long sought to substantiate, but objected instead to the empirical basis of the theories Long passionately defended. His calm criticism of Long was intended to center the adverse publicity accorded the scoundrel and diminish his popularity:

> It requires the briefest consideration of the fact that tens of thousands of Mr. Long's books have been sold for supplementary reading in the schools—where, judged only on their literary charm, they are almost uniformly commended by teachers—to realize their far-reaching influence for evil. . . . Is it not, then, the duty of naturalists to enlighten the general public, and especially those entrusted with the education of children, in regard to the real character of Mr. Long's efforts?

But Long had his readership and was popular with the press. Finally Theodore Roosevelt, one of the backstage strategists of the nature faker war, could remain silent no longer and in 1907 granted journalist Edward Clark an exclusive interview in which he condemned the nature fakers. The interview was published in *Everybody's Magazine.* This was a bold move for any president. Long was a private citizen and an attack launched by America's highest elected official was bound to become a David and Goliath confrontation. The press stepped in immediately to ridicule Roosevelt's claims as a nature lover, calling attention to the president's obsession with big game hunting. Roosevelt's heartless slaughter of innocent animals was seen in juxtaposition to the Reverend Long's benign woodland rambles.

Roosevelt's attack on Long was ineffective, because he limited himself to debunking Long's veracity and shied away from the larger issues of animal psychology central to the entire controversy:

> Men of this stamp will necessarily arise, from time to time, some in one walk of life, some in another. Our quarrel is not with these men, but with those who give them their chance. We who believe in the study of nature feel that a real knowledge and appreciation of wild things, of trees, flowers, birds, and of the grim and crafty creatures of the wilderness, give an added beauty and health to life. Therefore we abhor deliberate or reckless untruth in this study as much as in any other. . . .

Eventually the nature faker controversy petered out. As the science of ethology advanced, Long's sense of isolation waned, and his tone became less hysterical. Long was dedicated to philosophy and natural history but was without adequate training in scientific method.

Mabel Osgood Wright, associate editor of *Bird-Lore,* author of more than thirty novels, preeminent birdwatcher and educator, was presented to Mr. Long one evening during the nature faker controversy at a meeting of the Connecticut Audubon Society. Long is reported by Chapman to have said, "Wright, Wright, you're the bird woman, aren't you? It seems to me that I have a letter from you at home, but I haven't read it yet." "Well, it couldn't be from me," Mrs. Wright replied with icy clearness, "for I never heard of you before." With that she must be imagined as taking Chapman's arm and turning away.

Abbott Thayer's intense 1919 self-portrait in pencil. *Metropolitan Museum of Art, gift of Mrs. E. H. Harriman.*

*T*heodore Roosevelt was at the center of another controversy which swirled around an elaborate theory of concealing coloration in the animal kingdom, propounded with fanatical enthusiasm by Abbott Thayer, distinguished American artist and amateur ornithologist. Thayer, an eclectic and eccentric personality, had retreated around 1885 with his large family from Brooklyn to Dublin, New Hampshire, where they lived in an unwinterized, crudely built cottage. There the artist maintained a popular teaching studio and his students took up residence in this tiny utopian community. Abbott Thayer was a powerful patriarch, as committed to nature study as he was to painting. His oldest son,

Gerald, an able draftsman and painter, assisted in his father's ornithological experiments.

At first Thayer studied birds at random. He had thought to make his reputation as a painter of animal portraits in the manner of John James Audubon whose art he admired above all else. But he soon discovered a talent for portraiture, a lucrative pursuit which kept his growing family in food and clothes. Louis Agassiz Fuertes, destined to become a great bird artist, at an early age joined Thayer's atelier in Dublin to learn Thayer's remarkable technique for portraying the subtle textures and colors of birds. In return Fuertes sent his teacher bird skins and through correspondence with Fuertes, Thayer kept in touch with ornithological discoveries and theories. It is against this backdrop that his theory of concealing coloration appears most clearly.

Thayer perceived as early as 1895 that many natural forms, especially birds, appear invisible in their favorite haunts. He applied himself to discovering the basic principles of nature which he felt must underlie such a universal phenomenon as animal camouflage. Not surprisingly, his solution to this puzzle was grounded in a variation of color theory. Thayer's originality as a scientist lay in the sensitivity he brought not just to painting but also to natural history.

Thayer publicized his elaborate theories about animal coloration on two occasions: once briefly in an article for *The Auk* in 1896, and then extensively in a heavy tome attributed to his son Gerald, but largely by himself, called *Concealing Coloration in the Animal Kingdom,* published in 1909. Theodore Roosevelt apparently ignored Thayer's first essay but the obsessively argued book of 1909 so outraged the former president that he felt compelled to respond extensively and angrily to Thayer's theories, both in an appendix to his book *African Game Trails* of 1910 and in a book-length article in the *Bulletin of the American Museum of Natural History* for 1911.

Without Roosevelt's vigorous refutation it is likely that Thayer's theory would have been quietly culled by scientists for those points that were valid and the remaining absurdities would have died on the library shelf. But Roosevelt brought Thayer's theory into the unnaturally. strong light of his scrutiny, under which it certainly could not bear up.

Abbott Thayer's theory is one example of the intense interest in scientific discovery which characterized bird study of that time. Amateur naturalists like Thayer felt justified in inventing scientific models even though they lacked basic training in the discipline. Much of

Thayer's elaborate theory proved incorrect, but some of it did enter the body of scientific theory. Thayer based his theory of concealing coloration on a natural law which he compulsively formulated to apply to all animals. Had he argued more reasonably that concealing coloration serves effectively only in certain situations but not by universal rule, he would have been more convincing. But he was led astray by his obsessive personality.

Briefly, Thayer assumed that an animal's coloration affords protection in only two circumstances—when it is on the verge of catching food or of being caught for food by a predator. For Thayer, not one mark or pattern existed anywhere in the animal world that did not serve to conceal the animal. Alfred Russel Wallace, co-inventor with Darwin of evolutionary theory, had already adumbrated this view in 1867.

Thayer therefore demonstrated some acquaintance with Darwinian theory. He believed that natural selection must have determined the color patterns of all animals in a way that served the species rather than harmed it. The flaw in this argument is that coloration in animals is not always an aid against predation, nor does it enhance success for a predator, but often operates as a sexual signal or as a territorial marker in mating strategies. Some animals depend upon concealing coloration for survival but many do not. For those that do, Thayer's theory was valid but, for example, the male cardinal's bright plumage is a stratagem in attracting a mate and in staking out territory against males of his and other species. For safety the cardinal relies on quick reactions and concealment in dark shrubbery.

Thayer went on to establish the validity of his cherished assumptions with an extraordinary series of paintings, photographs, and live demonstrations designed to show that even the most brightly colored birds are at times invisible. The principle of which Thayer was most fond, and the only one which has stood the test of time, was that of countershading in animal coloration. Thayer declared that "the newly discovered law in its application to animals may be stated thus: animals are painted by Nature darkest on those parts which tend to be most lighted by the sky's light, and vice versa."

To demonstrate the truth of this law, Thayer would place several decoys at a good distance from the viewer, who saw the decoys as uniformly shaded and always failed to see those Thayer had painted lighter below. Thayer's law neatly explained the fact that so many ground-dwelling species are colored lighter below than above. By crouching close to the ground, the animal masks the shadow cast by its darker back with the light reflected from its lighter belly. Had Thayer been content with this law alone, his theories probably would not have elicited strong negative reactions. But he suffered from two flaws fatal to any scientist: he fell in love with his own theories, and he was too ready to generalize from incomplete data. He asserted that all animals evinced the same survival strategy of freezing when in danger, and his theories completely disregarded the element of movement. Concealing coloration operates only when an animal is still. A fleeing animal is never invisible.

One of Thayer's more controversial demonstrations involved the bluejay, which relies on rapid flight for protection. But according to Thayer, the bluejay's color helped it to avoid danger. The bird's blue color, he argued, exactly matched the shadow cast by a spruce tree on snow. Under such auspicious conditions the bluejay is in fact less visible, but as Frank Chapman wrote in his autobiography:

> On former occasions when I had witnessed Thayer's demonstrations, so overpowering was his personality that I lacked the courage to disagree with conclusions I could not endorse. But in this instance (the bluejay demonstration) . . . I felt I must speak my mind. . . . As an arboreal species bluejays do not often descend to snow-covered ground. . . . Thayer looked at me sadly, and I fear from that day he regarded me as a backslider from the ranks of his earliest supporters.

Thayer developed his theory more elaborately than can be usefully described here, defining types of camouflage and coloration strategies. His formulations became the great obsession of his later years. The book of 1909 is extensively illustrated and argued. One astounding plate shows a copperhead snake lying on a bed of dried leaves. The snake is so indistinct that a stencilled outline is superimposed upon the illustration to reveal the snake's form. Another ingenious plate reproduced three watercolor sketches of roseate spoonbills and flamingoes feeding in a marsh at dawn and dusk. The pink birds are shown camouflaged against the peachy tones of the sky. The drawings are charming but, as President Roosevelt pointed out, the birds move when they feed, obliterating any benefit they might derive from camouflage.

Thayer himself, his family, and sometimes his students devoted intense energy to preparing the numerous illustrations for the text of *Concealing Coloration*. The artist also boosted his theory personally,

Thayer painted blue jays concealed in shadowed snow, a demonstration rejected by Frank Chapman. *National Museum of American Art, Smithsonian Institution, gift of the heirs of Abbott H. Thayer.*

demonstrating his ideas for ornithologists in Central Park and defending his observations in long and obsessive letters to Theodore Roosevelt, who repeatedly refused to attend Thayer's demonstrations.

Until Theodore Roosevelt took up arms against his theories, however, Thayer had convinced some prestigious scientists to accept their validity. Frank Chapman, as we have seen, was at first taken in. Thayer was a bit of a sorcerer, conjuring up optical illusions for the delight of his audiences.

But Roosevelt refused to be enchanted. His knowledge of natural history was more systematic than Thayer's and his intellect more mature. He was so outraged by Thayer's success with his theory that he determined, as in the nature faker controversy, to air his views even at the cost of criticism from the press. His heavy-handed refutation of Thayer's theories brought him no joy. Chapman was again forced to mediate the dispute, writing an editorial in *Bird-Lore* designed to placate both sides.

Roosevelt rejected Thayer's theory at its weakest point when he stated in *African Game Trails* that "in sufficiently thick cover, whether of trees or grass, any small animal of any color or shape may, if motionless, escape observation." But Roosevelt went too far when he objected to the valid law of countershading that Thayer with his painter's eye had discerned.

In fact, Roosevelt often underestimated the importance of coloration as a strategy for species survival. His strong reaction against Thayer's emphasis on visual strategies may relate to Roosevelt's personal handicaps—he was myopic and all his life struggled with extremely weak eyes. For him objects at any distance were a blur, so that he came to rely more heavily than other naturalists upon perceptions of movement. Both Thayer and Roosevelt found themselves defending their own tactics as members of the species *homo sapiens.* Thayer, visually astute and with the color sensitivity of a born artist, stalked his prey exclusively through sight. Roosevelt, visually impaired, located his prey through movement and sound.

The concealing coloration controversy was of less importance to the average birdwatcher than the nature faker controversy, but it is an amusing part of birding's history. It demonstrates the popularity of science as a hobby at the turn of the century, when birdwatchers were better attuned than now to the developments in ornithological research. Thus, a former president and a respected artist stimulated other amateurs to test out theories and explore principles of natural history.

Chapter Eleven

Introduced Species: Cats, Starlings and English Sparrows

From being originally a keeper of cats—I will not say a lover of them, because one cannot really love anything of such inherent treachery of temperament,—I have come, through a long experience, to consider them the chief menace to bird life of the day. What warden can protect game birds, eggs or young from this velvet-pawed prowler, who blends its sinuous color-protected shape in the shadows of the two twilights, the time of its principal hunting?

Fight and kill them as I may within my own garden, each year has its tragedies. . . . Neither is this a wild, half-starved cat, with any plausible sort of excuse or need, but belongs to a neighbor, who calmly affirms that it never hunts and seldom leaves the house. We call this animal the *domestic* cat. There is no such thing in nature. The cat is a hunter, pure and simple, who is at times distorted into a kind of tameness, from which it quickly relapses.

Mabel Osgood Wright wrote these bitter words in *Bird-Lore* in 1911 during the plume wars and the first wave of bird conservation. Targeted as bird enemy number one, the cat—stray, feral, or domestic—was repeatedly vilified by bird-lovers. Cat-lovers everywhere were horrified. The Audubon societies had already entered the ring slugging, resolving at their annual conference in 1905 that "in the interests of humanity and bird protection the National Association of Audubon Societies endorses the movement to make owners responsible for their [cats'] acts and welfare."

The resolution was later tempered somewhat to placate the cat-lovers among the membership. Feral cats, rather than domestic cats, became the prime targets. Citing awesome statistics (the ASPCA in New York City destroyed 465,065 diseased, homeless, or injured cats in nine years, for example), the association argued that the millions of feral cats roaming the land led a pitiful existence and should be put down for humane reasons.

But the friends of the cat would have been unwise to relax. Mabel Wright never failed to include the pet cat in her frequent diatribes, and other contributors to *Bird-Lore* maintained that well fed domestic pets would still prey upon ground-nesting birds purely for sport. Supporters of cats argued that little concrete evidence had been gathered against the

Bird-Lore's propaganda enraged cat lovers.

domestic cat, whereas numerous studies had demonstrated the animal's usefulness in destroying rodents.

Bird-Lore published arguments on both sides. The Audubon association, fearing to alienate its cat-loving members, was forced to pull back from the extreme anti-cat rhetoric of the campaign's first thrust. T. Gilbert Pearson urged Edward Howe Forbush, state ornithologist for Massachusetts and noted student of economic ornithology, to systematically examine the habits of the cat. Hard evidence of its perfidious depredations might quiet the outraged cat-lovers among the membership.

In 1916 Forbush published his book-length pamphlet, *The Domestic Cat, Bird-Killer, Mouser and Destroyer of Wildlife. Means of Utilizing and Controlling It,* and in it came down hard on the pet cat, citing results of surveys and analyses of stomach contents. Forbush had little to say in defense of cats, which he considered an obnoxious species introduced into North America by man to the detriment of native wildlife. He

Audubon association president
T. Gilbert Pearson counts cat corpses.
Department of Library Services,
American Museum of Natural History.

devised a statistically persuasive method of tabulating cat predations and concluded that stray cats could be expected to kill at least 700,000 birds a year in Massachusetts, 2.5 million in Illinois, and 3.5 million in New York State.

In 1915 one of the Audubon society's fondest hopes was realized when Montclair, New Jersey, became the first municipality in the United States to enact a vagrant cat ordinance providing for mandatory cat licensing. All untagged cats would be destroyed as vermin. But even while Edward Howe Forbush was amassing his statistics and the Audubon association was pressing for cat ordinances nationwide, T. Gilbert Pearson somewhat hypocritically sought to placate the member cat-lovers.

After applauding the Montclair ordinance in *Bird-Lore,* he went on to say that "the Association is not at this time prepared to begin a campaign against cats, but we have undertaken . . . various investigations of the relation of cats to birds. We want to know the truth; and all readers of *Bird-Lore* are invited to forward to this office any evidence they may have bearing on the subject, either for or against cats as destroyers of birds."

No cat fancier could be fooled by the inconsistency of Pearson's plea for open-mindedness. And evidently the association decided to pull back from the issue for a few years since passions were being needlessly aroused. Instead, it quietly pursued a lobbying campaign in the state legislatures, leading to the first state cat ordinance enacted by New York in 1918. The bill gave permission to licensed hunters to shoot any cat found hunting or killing birds—a law not well conceived, for what constituted evidence of a cat hunting? But *Bird-Lore*'s editors were emboldened by this victory and increased their vituperation against cats.

In the spring of 1918, *Bird-Lore* said: "One of the greatest menaces to the bird-life of the country today is the house-cat. . . . We earnestly ask the owner of every house-cat during the next three months to assume the responsibility of seeing that the cat will not be given an opportunity to kill birds." But the adverse publicity the anti-cat campaign brought was intolerable and for the next fifteen years or so the organization maintained a low profile, restricting its comments to short notices about cat ordinances or reports of feral cat destruction programs.

In 1930 an aging Mabel Osgood Wright crankily reported in *Bird-Lore* that in the first sixteen years of Birdcraft Sanctuary, the ten-acre refuge she founded near her home in Fairfield, Connecticut, two hundred feral cats were shot. "How did they get in?" she wondered, "By pussy-footing between the spikes of the fence and dropping from overhanging trees; but *they did not get out.*"

Three years later, in 1933, T. Gilbert Pearson again reinstated the cat issue as a primary concern of the Audubon association. In his annual report as president he outlined the poor legislative response to the campaign. Only five states had included cat clauses in their fish and game laws. He had sent out a model cat ordinance to 4,000 towns but only sixty of those exhibited even a slight interest in the matter. "Nowhere in the country today . . . is there a concerted effort to reduce the numbers of vagrant cats, other than that put forth by sportsmen's clubs and the ASPCA. . . . We shall continue our efforts to seek a sane and workable method of dealing with this vexatious problem."

A famous instance of the society's failure to sway public opinion about the cat occurred in 1949, when the Illinois State Legislature passed a bill (Senate Bill Number 93) which would impose fines on owners who let their cats run at large. No less a liberal-minded politician than Adlai Stevenson, then governor of Illinois, vetoed this bill, stating:

> The problem of cat versus bird is as old as time. If we attempt to resolve it by legislation who knows but what we may be called upon to take sides as well in the age-old problems of dog versus cat, bird versus bird or even bird versus worm. In my opinion, the State of Illinois and its local governing bodies already have enough to do without trying to control feline delinquency.
>
> For these reasons, and not because I love birds the less or cats the more, I veto and withhold my approval of Senate Bill Number 93.

Time has not treated the Audubon association well on the issue of cat versus bird. Feral cats are still viewed as undesirable, and for good reason. A feral cat can be defined as an animal which breeds and feeds without the assistance of man. The feral cat is a wild animal which poses a threat in numerous ways. Untreated for rabies and distemper, it spreads both diseases to indigenous species wherever it lives. A formidable breeder, the cat replaces its numbers so frequently that it counters population reductions from the maladies it spreads. The census figures for feral cats are staggering, with an estimate of somewhere between 8 and 16 million animals in the United States.

The Audubonists erred, however, in their conviction that birds constitute the major portion of the feral cat's diet. Behavioral studies have resulted in evidence exonerating the cat as bird predator. Analyses of stomach contents reveal that cats infrequently eat birds. The overwhelming majority of them prefer a rodent diet for the simple reason that birds are much harder for them to catch than rodents. Cats, the biologists agree, have little impact on bird populations.

The Audubonists, then, were right to wage a war on the feral cat but did so for the wrong reasons. The feral cat population does not belong as an issue to bird conservation but rather to the broader field of wildlife management. It is unpleasant to come upon the remains of a bird beneath one's feeder, but in all probability the bird was caught because it was in a weakened condition. For defense a healthy bird depends upon flight, against which the cat has a limited hunting strategy.

*T*he grounds keepers of Tanglewood, the Boston Symphony's summer headquarters, have been battling an infestation of starlings. The gregarious birds nest in the vast roof supports of the open music shed, fouling the seats below them and whistling during concerts. Poisons, decoys, traps, and guns have failed to deter them. The bluebird has all but disappeared from its former haunts on the East Coast, driven out of its preferred nesting sites, the holes in old trees and fences, by English sparrows and starlings, more aggressive alien species which commandeer the nest holes of the easily bullied bluebird.

It is difficult to understand why a few amateur naturalists in the last century brought about the introduction of two species often considered pests in their homelands. How these birds were introduced is well known but why they were imported is harder to discover. These two introductions, one of the English sparrow and the other of the starling, were distrusted by conservationists. Their early forebodings were borne out by events.

The first attempts to introduce the English sparrow into America were instituted in 1851 by the Brooklyn Institute (now the Brooklyn Museum), a natural history academy and museum. The eight pairs of birds released at that time died. Undeterred by this failure, in 1852 the Institute's personnel freed fifty more sparrows from a ship in the harbor and placed another group in the tower of the Greenwood Cemetery Chapel in Brooklyn. After a period of acclimatization the birds were released at the cemetery, where a keeper encouraged their health with grain and their fecundity with nesting boxes. The much cossetted birds flourished. Soon thereafter flocks were released in Portland, Maine, Rhode Island, and other locations. The largest recorded release, in 1869 in Philadelphia, consisted of one thousand birds.

The English sparrow did well in North America, spreading rapidly across the continent and requiring no assistance to survive. Because it was thought to be primarily an insect feeder, the sparrow was at first welcomed as a possible control species for caterpillars. Instead, the English sparrow fed primarily on seeds and grains, choosing insects only when feeding its nestlings and encouraging leaf-eating caterpillars by displacing the orioles, cuckoos, and robins which did feed upon them. The English sparrows were particularly successful in urban areas where they gorged themselves on the undigested grain in horse droppings.

Initial enthusiasm for the English sparrow was so great that John Galvin, city forester for Boston, claimed that the birds had exterminated canker worms and yellow caterpillars in Boston's public parks. He then had his men destroy the bands of shrikes which fed upon the sparrows, insuring the birds' unrestricted increase. But by the late 1870s the tide had turned quickly against the English sparrow. Ornithologist Elliott Coues suggested an analysis of the birds' stomach contents. Scientists failed to find evidence of insects in the stomachs of fifty-six Boston sparrows, and war against this import was declared.

In 1886 the Boston-based Society of Bird Restorers mounted a clean-up campaign in the Public Garden, but it proved too costly and difficult. Following this the United States Department of Agriculture created a special task force to study the habits of the English sparrow and concluded that the sparrow was successful partly because of its ability to adapt to a diversity of physical and climatic conditions. The task force condemned the bird as a pest which damaged decorative plants and trees. It had destroyed the English ivy, for example, at the Smithsonian Institution and was known to ravage vegetable and fruit crops. It roosted in the eaves of urban buildings, blocking gutters with nesting materials. It was also noted that the English sparrow was an aggressor against native species, successfully competing for nesting sites with swallows, finches, and bluebirds.

The panel suggested several ways to exterminate the English sparrow: killing the bird and destroying its nests wherever it thrived; passing laws against feeding it or introducing it into new locations; and hiring municipal sparrow destroyers.

Trapping, shooting, or poisoning were unfortunately ineffective in controlling a bird frequently defended as a cheerful visitor from Europe or a dispatcher of harmful insects. Moreover, the sparrow is notoriously difficult to outwit. It avoids traps that are normally successful for other species and will not eat poisoned grain. For a short while an effort was made to introduce the English sparrow as a table bird. It was offered in restaurants and boarding houses as "reed birds" (bobolinks), a popular southern dish. That campaign was moderately successful, and in 1887 the birds were bringing one dollar per hundred in the Albany market.

Both ornithologists and the leadership of the Audubon societies welcomed what they felt was a long overdue campaign against the English sparrow. *Bird-Lore* frequently published letters and notes from readers describing methods for control of the sparrow and reporting its obnoxious habits. But an all-out campaign was avoided. As with the cat controversy, Audubonists found themselves pitted against sentimental pro-sparrow members who would find unpalatable a campaign to exterminate a songbird. The Audubon society had to be content with periodic hostile articles about the sparrow and with lobbying efforts in state legislatures. With the advent of the automobile, as horse droppings became less plentiful, the bird became scarcer and less a nuisance, and the campaign against it subsided naturally.

The starling has had a somewhat similar history and reception in America. The Society for the Acclimatization of Foreign Birds introduced the bird into the United States in 1877 by liberating a small flock in Central Park. The first try failed, but undeterred naturalists in Portland, Oregon, liberated another flock of starlings in 1889. Then in New York City in 1892 Eugene Scheiffelin, a wealthy manufacturer with a predilection for bird study who was a leading force in the American Acclimatization Society, determined to introduce into America all the birds mentioned by Shakespeare. A flock of starlings let loose by his group in Central Park immediately thrived and began nesting, among other places, under the eaves of the American Museum of Natural History.

Since then the starling has spread as far as British Columbia, and its success was closely studied by the Biological Survey and the Audubon association. Like the English sparrow, the bird had a remarkable ability to adapt to new conditions. *Bird-Lore* followed its steady march westward and southward, reporting, for example, that in 1912 two hundred starlings had taken up residence on the Princeton University campus,

ABOVE. Ernest Thompson Seton enjoyed the English sparrow's antics. *Seton Memorial Library, Philmont Scout Ranch.*

LEFT. Allan Brooks portrayed the starling as an elegant immigrant. *Department of Library Services, American Museum of Natural History.*

and in 1922 the birds had reached Tennessee and Louisiana. The National Association of Audubon Societies was cautious in attempting to villify the starling, a bird whose popular appeal was evidently connected to its rakish, intelligent sociability and its reputed effectiveness against crop-destroying insects.

As early as 1911 Mabel Wright recognized the bird's aggressive behavior toward nesting songbirds, and Frank Chapman a year later advised curbing its spread. But evidence for and against the starling's usefulness was sufficiently inconclusive to subdue the association's rhetoric. Convinced of the starling's potential destructiveness toward songbirds, Chapman and other conservation leaders opposed the introduction of any foreign species but felt constrained to wait until the Department of Agriculture established the facts of the starling's diet. The study, unfortunately, gave the starling a clean bill of health. Analyses of the stomach contents of more than two thousand starlings revealed that the bird appeared to be primarily an insect feeder and economically more useful than the flicker, robin, catbird, red-winged blackbird, or grackle. It recommended that the bird be protected by law.

Bird conservationists were powerless to lobby against a species beneficial to agriculture even though it was an enemy of more attractive indigenous species. The national association had been beaten on its own territory. In 1924, Edward Forbush prepared an educational leaflet for the national Audubon association, in which he pointed out that the starling is omnivorous, feeding frequently to devastating effect on such produce as cherries, grapes, strawberries, corn, and apples. He also noted that the bird was considered a nuisance in every country where it had been introduced, and concluded that nothing could halt the starling's increase in the United States. It was too late, he said. Forbush's prophetic words unfortunately proved correct. By 1962 the starling population had swelled alarmingly. The largest roost, in Virginia's Dismal Swamp, numbered 20 million birds. Modern bird biologists have established that the starling is harmful in myriad ways. In the West, especially in Texas, huge flocks consume enormous quantities of grain set out for cattle. They also carry and spread swine diseases.

Biologists and historians have suggested motives for the introduction of foreign species of birds, primary among them the immigrant's longing for the sights and sounds of home and the belief that the birds would aid in insect control. But neither of these seems sufficient explanation. The word "acclimatization," which occurs in the names of organizations dedicated to introducing foreign species (in France Le Société Imperiale d'Acclimatation, in England the Society for the Acclimatisation of Animals, Birds, Fishes, Insects and Vegetables, and in America the American Acclimatization Society), provides a clue to these introductions. These societies of mostly amateur naturalists were dedicated to applying Darwinian theory to suburban gardens and zoos. Above all other aspects of evolution, the acclimatization enthusiasts caught hold of Darwin's perception that geographic isolation often led to the development of new species—that space along with time played a major role in the evolution of species. Darwin was concerned with the effects of climate and geographic isolation on species such as the Galapagos finches, famous as one of the keys that unlocked the mysteries of evolution.

In his 1868 *Variation of Animals and Plants under Domestication,* Darwin described how species adapt to new climates, soils, or diets. Horticulturalists and zoologists began to use Darwin's theories to develop better domestic products. The acclimatization societies took up this work of moving useful species from one location to another as a hobby. When the American Acclimatization Society introduced Old World species of birds into North America it was undertaking an acclimatization experiment. Most of these introductions failed because the societies rushed the process, neglecting to follow patiently the selective breeding techniques which would ensure success. Of all the birds introduced— and there were over ninety species—only a few survived. But the starling and the English sparrow acclimatized too well.

The Audubon association and the Department of Agriculture were more or less powerless to stop the acclimatizers. It has always proven disastrous to relocate species without understanding what effect these introductions might have on native species. But man finds irresistible the manipulation of nature for his own benefit, and neither conservationists nor the United States government had any effect upon the acclimatizing efforts until legislation called a halt to it.

Chapter Twelve

The Literature of Birding

*T*he literature of nature in modern times starts with the works of Henry David Thoreau (1817–1862). Thoreau, with his trenchant writing style constantly refreshed by his searching genius, has become the model for writers pursuing the nature essay as a literary form in his own century and well into the next. The impact of his writing, his comprehension of the interwoven patterns of ecology, and his perception of the need to conserve the outdoors confirm his primary position as a nature writer. Thoreau's best writings on birds have been selected and compiled by Helen Cruickshank, and the discussion here uses passages from her *Thoreau on Birds*.

Nearly every day of his life Thoreau went out to visit in rotation his chosen sites of natural beauty in his home neighborhood at Concord, Massachusetts; every night, in a few words or in a polished essay, he recorded in his journal what he had seen. This record contained the naturalist's freshest and most revealing thoughts. It offered not just the jottings of a diary but the rounded prose of an idiosyncratic stylist nourished on the classics. Often Thoreau was content to describe a bird, tree, or flower factually, holding to essentials but exercising his habitual thoroughness. But he was also capable of transmuting an initial description into a profoundly personal expression of nature's inner power and its link to man.

The greater number of Henry's remarks on birds are found in his journal. One passage, first rehearsed in the journal and then polished in *Walden,* serves to recall the rich Victorian resonance of Thoreau's prose, moving from actuality to emotional appeal:

> The change from storm and winter to serene and mild weather, from dark and sluggish hours to bright and elastic ones, is a memorable crisis which all things proclaim. It is seemingly instantaneous at last. Suddenly an influx of light filled my house, though evening was at hand, and the clouds of winter still overhung it, and the eaves were dripping with sleety rain. I looked out the window and lo! where yesterday was cold gray ice there lay the transparent pond already calm and full of hope as in a summer evening. . . .

As a birder, Thoreau had some attitudes which inspire wonder in the eager lister of today. He was, and intended to remain, an amateur bird student. Although an experienced botanist and occasional surveyor of birds and most natural forms, he relied on his own powers of observation and on his unending curiosity. The bird books available to him were inadequate; Wilson, Audubon, Nuttall, and Brewer were pioneering ornithologists, but no one today would think of using their books for field work. Partly because of the limited scope of these sources, partly because of his own attitude of disengagement, Thoreau sometimes chose not to identify the species of a bird. "A new bird, probably an eagle," was most likely an osprey, and "the largest bird of the falcon kind I ever saw." He once spotted "a very slight and graceful hawk; . . . the Merlin it might be called; but I care not for its name." He confounded his readers with a bird he called the "seringo," which may have been the Savannah, grasshopper, or perhaps the vesper sparrow. The "night warbler" was a bird name of his own genial invention, which like the possible merlin, he seemed content not to pin down, and it has confounded his admirers ever since. For Thoreau it was enough to know that this species had an air of evocative mystery. He heard "the night warbler breaking out as in his dreams, made so from the first for some mysterious reason."

Thoreau was not at all interested in the specific bird as a taxonomic specimen. His transcendental insights stimulated him to explore a wider sphere, and he wanted to know not just the bird's name, but what it meant in the cycle of beings, what it did and why, and how it related to man. His description of migration in the journal provides an example of his vision of birds. "Now about the first of September, you will see flocks of small birds forming compact and distinct masses, as if they were not only animated by one spirit but actually held together by some invisible fluid or film, and will hear the sound of their wings rippling or fanning the air, as they flow through it. . . ." Thoreau perceived how birds surge through a world they alone can know, impelled by flickering nervous impulses beyond human comprehension.

When he focused on one winged specimen, Thoreau could bring stunning precision to his observations. Marsh hawks, he perceived, "flew in their usual irregular low tacking, wheeling, and circling flight, leisurely flapping and beating, now rising, now falling, in conformity with the contour of the ground." He knew that grouse burrowed into the snow for shelter and how deep and wide a tunnel they made, how they walked over the snow before plunging into it, and how on emerging again they left impressions of their wings like a memory image. Chickadees, "picking up the crumbs the squirrels had dropped, flew to the nearest twig, and, placing them under their claws, hammered away at them with their little bills, as if it were an insect in the bark, till they were sufficiently reduced for their slender throats." Thoreau's capacity to see and by seeing to learn proved that his know-nothing pose was ephemeral. If from time to time he chose not to identify some bird, it was because he wished to go beyond phylogenesis and to contemplate a creature of God as a unit within nature's entity.

He perceived any bird not isolated as in a bird book portrait but as a working link in nature's design responding to an environment and attuned to the flux of its surroundings. This concept of ecology underwent further development just after Thoreau's death in 1862 with George Perkins Marsh's influential *Man and Nature*. Ethology, the study of animal behavior, only matured as a science between the two world wars. Thoreau prophetically anticipated both these modern fields. He saw the bird not as a specimen skin stored in a drawer, but as both shaping and being shaped by its surroundings. For example, pine grosbeaks, visiting New England in winter, suggested an inverted ecological lesson to Thoreau because they predicted relief from winter's dimness while their bright plumage against a muted backdrop reminded him that this harsh season was as much part of nature's cycle as these lively birds. On one of his visits to Cape Cod Thoreau, puzzling at the barren ecology of the dunes, characteristically turned to the question of what birds could find a home in these surroundings. The mackerel gulls

(common terns), he concluded with his familiar sense of nature's wholeness, "were adapted to their circumstances rather by their spirits than
their bodies. . . . Their note was like the sound of some vibrating metal,
and harmonized well with the scenery and roar of the surf. . . ."

Thoreau's incisiveness as a writer, his preference for the larger view,
his power as an observer and sensitivity to the environment all contributed to his finely focused but far-sighted vision. His abstract and
speculative concept of nature owed much to his Concord mentor, Ralph
Waldo Emerson, whose transcendentalism Thoreau embraced eagerly.
Transcendentalists saw nature as a unity, its creatures as links in a chain
forged inseparably together and acting in harmony. Man was part of this
continuum and, while the Concordians did not think of birds and other
animals as living like humans, they discerned parallels that opened up
the study of avian behavior.

Thoreau brought humor to the world shared by bird and man, as
when he said, "I rejoice that there are owls. Let them do the idiotic and
maniacal hooting for men. . . . They represent the stark twilight and
unsatisfied thoughts which all have." With other birds Thoreau formed
ties of sympathy, recalling the Indian rituals which interested him. The
kingbird, for example, could lift his thoughts to the clouds, and in his
journal entry for January 11, 1855, Thoreau evoked the common crow
in surprisingly devotional ecstasy: "What a delicious sound! It is not
merely crow calling to crow, for it speaks to me too. I am part of one
great creature with him; if he has voice, I have ears. . . . Ah, bless the
Lord, O my soul, bless him for wildness, for crows that will not alight
within gunshot!"

Everywhere in his Concord half-acre Thoreau saw evidence of the
interlocking forces in nature. In September 1860 at Walden Pond he
noted how cherries fell so that birds could easily get their pits which,
dropped from many beaks, sprouted new cherry trees. And in another
passage Thoreau wittily conjures up a breathless cosmic overview:

Vegetation starts when the earth's axis is sufficiently inclined; *i.e.* it follows
the sun. Insects and all the smaller animals (as well as many larger) follow
vegetation. The fishes, the small fry, start probably for this reason; worms
come out of the trees; buffaloes finally seek new pastures; water-bugs
appear on the water, etc., etc. Next, the large fish and fish hawks, etc., follow the small fry; flycatchers follow the insects and worms. . . . Indians
follow the buffaloes; trout, suckers, etc., follow the water-bugs, etc.,

reptiles follow vegetation, insects and worms; birds of prey, the flycatchers, etc. Man follows all, and all follow the sun.

What is the meaning of the frenzied movement, this endless dance of pursuit and confrontation in nature? Wild creatures, Thoreau said, must strive first to find food, then search for shelter, and third for security from foes. What Thoreau saw in the microcosm of Concord's fields and woods was akin to the layered human cosmos of Dante, one of the many classical sources Thoreau often mentioned.

Thoreau's feeling for the outdoors also brought him to an applied practice of natural history. He was the first American to take a vigorous stance on the need to conserve nature. He originally emulated Audubon and Wilson in shooting any bird he wished to study, but he eventually renounced this method, as did later bird students like Burroughs and Chapman. As his interest matured, he recognized that while a dead bird was convenient for identification of a species, "you can study the habits and appearance best in the living specimen." Thoreau tormented himself with guilt when he killed an animal, for example, when "collecting" a box turtle for Professor Louis Agassiz. "I cannot excuse myself for this murder," he wrote, "and see that such actions are inconsistent with the poetic perception—No reasoning whatever reconciles me to this act. I have lost some self-respect." Thoreau once tried to dissuade a farmer, who was afraid for his hens, from shooting red-tailed hawks because "it was worth more to see them soar especially now, that they are so rare in the landscape. . . . I would rather never taste chicken's meat or hens' eggs than never to see a hawk sailing through the upper air again."

The Concord naturalist also had his say about the destructive custom of collecting birds' eggs, then a popular pastime for both boys and men. He praised the eggs' beauty and meaning in their proper setting and made a brief appeal which ends, "And is not that shell something very precious that houses winged life?" Thoreau censured most forms of depredation against nature common in his time. He foresaw the important steps which conservationists were eventually to take. Thus he wrote: "Each town should have a park, or rather primitive forest, of five hundred or a thousand acres, where a stick should never be cut for fuel, a common possession forever, for instruction and recreation. . . . Let us keep the New World *new,* preserve all advantages of living in the country."

After Henry's tragic death in 1862 from tuberculosis at the age of forty-four, a diffuse school of nature writers grew up in his wake. None of these authors, though many were talented, attained the heights of Thoreau's intellect or the near mystical idealism he brought to nature study. Inspiration was available, of course, in his published books. Selections from his journals, rearranged in seasonal order, began to appear in 1881, edited by his friend H. G. O. Blake, who had inherited the forty volumes from Thoreau's sister. Bradford Torrey, a nature essayist in the Concord tradition, and Francis H. Allen, an editor and ornithologist, brought out a more complete edition in 1906, but it still had many omissions. Torrey and a good many of Thoreau's emulators were New England idealists like the Concord naturalist. Despite the dilution of transcendentalism by later derivative interpreters, Thoreau's idealism had an inspiring impact on many subsequent bird writers.

The first of these in time and importance was John Burroughs (1837–1921; see Chapter Four). Burroughs acknowledged that his perceptions of nature derived from New England transcendentalism and so he recognized his direct debts to Emerson and Thoreau. Burroughs discovered Emerson's writings early, and in juvenile articles followed the spare style of the Concord essayist before finding his own way. It may be that Burroughs turned to the nature essay in an effort to expunge his dependence on Emerson's abstract epigrammatic formality. Burroughs's relation to Thoreau was more oblique, as shown in the two late essays he wrote about the naturalist. These are oddly restrained in praise and even somewhat critical, a surprising assessment from a writer revered for his benign tolerance. Both Burroughs and Thoreau attended the temple of transcendentalism but took care to worship in a way that preserved their individual souls. Both accepted no narrow bounds but sought to study all of nature, and both were honest, penetrating observers who rambled outdoors with receptive eyes and a disciplined absorption. But as Burroughs pointed out, with the asperity of a critic from another territory, Thoreau was an austere and inward son of New England, for whom the chain of being had a logical, even a predetermined imperative.

Burroughs was a farm boy brought up not in luxury but in some ease among the fertile fields of the Catskills' western slopes. He saw nature as a divinely conceived unity that was permanently benign and protective. Like Thoreau he may not always have been interested in identifying a bird, but he never tried to make one an abstract symbol. It was enough for him to absorb a creature's beauty passively. Thoreau and Burroughs shared passionate desires to embrace nature by studying it, but, as different personalities from different backgrounds, went about their quests in different ways. It is typical of Burroughs that his old-fashioned devotion to nature's goodness led him to doubt the harsh mechanics of Darwinian evolution, whereas, had Thoreau lived a little longer and gotten into Darwin's theories, he doubtless would have accepted them eagerly as clarifying his own inferences from nature.

John Burroughs's writing style reflected the meditative calm he found in his daily strolls outdoors, a ritual he followed as faithfully as Thoreau did. Burroughs also kept a journal, obsessed like so many nineteenth-century intellectuals with preserving memories, and like Thoreau's journal, it formed the basis of his more formal writings. Burroughs's essays poured forth incessantly and with dogged consistency. He worked at them like a farmer taking crop after crop of hay from a good small field, and in the end they made up twenty-four volumes. Burroughs aimed to do away with style as much as possible and to find an easy country way of writing. Faithful to his view of the world as an earthly paradise that basked under one smiling intelligence, he held himself to plain descriptions of what he saw. Elaborations would be dishonest, he felt, and his essays contain neither Thoreau's epigrammatic impact nor the polished charm of Torrey or Sharp.

Burroughs's prose is by no means without personal appeal. He reached a larger audience than had any other nature writer, and his books even came to serve as school readers. Later in life, confident of his position as the national nature guru, Burroughs expanded his scope by attempting intellectual comment on such topics as geological pre-history, evolution, Henri Bergson, and recent literary trends. These are his least convincing essays, because in them the country man and lover of nature wandered out of bounds.

Burroughs's first nature book was written about 1870 and largely concerned birds. It was called *Wake-Robin,* not after the familiar rusty-breasted thrush but for the early blooming white trillium that announces spring. Here in unadorned descriptions of birds he attained his best mode, simple, honest and brief. He writes this of the catbird:

> She is the parodist of the woods, and there is ever a mischievous, bantering, half-ironical undertone in her lay, as if she were conscious of mimicking and disconcerting some envied songster. Ambitious of song, practicing and rehearsing in private, she yet seems the least sincere and genuine of the sylvan minstrels, as if she had taken up music only to be in

the fashion, or not to be outdone by the robins and thrushes. In other words, she seems to sing from some outward motive, and not from inward joyousness. She is a good versifier, but not a great poet. Vigorous, rapid, copious, not without fine touches, but destitute of any high, serene melody, her performance, like that of Thoreau's squirrel, always implies a spectator.

He also linked birding with travel, as Thoreau and many subsequent writers did, relating a hunting trip to the Adirondacks and fishing in the Catskills. These recreations allowed him to describe further bird species but, more important, to record his unusual sensitivity to differing environments, as if again in homage to Thoreau. He admitted that he used a gun early in life but he later put it aside and converted to passive observation of living nature.

After publishing *Wake-Robin* Burroughs settled permanently at West Park on the Hudson near his beloved Catskill foothills. Devotion to his home region was his cherished inspiration and enabled him for a time to sustain the purity of *Wake-Robin*. But soon ambition pushed him to seek more sophisticated audiences, as he did in *Birds and Poets* published at the end of the 1870s, where the theme was more literary than nature-loving, chronicling what poets had said of birds. With this volume Burroughs began to lose his one-to-one relation to the outdoors and give way to dabbling in intellectual abstractions.

After the Catskills—perhaps because of the similarity of environment —John Burroughs loved England best. As a result of a second more leisurely trip there in 1882 he devoted a book to Britain, entitled *Fresh Fields.* His sympathy for a new place was first engaged by the topography itself. The calm pastures well wetted and green, the lanes inviting strolls and the dense hedgerows seemed ideal happy haunts for his favorite English songbirds, the chaffinch, wheatear and linnet. But while reveling in this idyll, as so often, he let himself become a victim of memory's tyranny and went off to relive the homage he paid earlier to Carlyle, this time by visiting his grave. *Fresh Fields* also contains extensive comparisons of British and American field birds and their songs, a trumped up argument which concludes by giving a slight edge to birds at home. The book on England again shows the author meandering away from a focus on nature to dip into history and literature.

In late works, "The Gospel of Nature" in *Time and Change* published in 1912 and "The Faith of a Naturalist" from *Accepting the Universe* of 1920, Burroughs began to ponder his lifetime experience of absorbing nature. He now found the outdoors no longer so seductive but rigorously balanced in its ordering. He still found nature vital in its wholeness and fruitful to prodigality, yet it wasted nothing as it changed of its own momentum and diminished man to insignificance. He wanted, and wanted us, to confront nature without notebook or glass, for its study was a moral lesson that expunged the vanities of life. In "The Gospel of Nature" from *Time and Change* Burroughs wrote, "Nature is not benevolent; nature is just, gives pound for pound, measure for measure, makes no exceptions, never tempers her decrees in mercy, or winks at any infringement of her laws. And in the end is not this best?"

God and evil, Burroughs declared in the philosophic vein of his late style, are also creations of man. Any religion that offers comfort is to the good, but do not expect to judge good and evil in nature where their balance gives them mute equality, where predation or infestation find ordained antidotes of renewal. Such deistic and vaguely transcendental thoughts may have earned Burroughs the reputation of a sage which he enjoyed in his time, but the pedestrian nature essayists who came after him may have looked more to the earthier mode of unspeculative nature watching in an early work like *Wake-Robin*.

The nature essayist perhaps closest to Burroughs in style was Bradford Torrey (1843–1912), author of some of the best writing on outdoor New England at the turn of the century. Torrey had a many-sided career, first in missionary work, then as an editor of *Youth's Companion* and of Thoreau's journals, and as a prolific essayist. He traveled widely within the United States, to North Carolina, New Hampshire, Tennessee, and Florida, and finally to California, where he retired in Santa Barbara. Most of these journeys had reverberations in his books.

Torrey was a gentle spokesman for nature and the birds, modest in recounting his difficulties with identification and reluctant to display his impressive knowledge of avian life. His style was personal, digressive, and chatty. Incidents about himself and intimate encounters with birds seen as neighbors gave his essays something of the tone of a newspaper column of local gossip. As a late Victorian, Torrey did not shy from sentimentality, and he unabashedly attributed human traits to birds. Yet occasionally he could be amusing and even ironic. An optimist who found hope in the outdoor world, much as Burroughs did, Torrey believed that birds lived in happy innocence, some of which they could bestow on their observers. In his essay "Phillida and Coridon" from the 1884 *Atlantic Monthly* he admitted that evolution forces birds to compete but cited many instances of the delight he felt they could find in courtship and love. His message was blatantly anthropomorphic, almost maudlin, pointedly unscientific, and anti-Darwinian, growing from vernacular ideals of nature enjoyment.

Bradford Torrey's essay "Scraping Acquaintance," from *Birds in the Bush* of 1885, is rambling and diffuse, but appropriately so, for here he diffidently recounts his first trials as a birder. He tells of sorting out the thrushes and warblers and compares the red-headed and red-bellied woodpeckers. In another essay, "Character in Feathers," he gives way to human bias as he sketches the character of some birds, as if in the Dramatis Personae preface of a play. He sees the blue jay as a minor rowdy, the towhee as self-reliant and contained, and chickadees are trustworthy, applied, independent, friendly, and merry.

Within the next ten years Torrey learned to perceive bird behavior more sharply. His close scrutiny of nesting vireos, told in "A Woodland Intimate" in the *Atlantic Monthly* of 1887, is not only touching but informative, and his observations in *The Foot-Path Way* of 1892, perhaps his central work, are sober and objective. His report in the essay "Widow and Twins" of the brooding and fledging of hummingbirds is documented hour by hour, the kind of sensitive behavioral study Thoreau would have approved. Torrey like Burroughs developed over time but in a different direction: he started as a light, almost flippant bird essayist, but matured into a serious devotee of ideal nature study in the transcendental tradition.

Another endearing late Victorian author was Dallas Lore Sharp (1870–1929). He was a generation younger than Torrey, and he felt free to follow that writer's lead toward informal ease in narrative. His essays are breezy, colloquial, and fun, as if he was reacting against the scholarly limits of his earlier calling as an English professor at Boston University. From this career he withdrew early and settled in the quiet village of Hingham, Massachusetts, where he could spend more time in the outdoors. His books of essays were published in rapid succession from the turn of the century until the mid-1920s. One of the earliest, in 1901, illustrated by Bruce Horsfall, was appropriately called *Wild Life Near Home,* for Dallas Sharp treasured the Victorian values of domestic well-being, both in the birds and in his readers—one reason, no doubt, for his popularity. In his essay "Feathered Neighbors" Sharp described a variety of birds gathering in easy familiarity about a human habitation. A flicker made a hole in a tram wire pole, and redstarts moved into the apple tree by the kitchen door. "From May to September, is there a happier sight than a flock of chimney-swallows, just before or after a shower, whizzing about the tops of the corn or coursing the river, like so many streaks of black lightning, ridding the atmosphere of its charge of gnats! They cut across the rainbow and shoot into the pearl- and rose-washed sky, and drop—into the depths of the soot-clogged chimney."

Sharp saw the bluebird as neither a fine singer nor boasting beautiful plumage but admirable for its spirit. (The perilous state of this species today might make modern birders disagree.) While these portrait sketches of home birds are delightful and entertaining, Sharp could also display a greater comprehension of nature in the tradition of Thoreau. He had a good sense of conservation and deplored the threat to the bobwhite from hunting, and he asked worthwhile questions about behavior, such as why some birds prefer to nest near paths and roads. In "Second Crops" he implies a feeling for nature's continuity when he asserts poetically that nature abhors death and never lets a living thing die definitively without promise of metamorphosis to some new form of life. In *Wild Life Near Home* he says:

Part of the answer, at least, is found in nature's hatred and horror of death. She fiercely refuses to have any dead. An empty heaven, a lifeless sea, an uninhabited rock, a dead drop of water, a dying paramecium are intolerable and impossible. She hastens always to give them life. The succession of strange dwellers to the decaying trees is an instance of her universal and endless effort at making matter live.

Frank Bolles (1856–1894) was another member of the New England group, twelve years younger than Torrey and fourteen older than Sharp. A giant, friendly man, he was the secretary of Harvard College and much loved by students. Bolles died of pneumonia at thirty-eight, and most of his writings were published just before or after his death. His essays, necessarily few in number, cover an eclectic spectrum: from endorsing Thoreau's willingness to face nature's more brutal moments, to the inventive play of "Bird Traits" in the *New England Magazine,* where in a kind of reverse anthropomorphism humans are wittily given the traits of birds. Bolles had the habit of walking out on Sunday to the environs of Cambridge in all kinds of weather. A record of these walks is the subject of *Land of the Lingering Snow: Chronicles of a Stroller in New England from January to June,* 1893. Bolles's observations were sensitive, but his telling of them sometimes lacked the freshness of his field experiences. However, he could focus effectively on an isolated instance of bird behavior, and in this book provided several descriptions of a bittern's call which were just right, not an easy undertaking:

> . . . It suggested the choking and gurgling of a bottle from which liquid is being poured, the bottle during the process being held inside an empty hogshead. . . . At a distance the sound seemed like two words, "pung chuck," but nearby there seemed to be a third syllable, and several minor sounds, inaudible at a distance, were made while the bird was getting up steam. It seemed to me at the time, knowing nothing of the nature of the process, that the bird produced the second by a mechanical use of a column of air extending from its open mouth to its stomach.

Bolles's story of raising two captive barred owls in *From Bromidon to Smoky, and Other Papers,* 1894, seems to mingle boyish play with a hunter's urges and scientific curiosity. That the author could observe systematically was demonstrated by a mechanism of mirrors he devised to study swifts nesting in a chimney. "Individuality in Birds" ventures some intuitions which look toward today's behavioral studies: man always desires to get near wild animals, but a gap between two-legged and four-legged or winged creatures ultimately prevents closeness. Yet beasts and birds show much intelligence; an example is the use of warning cries by crow and jay sentinels. Such insights into bird psychology as those expressed by Bolles were rare at this early date.

*V*ictorian literature inviting a new look at nature was not of course confined to New England, though it began there. A bird writer from another sector with a viewpoint of his own was the Reverend James Hibbert Langille (1841–1923), a Nova Scotian educated in America who served as a Baptist minister in and around Washington, D.C. Langille wrote religious tracts, history, and a number of children's books. His principal work on birds was *Our Birds in Their Haunts: a Popular Treatise on the Birds of Eastern North America* issued in 1884. The body of the book contains thorough entries on species, arranged in the seasonal scheme, by now customary, and drawn from personal observations, correspondents, and published sources like Elliott Coues, to whom the volume is dedicated. In his preface Langille reveals his clerical bias and defines his purpose in introducing the birds as God's creatures, clues to his power and glory. "Particularly do I note the many evidences of a Designing Intelligence in the department of nature," he says, as he urges fellow pastors to show children the wonders of the bird kingdom, which are at once a way to God and to the hearts of the young. Langille's application of a Christian ethic to bird study seems a long way from the transcendentalists' cult of nature, but both approaches found their own spiritual values in the outdoors.

Two women writers at the end of the century deserve more literary recognition than they have received so far. Mabel Osgood Wright (1859–1934) benefited from contact with both the New York intelligentsia and the best circles of bird lovers. Her father was an Episcopal clergyman with literary interests and her husband a British antiquarian bookseller in New York. Elliott Coues, Frank Chapman, and T. Gilbert Pearson were her close colleagues; Louis Agassiz Fuertes illustrated her children's book, *Citizen Bird;* and she held key editorships in Chapman's *Bird-Lore* for fifteen years, setting a lively pace in the wit and energy of her writing.

Mabel Osgood Wright's principal nature book that aspires to literary ambitions is *The Friendship of Nature, a New England Chronicle of Birds and Flowers,* dated 1894. It is rich in verbal texture, written precisely but in a self-consciously elegant decorative style. Vaguely adopting the customary seasonal scheme, she aimed to lay before the reader nothing less than an appreciative inventory of all nature's wealth. Despite an overlay of dazzling language, Wright's assessment of nature has objectivity and discipline. Behind it lies a respectable knowledge of birds, and underlying all a cheerful Victorian faith that the world of nature works in good order under a benign rule. Here is how Wright sees some backyard birds in their settings in *The Friendship of Nature:* "Precious is the solitude and the song of the water thrush, for they soothe the spirit; precious are the orchards, the sunlight, and the home-going cattle, for they warm the heart. The red thrush perching high pours out his voluble song, while the lilacs sway over the wall. Still querying in an elm swings the oriole: is he a bird, or a flower, or cloud, or the transmigration of all?"

An older contemporary of Wright and an equally talented bird writer was Olive Thorne Miller (a nom de plume for Harriet Mann, 1831–1918). She was born in a well-off family in upstate New York, married a Chicago businessman and lived in Brooklyn, becoming the mother of four children. From childhood she was a tireless writer. As a young matron she wrote popular juveniles and did not take up nature writing until she was in her fifties and free from domestic ties.

Miller's *A Bird-Lover in the West* of 1894 as a travel-and-nature book relates to typical interests of her time. Its first purpose is to tell how escape to nature can dispel the burdens of city life and how outdoor contemplation can help to inspire moral uplift. Miller's *Little Brothers of the Air* in 1892 may be a more revealing product of her pen. At first glance it seems a children's book, but like Ernest Thompson Seton's stories it reaches far enough toward nature's complexities to be enjoyed by adults. Here Miller gathers birding incidents from the Great South Bay of Long Island and the Adirondacks, most of which are about nesting, a typical preoccupation of bird books in her time. Searching for nests seemed to satisfy this author's desire to participate vicariously in avian domestic activity. Though she was a patient and tactful nest watcher, nothing seemed to come of her searches but her own pleasure in discovering breeding birds. Her appreciation is unquestioning but inconclusive; for while she relates her pleasure charmingly, she holds back from formulating the insights that her clear perceptions might inspire.

In the twentieth century man has often played a tragic role, and modern art and literature have sometimes turned inward in response to darker feelings. But love of nature can provide an antidote to pessimism, and some, but not all, modern writers on the outdoors have rediscovered the ideals of nature that flowered in the last century.

Several scientists who wrote popular books, often late in life, have enriched the idealistic literature of nature for all. An example is Aldo Leopold (1886–1948), whose career began with the Forestry Service in the Southwest. Always in the forefront of thinking in conservation, he conceived and successfully advocated the idea of wilderness areas, sometimes called "roadless," portions of national forests and parks set aside as untouched and closed to all motorized entry. After this initiative he held a research job in forestry, and later he developed a still more sweeping innovation in conservation, his theory of game management. The University of Wisconsin established a chair for Leopold and a department under his direction so that he could formulate and teach his theory. As the conservation movement gained momentum, the influence of his teaching and writing spread and in time became almost legendary. While living in Madison Leopold bought a run-down "sand farm" as a retreat, which he and his family restored with their own hands.

His popular book, *A Sand County Almanac and Sketches Here and There,* published in 1949 just after his death, begins with a month-by-month account of animal life in the farm's environs, then looks more broadly at wildlife from other regions and ends with some general thoughts on conservation. As a lifetime defender of nature, Leopold speaks with passion yet with the clarity of a thoughtful professional; his style is both simple and subtle, partly because of his restrained humor. Recalling Thoreau, Leopold is a loving student of nature who finds more than ordinary eyes can see; but unlike Thoreau Leopold does not fall into a trance at outdoor mysteries but comprehends most of what he sees and can explain it with a scientist's authority. How well he perceives and understands is made clear in a passage about the annual spring return of the Canada geese, one of the turning points that measures time on his farm's calendar:

> On April nights . . . there are long periods of silence when one hears only the winnowing of snipe, the hoot of a distant owl, or the nasal clucking of an amorous coot. Then, of a sudden, a strident honk resounds, and in an instant pandemonium echoes. There is a beating of pinions on water, a general shouting by the onlookers of a vehement controversy. Finally some deep honker has his last word, and the noise subsides to that half-audible small-talk that seldom ceases among geese. Once again, I would I were a muskrat.

A writer on the outdoors in the humanist tradition who carried the ideals of nature appreciation almost to obsessive devotion was Edwin Way Teale (1898–1986). Teale found inspiration in the pastoral landscapes of Long Island and Connecticut. He wrote devotedly about the birds and other creatures he studied every day throughout a long life. His patent love of nature expressed in an easy style suited a range of subjects, and his genial personality gained him recognition as dean of modern nature writers. Few of his contemporary colleagues have failed to acknowledge a debt to Teale.

Teale published historical editions of Thoreau's *Walden* and of writings by Audubon and Muir, but representative of his own works drawn directly from nature are *Circle of the Seasons, the Journal of a Naturalist's*

Year, set on the Long Island shore, and *A Naturalist Buys an Old Farm,* where the locale shifts to upland Connecticut. A passage in *A Naturalist Buys an Old Farm* reveals Teale's complacent pleasure in the outdoors:

> Sitting there in the twilight, watching the fireflies and listening to the whippoorwill that first evening, we seemed in a perfect habitat for a pair of naturalists. We felt as comfortable as a rabbit in its form. Here, in every season of the year, we would be living on the edge of the wilderness. All these acres around us, all these fields and woods fading into the night, would form a sanctuary farm, a sanctuary for wildlife and a sanctuary for us.

Emulating Thoreau, Teale walked his personal refuge daily and always found some natural event of interest for his journal. Often what

Aldo Leopold contemplates a pine tree. *Division of Archives, University of Wisconsin-Madison.*

he saw was not an ordinary occurrence but an odd one where nature was caught off guard, and even the informed reader of his report is pulled up short. Unlike others with the journal habit, Teale published his daily sightings with little reworking, giving the reader a spontaneous revelation of outdoor life as first beheld. Insects, wildflowers, birds, and small animals—any display of nature's wealth—came into Teale's encompassing focus on the humble acres described in these books. Not once in exploring the natural happenings of his elysium did Teale hint that nature could be harsh or destructive. That threat he blandly filtered out to leave a laundered outdoors always benign and joyful, the same pure and welcoming idyll in which Burroughs and other idealistic naturalists rejoiced.

Edwin Way Teale, guiding spirit of American nature writing. *Massachusetts Audubon Society.*

*T*ravel, as every birdwatcher and every reader of Thoreau knows, is a *sine qua non* of birding. Once a birder is familiar with species at home, he gets an urge to find new and more exotic birds. Travel has fed the literature of birding richly, and some attention is due these writers, whose journeys in America or beyond have led them to tell of faraway bird adventures. These authors cannot be typed as idealists or realists, since they tell where they went and what they saw with little concern beyond their own experience.

Robert Porter Allen (1905–1963) was a professional ornithologist, a field researcher and director of sanctuaries for the national Audubon association. His specialty was studying endangered species along the southern U.S. coasts, especially the flamingo, roseate spoonbill, and whooping crane. For each he produced a scientific life history that helped to define the problems in its conservation. In every case, aware that a bird's well-being partly depends on man's good will, Allen supplemented his technical report with a popular account of his research, strategy, and findings in separate books such as *On the Trail of Vanishing Birds.*

His method in the field was simple, bold, and strenuous: he went to live with the birds, observing them day and night while camping nearby, often in discomfort. In order to study the whooping cranes of the Aransas refuge in Texas, Allen needed a blind, and with as much wit as ingenuity he constructed one of wire and red-brown canvas in the form of a Santa Gertrudis bull, the largest animal in Texas outside zoos. There was enough room to stand up inside even with cameras, optical equipment, and notebooks, the perforated nostrils provided viewing ports, and interior handles allowed the thing to be picked up and moved as if it were grazing. "I hate to say this," Allen said, "but it was a bum steer! . . . The expression in the eyes was quite demure and unbull-like. In fact, everyone came to refer to my artificial beast as a 'cow.' " And did the bull-blind, or *bovus absurdus* as Allen called it, work out? The cranes stayed well out of visual range, but—who would not suspect it?—a breathing, snorting Santa Gertrudis bull soon turned up to see what rival was invading his territory. Allen had some bad moments as he thought about a massive angry charging animal, but the real bull, after a few suspicious and then bored sniffs, ambled off. Robert Allen was blessed with energy and enthusiasm, which he brought to an unusually close relationship with his subjects. The appeal of his adventures comes from the dramatic actuality of what he did, and his verve and sustaining humor enliven the story.

Roger Tory Peterson is known to all birdwatchers as America's senior birder, artist, author, and master of the bird guide. His principal discursive book is *Birds over America* of 1948. Peterson has an anecdotal approach that draws upon his own large experience, and to a considerable extent the book becomes an unintended autobiography. The author constantly reports the finding and identifying of birds, more than their behavior, and he expresses a genuine appreciation of what he sees outdoors. Peterson's writing style is restrained but salted with an occasional literary phrase or extended simile. He takes the reader to many birding spots—some hot, some cool—as an informed and genial guide, but his book is less a tourist's view than a field guide to the author himself, a knowledgeable birder who has been everywhere and seen nearly every bird in America.

Among living writers on nature most critics agree that Peter Matthiessen has attained the highest point of accomplishment. His versatility is dazzling; his range in interpreting nature takes him from poetic invocation to precise scientific description. Besides half a dozen novels, he has written travel books about such exotic places as the South American wilderness *(The White Clouds)* and the Selous Wildlife Reserve in Tanzania *(Sand Rivers),* as well as two books presenting intense research on American animals, *Wildlife in America,* dealing with threatened species, and *The Shorebirds of North America,* a technical survey. He also wrote a popular descriptive sequel to the latter book, *The Wind Birds.* His scientific work on shorebirds commands ornithological detail with professional precision, and each of these books adopts a style of easy and appropriate sophistication, factual, lyrical or both together, according to its subject matter. Central to all is Matthiessen's most revealing book, and his most powerful and moving one, *The Snow Leopard,* on its face a travel book about a trek into the Himalayas but offering far more, including deep revelations about the author, the rest of humankind, and how one lives in nature. The background to the book, as Matthiessen explains, comprises three circumstances: that he has just lost his wife to cancer; that he is a recent convert to Buddhism; and that he and his colleague, George Schaller, a New York Zoological Society scientist studying bharal, must travel under pressure after a delayed start in order to reach their mountain goal before the winter snows shut it off. For Matthiessen the trek increasingly became a visionary self-exploration as he entered an unreal world of surprise slopes with snow swirling upward, lunar light reflections, and deserted villages traversed by gloomy trading caravans of yaks. After several conversations with a weathered hermit living in a cave, he was shocked to discover he had been talking with no less a sacred personage than the lama of the great but abandoned Shey Monastery. It is characteristic of Matthiessen to elevate the actuality he experienced toward a distant mystical sphere. He never saw the rarest and most ephemeral animal of the Himalayas, the snow leopard, although his colleague happened on it at the last minute. Matthiessen's title is itself an apparition, referring to a mythical beast that tantalized him but never came forth in the flesh.

Several women have written of distant birding adventures in wild places where they went either with ornithologist husbands or on their own. The most dedicated of these may be Helen Gere Cruickshank, wife of Allan Cruickshank, an Audubon association staff member and brilliant bird photographer. Allan's work directed their steps and he illustrated her books, but Helen is a knowledgeable birder herself and has written a variety of works useful to avian study. In books of travels with her husband, such as *Bird Island Down East* (1941) and *Flight into Sunshine, Bird Experiences in Florida* (1948), she focused on coastal birds in Maine and Florida, and she also edited useful anthologies on the two Bartrams, father and son, and on Thoreau's bird sightings. Despite desolate stinking cormorant colonies, giant snakes, and inch-deep lakes in Florida where she and her husband had to push their skiff loaded with equipment through the mud, the Cruickshanks persisted in reaching isolated bird outposts with their spirits undaunted. Helen recorded these adventures in straightforward prose, gracefully and without embellishment. She delineated the natural settings in her books, whether lovely or intransigent, with honesty and a respect which validates her pleas for their conservation.

A writer whose life took a parallel course to Helen Cruickshank's and who was one of her mentors was Florence Page Jaques (1890–1972). She also came to know birds through a professional husband, Francis Lee Jaques, a bird artist of the first rank (see Chapter Thirteen). Like the Cruickshanks, the Jaques traveled together, and she wrote books about their journeys, illustrated by him, such as *Birds Across the Sky* of 1942. The land of their desire was the canoe country of northern Minnesota, where they went to live permanently in mid-careers. Jaques's reporting of outdoor adventures with her husband was not as knowledgeable as

Cruickshank's; Florence preferred to remain an apprentice birder and made a game of playing her inexperience against her husband's expertise. While she eloquently conveyed her deep love of the northern lakes and woods, she tended to hide her feelings behind a facile, entertaining style. Whenever she saw a crow, she habitually asked, "What is that big black bird?," assured of arousing her husband's mock disgust. With humane illogic she decided she liked hunting and would go out with a gun, which she never fired, since she just liked to walk outdoors.

Humor has rarely entered bird writing. Thoreau used a dry irony in the privacy of his journal, his successors Torrey and Sharp had ample good humor if not much wit, but it was a woman birder, Frances Hamerstrom who, pursuing the comic flounderings of Jaques, found that birding could be both fun and funny. Her *Birding with a Purpose, Of Raptors, Gabboons and Other Creatures,* 1984, takes a bold tack toward more youthful, sometimes bawdy humor. Hamerstrom, once a New York fashion model, is a graduate wildlife biologist and retired research associate at the University of Wisconsin, where she studied under Aldo Leopold. She and her husband, also a wildlife scientist, studied the endangered prairie chicken over many years. She also runs a program of raptor banding, scooping the hawks up from roadside traps into her minibus laboratory. Hamerstrom is an experienced professional naturalist with a knowing love of wild creatures, a commitment which the jocularity of her quick-paced book does not altogether conceal. A book about birds which is not just amusing but hilarious, sometimes riotous, is a new concoction and welcome. Hamerstrom is more intrigued than dismayed by a bunch of ungrammatical, scruffily dressed teen-agers who turn up in their van always unexpectedly and leave as suddenly, called the Rockford Gang or the Gabboons. Regardless of appearances, she tunes in to their adeptness as banding assistants, who like her have a passion for hawks as the wildest of the wild beings.

*S*ince the first Europeans landed writers viewed the natural world as an idyll, a vision created whole and to be kept pure. But then some began to see nature as a staged festival, a mundane arena where the joy and pain of life mingle, sometimes chaotically. A leader of this more down-to-earth school of thought was the animal artist and author Ernest Thompson Seton (1860–1936; christened Ernest Seton Thompson, though his family later chose to rearrange his names). Seton had about him an aura of genius, sometimes recalling Audubon, manifested in a fierce energy, a restless urge to break into new fields, and in equal brilliance as draftsman and storyteller, zoologist and, perhaps above all, as a lecturer, the chief means by which he earned his way. He was also socially ambitious, marrying into the New York 400, and late in life had homes in Greenwich, Connecticut, and Santa Fe, New Mexico. Though acquainted with Theodore Roosevelt, he failed to gain membership in the prestigious Boone and Crockett Club, a snub which always stung his pride.

Seton was a broad-based naturalist in the tradition of Bartram, Audubon, Burroughs and, in this century, Teale and Matthiessen. The Canadian naturalist's affinity for wild creatures focused on the best known groups of large vertebrates, the mammals and birds. He made a profound contribution to mankind's further comprehension of the animals already understood best. True, Ernest Thompson Seton was an artist before he

Ernest Thompson Seton with Mary Austin at her home in Santa Fe. *Museum of New Mexico, Carol Stryker.*

became a nature writer and, as a Canadian in part educated abroad and in any case by nature a rebel genius, he was outside the mainstream of thought about natural history. Yet he was able to perceive and express, whether in his drawings or in stories, a new sense of how animals think and act on their mental signals. If Henry Thoreau was innately but unconsciously the founding father of modern environmentalism, then it can be said that Seton was the advanced prophet of ethology, the study of animal psychology that has recently proved so fruitful, even in perceptions about human life. Far ahead of his time, Seton had insights into animal thought and behavior that marked a turning point in man's view of the natural world and helped to lay the foundations for current ecological knowledge. But however farseeing his ideas about the animal world, Seton was also in many ways a typical turn-of-the-century thinker whose work seems broadly related, to cite just two parallels, to the psychological tenets of William James and the humanistic speculations of Henry Adams.

Seton's family immigrated from northeastern England to Ontario when he was a boy, and he remained a Canadian citizen for most of his life, partly to retain a title he prized as naturalist consultant to Manitoba, the province he became acquainted with as a teen-ager on a camping trip with his brother, when he first discovered his love of wildlife. After determining on a career in art, he won a fellowship to the Royal Academy in London. But he disliked England and suffered from poverty while there; he later went to Paris, where he attracted the tutelage of Jean Léon Gérôme, the late romantic academic. Once again lack of funds wore the young art student down and he retreated to Canada, ill and discouraged. After recovering at home he went to New York and easily found work there as a book illustrator. His flexible, spare and often witty graphic style soon proved a valued asset.

Seton brought out his first book of animal stories, *Wild Animals I Have Known,* in 1898 when he was nearly forty. Illustrated by him, it features full page wash drawings supplemented by lighthearted marginal ink sketches. While the stories are at first glance quick paced and entertaining, especially for the young, they also embody Seton's idiosyncratic and insightful thinking about the animal world. The title stresses that the author has *known* these animals—some personally, some through study of their cousins. Each is named, each has a memorable personality not borrowed from human traits. Most important, each heroically leaps or flies into motion ordained by instinct or circumstantial reaction or both together, and most of them, as heroes must, meet tragedy in the end. These animals' lives, though lifted at one moment to joy, must conclude in terror. Perhaps Seton's most popular and characteristic story is his first, "Lobo, the King of Currumpaw." Lobo was a wolfpack leader, tough and wily, who maintained his hostility to man, in the form of the author, until his strange self-willed death.

Ernest Thompson Seton's other stories often focused on themes of animal tragedy similar to "Lobo." A story in the same book tells of the fate of Silverspot, a crow known by a coin-sized light patch on his cheek. Silverspot was the leader of his flock, a crow's crow, smart as only a crow can be. Constantly he warned his fellows about owls, a crow's most dangerous enemy after man. And when Silverspot met his end, as all the strong must do in Seton's tales, it is of course an owl that serves him with death.

Entertaining as these stories are, told in a swift but low-keyed style suggesting the intimacy of an evening campfire, they are most important for their point of view on animal life. All earlier nature writings depended on the observer's position as he looked out and saw some

LEFT. Seton's sketches of Silverspot, leader among crows. *Seton Memorial Library, Philmont Scout Ranch.*

OPPOSITE. Seton's drawing of Silverspot's last moments.

creature in action; Seton, in contrast, inserted himself into the animal's brain so that he could reconstruct his subject's loves and battles from within as they developed. It followed from Seton's views of animal motivation that wild creatures must have emotions and thinking power, not like man but in their own measure. In physical beauty, in grace and power of movement beasts and birds find joy in themselves and arouse the admiration of man. But as with Greek epic heroes fate always unpredictably sends some hostile force—the creature's most relentless enemy, man, or a foe of their own world—that is destined to destroy them.

Seton's second book of stories, *Lives of the Hunted*—note the title—shows him as much the conservationist as most nature lovers, and here he points an accusing finger at man as ravager of nature. Seton dedicated the book "to the Preservation of our Wild Creatures," and he ended it with a bitter drawing showing a handsome nude man posed like a hero on a Greek pediment raising a huge broadsword to strike at a bird perched on his toe. Undoubtedly he will kill the bird and just as surely wound himself.

Seton's revolutionary thinking grows out of Darwinian theory and

the more objective side of Thoreau's explorations, but his ideas ran counter to the ideal conventions of late nineteenth-century American writing on the outdoors. Seton drew little from others and depended mostly on his own knowledge of animals, displayed in his technical books. The impact of his views on animal psychology were, as usually happens with an innovative theory, slight at first, but the present century has come to see his insights as significant, even astounding. Only recently has the promise of Seton's rebellion been fulfilled with the exploration of the thinking and feeling capacities of wildlife by modern ethologists like Konrad Lorenz.

A more modern writer who fuses science and poetry as Seton did is Rachel Carson (1907–1964). Critics justly place her among the most brilliant nature writers of the twentieth century. In her tough-minded polemic *Silent Spring* (1962), she spared no brutal fact that could speak for conservation, and in *The Sea Around Us* of 1951 she penetrated the ocean depths to show the reader a life unimagined before. But these works are not so much literature as explication; in contrast, her first book, *Under the Sea Wind* of 1941, is a poetic unveiling of the sea that synthesizes the knowledge of an experienced marine biologist with the creative mastery of a lyrical writer. Like Seton, Carson gives names to

Rachel Carson was honored by the Postal Service. *United States Postal Service.*

principal animals and birds—Rynchops the black skimmer and Scomber the mackerel—derived from their scientific names, an old-fashioned custom that did not diminish either the up-to-date accuracy of her information or her modern approach to nature study. Again like Seton, she was able to enter the life of her animal subjects and describe in knowing detail what they do and see through their own eyes. Drawing on her position as a marine scientist, Carson could recapture the vivid actuality of life in and around the sea, not in the formulaic language of science but with a grace and sureness that echo the rhythms of cyclical nature. Her opening chapters on the shore dwellers give new insights about familiar creatures, such as the activity of black skimmers at night:

> [Rynchops] joined a flock of other skimmers and together they moved over the marshes in long lines and columns, sometimes appearing as dark shadows on the night sky; sometimes as spectral birds when, wheeling swallowlike in the air, they showed white breasts and gleaming under parts. As they flew they raised their voices in the weird night chorus of the skimmers, a strange medley of notes high-pitched and low, now soft as the cooing of a mourning dove, and again harsh as the cawing of a crow; the whole chorus rising and falling, swelling and throbbing, dying away in the still air like the far-off baying of a pack of hounds.

For Carson the ocean world was by no means a gentle and idyllic place; she did not flinch from describing the bitter rule of hunger and death in the marine world. Shad struggle upriver to lay 100,000 eggs, which, if not eaten by fish or birds or destroyed by currents, may produce one or two offspring; a grebe ensnarled in a fish net thrashes helplessly and soon dies. She writes about the food chains at sea, which she makes seem more inexorable than those that rule land creatures. With nearly shocking actuality she depicts underwater life as not just a well-meshed mechanism but as subject to relentless rhythms that harshly grip marine life. In some passages the author wrote in short sentences of similar length, as if she too had absorbed the rhythmic patterns of the sea and let them flow across her pages. She lets a shadow of surrealism fall over her writing, appropriate to invoking the murky depths where life and death rub together. Rachel Carson's commitment to a modern approach to nature is well recognized both in her style and in her understanding of the ocean as a stage for nature's drama. She synthetically used science and personal insight to make her sensitive prose respond to the power of the sea.

An author as contemporary in point of view as Carson but more private and idiosyncratic in imagination is Leonard Dubkin (1904–). Dubkin, an insistently amateur nature student, professionally a journalist, sets himself apart by a bold choice of locale for outdoor exploration; he chose to study nature in a big city, Chicago, and nowhere else. His first book of 1947, *Enchanted Streets, the Unlikely Adventures of an Urban Nature Lover,* somewhat self-consciously tells of his personal conversion to full-time love of nature at a time when he needed consolation because he had lost his job as a reporter. As Dubkin strolled around the city in jobless leisure, he tried hard not to seek out natural events but to let them catch his eye where and when they would. He is careful to claim no precise knowledge of wildlife, yet in fact he is a perspicacious observer who writes with a good grasp of what he sees in the dense canyons of the city streets. Hardly meaning to let himself look, he watches a weasel take a gull on an ice floe in Lake Michigan, and the number of insects, birds and animals he happens upon in the concrete jungle is no less than astounding.

His *Natural History of a Yard* of 1955 makes a bolder claim to virtuosity by further limiting the milieu to a tiny grass plot in front of his apartment house. Despite the unpromising setting Dubkin, assisted by his young daughter, found enough pocket nature to fill a book with descriptions—mostly such common lawn creatures as carpenter ants and larvae, house sparrows and robins. These events the author reports in terse journalistic prose, somewhat in the style of a tabloid, an appropriate choice for city nature writing. Dubkin is a rare breed—an apparently comic outdoor writer—who comments on a native American tradition by arbitrarily limiting his field. But his books are entertaining, diligently observed, and well informed, and it is possible to view him as a serious contemporary specialist who chose to focus on one place in order to achieve depth of perception in the tradition of Thoreau in Concord, Dallas Sharp at Hingham, and Leopold in Sand County.

Louise de Kiriline Lawrence is a nature writer of strong intellectual commitment who discovered wildlife late in her exceptional life. She made up for the delay by the logical insights of her outdoor explorations and her clarity in presenting them. Lawrence was born to well-to-do parents in Sweden, where her family's extensive estate and her father's affinity for the outdoors gave her a first taste of nature. She served with the White Russian army as a translator and nurse during World War I, and lost her young husband in that war. She later immigrated to Canada and continued nursing until she and her second husband went to live in an isolated cabin in the forest near Pimisi Bay, Ontario. Here the appeal of bird life slowly grew on her, and her book, *The Lovely and the Wild,* published in 1968, gains an added dimension in following her growth as a self-taught naturalist. Despite its lyrical title Lawrence looks beyond old-time nature appreciation toward an urge to know what birds do and why. Her mentor was the astute behaviorist Margaret Morse Nice, to whom her book is dedicated.

Lawrence took up banding only to find that the statistics of trapped birds and returns meant little to her, but the work stimulated her to look more closely at the birds and to try to deduce their psychology. Soon her observations went far beyond those of a beginner. She perceived that squirrels and birds are driven to predation not only by hunger or hostility but sometimes when fear forces them to panic, and she intuitively grasped the ethological concept that bird calls are not simply functional but ritualistic, and even symbolic. She described how chickadees survive in sub-zero weather by generating warmth through the stimulus of movement, sun-bathing, and food, and how they peaceably work out a pecking order by slanting their bills up or down—an astute microscopic perception. Lawrence was no casual student even without training in scientific method, a lack she made up with her innate intelligence and sharp eyes. Her curiosity enhanced her sense of discovery in whatever she saw, and she analyzed each new sighting until it was absorbed into her growing knowledge of bird behavior. Louise de Kiriline Lawrence deserves a place alongside Thoreau, Rachel Carson, and Aldo Leopold, for these were the finest minds that contributed to bird study.

The bird writer intentionally placed last in this short survey excels for the grace of his prose, but he also seeks new meanings beyond the range of any other bird student. With originality and insight he finds these by analyzing how the human and animal worlds interrelate, a persistent theme and a fresh and thoroughly modern one in all his essays. This writer is Louis J. Halle, Jr., who has published widely as a scholar of international relations but also writes on birds, his avocation. Halle's two principal books of bird essays, the first in 1938, the more recent in 1970, are *Birds Against Men*— the title reveals the theme—and *The Storm Petrel and the Owl of Athena.* Halle's momentum as a writer leads him beyond description to analysis, even to philosophic speculation. Despite this intellectual bent he is capable of narration as vivid as any in the past century of bird writing. His close-up vignette of a falcon stalking a flock of pigeons in the essay "A Hawk at Dusk" in *Birds Against Men* and the opening description of the summer birds of Shetland in *The Storm Petrel* invite comparison with the delights of Torrey or Teale but the younger author has an edge in solidity of detail. Characteristically Halle is not content with a brilliantly distilled description of the birds of Shetland but pushes on to a thoughtful comparison of those in one group, the *alcids.* Without aspiring to scientific completeness he selectively compares the members of this look-alike family with a clarity that identifies them for the birder more precisely than could any illustrated field guide.

Halle's fundamental recurrent theme, one seldom taken up before, is how birds relate to man. He circles around this question and haunts it from every angle: birds have been known to attack man, and man to wipe out a species like the great auk; real birds told Columbus when

Louis J. Halle, thoughtful bird writer for our time. *Louis J. Halle.*

he was near the New World, but humans may feel more akin to a symbolic and legendary bird like Athena's owl; some birds, such as the house sparrow and mute swan, live near man, but others like the loon and petrel seek a remote life. Halle tells a provocative eye-opening parable of bird freedom and man's bonds: when living in Switzerland on Lake Geneva he became acquainted with a flock of ducks which swam before his house. One day they set off to paddle across the lake and so to end up in France. Halle, on an impulse, decided to follow them to see what they were doing. His decision involved packing some provisions, gassing his car, circumnavigating the end of the lake through traffic, and passing through two customs posts where he had to show his documents and give an unlikely explanation of his purpose. So man encumbers himself with material needs and bureaucratic boundaries, while the ducks just paddle across to France.

Another allegory of a bird set against man is the story of Akbar, which Halle narrated with much exactitude. Akbar was a red-shouldered hawk with a broken wing. The author adopted, cared for, and fed him, but throughout the hawk remained inherently tough, aloof, and disdainful of the human help. A pet crow, in contrast, was all ingratiating sociability. Akbar in time recovered enough to learn to hunt by playing at it and was able to capture large insects on the ground, but he was not quick enough to take a chipmunk. The final irony of this bird's rebellion against accommodating to man came when it was released and then shot by a hunter.

Halle's original and thoughtful viewpoint provided the intellectual scope to offer fresh insights on birds. Describing the kingbird in depth, he concluded that it is a kind of instinctual hero, never pausing to think, knowing and acting in response to some inscrutable inner drive—in short, nothing less than the paradigm of an existential being. Halle's analysis of men and birds led him even to question the sacred structure of species. The proliferation of subspecies, variations due to location, the crossbreeding of domestic birds—all suggested to him that the systematics of species may not be as consistent with nature as science assumes. After thus giving nightmares to a few ornithologists, Halle then tossed a bone to the conservationists: could not endangered species, Akbars excepted, sometimes be saved by massive partial domestication, like the buffalo, the swans and ducks in parks, and birds in zoos? These creatures, kept by men and bred for larger numbers, might contribute to the conservation of their kind.

Most bird writing has stressed wide-eyed appreciation, inspired by whatever delight attracted the observer; such subjective responses generated some fine lyrical writing but not many new thoughts. It is refreshing to find in Louis Halle a modern and bold approach that looks beyond the surface of nature for meanings too often passed over.

Chapter Thirteen

Artists of Bird Life

*P*ainting in nineteenth-century America was resolved into conventionally determined types. Portraitists, landscape and still life artists, and painters of everyday life tended to keep to their own bailiwicks. Bird artists were further constricted because they owed allegiance to the factual precision sought by science. Often they served as scientific illustrators, and few could put aside the demands of bread-and-butter commissions to produce their own designs.

The dilemma of the bird artist is shared with the portrait painter: both must satisfy recognizability and the patron's demands while tactfully arranging artistic pose and expression. Most bird painters were all too aware of their conflicting obligations. Louis Agassiz Fuertes endured the only setback of a happy career when Frank Chapman and Gilbert Grosvenor rejected his illustrations for the *National Geographic Magazine* as inappropriately artistic. Fuertes longed for a period free from commissions to explore his own ideas but could never manage it. He and others painted bird portraits, as they are accurately enough called, most often in profile, echoing the formula of early Renaissance portraitists, since the side view most clearly presents shape and color. The paradoxical restrictions placed on the bird artist limit his stylistic expression and make his art hard to analyze formally. But twentieth-century artists have resolved the dilemma of bird art by adopting a realism that rivals photography and responds to a technological age.

Of all nineteenth-century nature artists Audubon brought the most flair and force to his art, pushing it to new frontiers and leaving old restrictions behind. Audubon had predecessors such as Mark Catesby, an Englishman who spent some years in the Southeast during the early eighteenth century, and Alexander Wilson, the striving Scottish immigrant and author of *American Ornithology* (see Chapters One and Two). But as artists both Catesby and Wilson were self-educated, and lacking the experience to reform conventional bird drawing, they were constrained to accept its stiff stylizations. The story of American bird art only began in earnest with Audubon.

Audubon's drawings, all but a few kept today in the New York Historical Society, to which his wife sold them in 1863 for $2,000, and the prints after them in *The Birds of America* were formed in a strong personal style. Yet it is surprising that little has been written about this artist's style in its own right. The colorful display of the birds he drew, along with his dramatic personal story, have conspired to distract attention from the elements of his art. Frontiersman, failed merchant, narrator of American life in his charming episodes inserted in *Ornithological Biography* and creator of a masterpiece of bookmaking, Audubon was first and last an artist. From boyhood till his eyes failed in 1846 he drew. Even the black chalk portraits he made for spare cash when hard up have a remarkable quality.

Audubon's life story makes a romantic tale of talent vindicated, and his art is no less a vivid statement of the romantic age. In high art the best analogy to his work seems to be the baroque romanticism of the young Delacroix, thirteen years his junior. Before Audubon and even in his own youth, bird portrayal achieved no more than a dry standard; the bird was almost always presented in profile silhouette, unable to move and imprisoned in compressed space. Only a few of Wilson's birds flex enough to turn head toward tail. The teen-aged Audubon in drawings done at Mill Grove and in France had not yet conceived the means to break this flat formula. But once he perfected his technique of wiring dead birds in selected poses and as the bounty of American nature unfolded and inspired him, he broke the bonds of tradition once and for all. He rapidly learned to electrify his birds with all the life force that nature grants them. The driven energy which he personally shared with outdoor creatures was transmitted through his brushes to the swirling, tumbling forms on his drawing pad.

For his drawings Audubon logically chose a light technique, a variable combination of gouache, pastel, and watercolor. This permitted him to capture the birds' wealth of color with no loss of detail. The artistic obverse of Audubon's drawing is the heavy, slow, and thick medium of oil painting, a technique he had difficulty learning even after lessons from colleagues like Thomas Sully. Oil painting did not suit his mercurial personality. In England, responding to local taste and his usual need for cash, he did a number of bird and animal paintings in oil, but had to confess his dissatisfaction with them as potboilers. His discomfort with the oil medium is another indication that Audubon was self-taught and never, as he claimed, studied with David. The delicate means of his drawings allowed him to capture both the flashing motion and the exquisite details of bird life. The browser first senses in *The Birds of America* a tumult of spontaneous activity; a closer look reveals that the artist was also a disciplined observer of natural particulars.

With his mercurial temperament and buoyancy of style, Audubon seemed likely to be a quick draftsman, but in fact he worked laboriously. To portray a captive golden eagle he persisted until he became ill, first studying the bird for two days, then devoting a painful day to killing it mercifully, finally drawing for two weeks. During the seven weeks' journey to Labrador he produced twenty-three drawings in working days that often stretched from 3:00 A.M. to dusk, not a facile production even in adverse conditions. The synthetic genius of Audubon's style assured fidelity to his subjects but also an imaginative release of their vitality.

No artist can ignore trends in art, and Audubon was a surprisingly typical product of high romantic art. He must have known what was happening in both the European and American art of his era. During visits to Philadelphia he was in touch with such artists as Sully, Vanderlyn, and the Peales, and during his sojourns in England and Paris he must have seen some of the great collections. In his own drawings Audubon frequently refers to romantic concepts of design. He used an ingenious variety of compositions for his bird drawings, from the simplest profiles to swirling groups of a dozen forms. A favorite design was a spiral, often moving from the bottom right of the sheet to the middle left to top center or right. This geometry was useful for presenting larger groups of birds, like the Carolina parakeets or painted buntings, but could serve for a charming pair like his passenger pigeons, where the male bends down to feed the upreaching female, or even for a single bird like the plummeting common tern.

The dynamic swirl is not Audubon's invention, but a tradition in western art during the baroque, rococo, and romantic eras. Contemporary parallels to Audubon's dynamism can be found in the art of Delacroix, Gericault or Blake, and the helical movements in his designs could even find sources in hundreds of eighteenth-century ceilings and altarpieces descending from such an ancestral figure as Rubens. John James Audubon belongs to the family of romantic artists, although he remained somewhat outside the accepted tradition because of his special subject matter, his peripatetic life, and his volatile personality. His art nevertheless finds a place in the historical context of other leading romantic painters like Alston, Cole and Vanderlyn in early nineteenth-century America.

LEFT. Audubon's calisthenic great blue heron. *OPPOSITE.* The feeding ritual of the passenger pigeon, as gracefully recorded by Audubon.

*S*tarting with Audubon, bird art, involving a commitment to travel and to the ideals of nature, often attracted a talented elite. Agreement is widespread that one member of this clan stood out in human qualities, in sympathy with man and wild creatures alike. This paragon was the beloved artist-naturalist Louis Agassiz Fuertes. Fuertes was fortunate in background, born of educated parents. His father was an engineering professor at Cornell who fortuitously named his son after the great Harvard naturalist, and his mother was a fine musician who bequeathed Louis an avocation that helped him perfect his imitations of bird calls. Louis was fortunate also in knowing from school days, when he made his first bird drawings, that this art would engage him for a lifetime, even though his father doubted that the pursuit could pay enough and tried to guide his son toward architecture.

While still in college at Cornell, Fuertes met Elliott Coues, the most respected ornithologist in America, during a Glee Club trip. Coues

LEFT. Louis Agassiz Fuertes, the bird artist as a young man. *Department of Manuscripts and University Archives, Cornell University Libraries.*

OPPOSITE. Fuertes' studio was filled with souvenirs of his field trips. *Department of Manuscripts and University Archives, Cornell University Libraries.*

recognized Fuertes's talent and forcefully adopted his cause, displaying his drawings and touting him at AOU meetings. As a result the young artist, still an undergraduate, found himself with several major commissions, including the illustrations for Coues's and Mabel Wright's *Citizen Bird* and Florence Merriam's *A-Birding on a Bronco*.

Fuertes's precocious entry into the birding world also put him in contact with the eccentric New England artist Abbott Thayer. Thayer accepted Louis wholeheartedly and Fuertes spent the summer after his graduation, and other times thereafter, with the Thayer family in New Hampshire as a guest student of both art and nature. Thayer was in those years evolving his theory of concealing coloration in the animal world (see Chapter Nine). A domineering personality, he insisted that Fuertes portray birds absorbed in a setting. Thayer's obsession with his camouflage notions brought Fuertes one of the few conflicts of his sunny life, since he owed the older artist loyalty and gratitude, but patrons such as Frank Chapman and Gilbert Grosvenor of the *National Geographic*

demanded bird portraits of clear legibility that stood out from their settings.

Fuertes's frequent travels into the field began in 1898 when he went to Florida with Abbott and Gerald Thayer. The following year he was one of the youngest men on the Harriman Alaska Expedition and helped illustrate its report. He explored Texas with Vernon Bailey of the Biological Survey, whose Spartan style of travel made him more grateful for Harriman's luxury tour. Trips with Frank Chapman to help him expand the American Museum habitat groups took Fuertes to the Bahamas, then to Cape Sable, Florida, the Magdalen Islands, Yucatan, the western Canadian plains, and twice to Colombia. Fuertes's last journey in 1926, the year before his premature death in a railroad crossing accident, was to Abyssinia with Wilfred Osgood of Chicago's Field Museum. The stimulation of this new territory inspired his most incisive drawings.

Louis Fuertes is often called a naturalist-artist; with him the two roles are indistinctly fused. His love for birds was passionate, instinctive, and sensual. Having shot a specimen, he sometimes held it in his lap stroking and preening it to reorder the plumage, an act of empathy that put him in a trance beyond reach of his field companions. Painting birds, which Fuertes did more readily at home, and learning of them in the field were equal and interrelated expressions of his love for them. While traveling he worked as an ornithologist. In the morning, starting early, he collected specimens until about 11. After lunch he prepared his own skins, following a personal standard that looked to later portrayal. Only in the evening did he take time for some sketching, along with correspondence and keeping up his journal.

Fuertes's method for making a bird painting was not much different from the procedures of the old masters. Always confident, he worked rapidly and surely. He would refer first to field sketches, rough but lively annotations of the bird in action. Infrequently he used photographs or even the living bird, and the skin was always at hand. He outlined the portrait first in pencil, then leaving the bird in that flat state, washed in the background, often using one brush for several colors. He sometimes dunked the work in water at this point, then left it to dry for some hours or several days before he painted the plumage, submerging its flatness and building up sharp relief from the setting.

Fuertes' major tool was his acute memory for any bird. Field companions have described how he studied a bird in the wild, then returned to camp hours later to draw it in every detail. This empathy was the source of an added dimension often noted in his bird paintings: not only are they ornithologically sound but they hint subtly at the inner life of the wild being, which takes on a tinge of mystery after passing through the filter of the artist's memory.

For several reasons Fuertes focused intensely on the bird in isolation: one was his empathy with the wild creature, and another was that the commissions he lived by were most often guide books and state bird books treating species singly. Abbott Thayer, Fuertes's teacher, was chiefly a portrait painter and only a nature artist later in his career. Recalling Thayer's portraits, Louis Fuertes preferred to concentrate on the subject bird and more often than not omitted its setting or sketched the background loosely. The exceptions to this rule may help to prove it: Fuertes's gyrfalcon in the Charles Ferguson Collection has an icy blue seascape that echoes the bird's winter plumage, and the mammals he did for the *National Geographic Magazine,* which demanded an effort of will to succeed in an alien field, each dwelt in its appropriate environment. Fuertes was constrained to abandon Thayer's dictates that the bird lives concealed by its surroundings, and to follow the wishes of clients who insisted on seeing a species isolated and sharply delineated as through binoculars. Later in life the bird painter and the New Hampshire artist drifted apart because of the pressures on Fuertes and Thayer's obsessive advocacy of his theory.

Freed from his teacher's impressionist vision, Fuertes became more and more the authoritative recorder of species, succinctly observed. He showed his subjects living in space, turning or foreshortened as seen in the field. He adopted the habit of doing just the head of the bird, perhaps because this method allowed the artist to focus more sharply on his subject's essence or perhaps merely as a practical shortcut to capture what remained of a fading skin. But Fuertes was not content to do just portraits of isolated birds; he hoped to take a protracted leave from book illustration to pursue larger designs, but he never found the time.

Fuertes did not often undertake compositions of birds in groups, but when he did his artistic mastery did not fail him. Whether he painted a mated couple like the Texas canyon wrens in 1901 now in the Herbert Johnson Museum at Cornell, or a more ambitious design like the mural of flamingoes in the American Museum of Natural History, the rhythms seemed to grow from nature but with artifice enough to give pleasure to the eye. Most bird artists prefer large, visible birds and Fuertes's favorites were the raptors. Almost invariably, when depicting a hawk or owl, he showed the bird grasping its prey, often a small bird or rodent, in its talons, a motif enabling the artist to relate contrasting textures of fur and feather.

Fuertes was a master at reproducing plumage. He directed all the tact of his brush and his superhuman sensitivity to finding the most convincing equivalents in paint to simulate feathers. His sole American rival as preeminent bird artist, John James Audubon, was also famous for his illusionistic plumage, though Audubon worked slowly and Fuertes was a facile virtuoso. Some have questioned whether Audubon or Fuertes deserves to be rated first among bird artists. The issue is moot because

Northern shrike for Mabel Osgood Wright's *Birdcraft*, Fuertes' first commission. *Laboratory of Ornithology, Cornell University.*

the contending personalities are so variant; Audubon's art poured from his impulsive romanticism, whereas Fuertes was a disciplined observer holding to what he saw and knew.

*F*uertes had a particular friend in the bird artist fraternity, Allan Brooks of British Columbia, who was five years his senior. Brooks visited Fuertes in Ithaca in 1920 before they left on a trek to Florida. Resident all his adult life in British Columbia, Brooks knew the world beyond and kept in touch with England, America, and far-flung birding out-posts. Born in India, first educated in England before his family immi-grated to Ontario in 1881 and later to British Columbia, Allan Brooks thought of himself as English. A hunter all his life and never renouncing the sport as other American naturalists did, Brooks generally went into the field in a three-piece tweed suit with plusfours, stockings, and cap to match. When World War I broke out he was in England and eagerly joined a British regiment but was shipped back to Canada when it was found he was a reservist there. He reached the trenches anyway and won decoration as a sniper. He went home a breveted colonel with permanent rank of major.

Brooks knew the northwestern wilderness best from Alaska to the Columbia River, but both for birds and patronage he turned to Amer-ica. Besides Florida he traveled in all the southwestern states and fre-quently to California, free to do so as a single man until age fifty-seven. Later with his wife he went to Australia and England again. Though a naturalist of the West, he surveyed the coasts of Nova Scotia and New Brunswick for comparison. Most of his commissions came from Amer-ica, including the illustrations for Dawson's *Birds of California,* complet-ing the final volume of Forbush's *Birds of Massachusetts* following Fuertes's death, and a series of paintings for *Bird-Lore* and the *National Geographic.*

Allan Brooks was not so facile and productive an artist as Louis Fuertes nor so fervid in absorbing the character of birds. Self-taught like many bird artists, he kept a cooler distance from birds than Fuertes. Brooks, a hunter, military hero and bachelor outdoorsman most of his life, was the most delicate of bird artists—subtle in technique, restrained, and never violent. His forms are soft and sometimes a little blurred, as if seen through the mists of Victoria Island in British Columbia. The foreground birds have more focus than their setting—a device used by

Fuertes and others—but the backgrounds shimmer impressionistically. Shorebirds often appear in an ambiguous habitat where no horizon separates their two worlds of sky and water.

Brooks's birds move naturally enough if not as compulsively as Audubon's but, as with Fuertes, the larger number are posed in profile. The artist's sketches, most in soft pencil consistent with his style, a few in pen, allow further insights into the fluidity and charm that enliven the conservatism of his reserved style. While Fuertes animated the bird's inward motivation, Brooks's soft touch gently reveals the life of wild creatures behind the veil that falls between their realm and ours.

Frank Chapman, determined entrepreneur of birding and its art, induced the best bird artists early in this century to contribute illustrations for *Bird-Lore,* among them Louis Fuertes, Edmund J. Sawyer, and Robert Bruce Horsfall from Iowa, an exact contemporary of Allan Brooks. Horsfall lived a migratory life, shifting residences from Cincinnati to New York City, Washington, Princeton, New Jersey (where he did scientific illustrations), the Jersey shore, and Rochester. He traveled with William Beebe to Borneo, India, and Ceylon, to Oregon for a short stint as state biologist, and with his Princeton colleagues to prehistoric sites in the Dakota Badlands. A competent portraitist of birds but seldom innovating or penetrating, Horsfall had a genial talent without high aspirations in art. Of all the bird artists, who were mostly self-taught, Horsfall had the best formal training, first at the Cincinnati Art Academy and later in Paris and Munich. His academic background may have encouraged the conservatism of his art, but it also supported his versatility as impressionist landscape painter, formal portraitist, and recorder of every type of wild creature. Equipped with a style that spoke to all, Horsfall enjoyed a successful career. He painted diorama backgrounds for several museums, including the American Museum of Natural History, where he worked with Chapman, and illustrated over two dozen books with drawings that ranged from the scientific to children's fables, a humorous genre at which he excelled. Horsfall also found steady work not just with *Bird-Lore* but at *Century* and *Nature* magazines as draftsman and art editor.

Bruce Horsfall was less a bird painter than a book illustrator. A small scale suited him, and he rejoiced in the passing, or sometimes the humorous, incident. His most common works were delicate monochromatic wash drawings designed to grace a page. Horsfall's knowledge of birds, their anatomy, plumage, and behavior was extensive. He

Bruce Horsfall provides a rich setting
for the white-crowned sparrow.
Jane Voorhees Zimmerli Art Museum,
Rutgers, The State University of New Jersey.

chose a correct setting for each species, and in the manner of Brooks and Fuertes, whom he sometimes copied, he diligently modeled his bird portraits for a strong foreground focus while allowing the background to fade amid loose impressionistic strokes. Horsfall's independent landscapes have a cheerful high-toned spontaneity linked to advanced impressionism that informed the style he used for the settings of his birds. Otherwise Horsfall was little committed to depicting the action of his subjects in space. His favorite formula showed two birds in front, male and female or adult and immature, and a small flock beyond, diminishing diagonally to measure the setting. This formula does not ring with energy and lacks Audubon's dynamism or Fuertes's intensity.

One bird artist and critic, Robert Mengel, has dismissed Horsfall's art as saccharine sentiment. His casually stroked backdrops may contain bursts of unbotanical flowers, recalling the jubilance of a pre-Raphaelite scene. But Horsfall, a successful artist in touch with his time, was a late Victorian and sympathetic to the sentimental, which he indulged most in his drawings for children. Yet he could be a knowledgeable and even scientific recorder of nature. Just before Horsfall's death in 1948 the bulk of his remaining works were transferred to Rutgers University. In 1974 Rutgers held a selective exhibition of this rich material to introduce this little known and talented, if seldom brilliant artist.

A nature artist who shone with brilliance was Ernest Thompson Seton. He sensed the vibrancy of animal life and caught it with his facile pen. Seton drew with spontaneous ease, and all his life drawing remained his prime means of expression. Famous as a storyteller through his books and lectures, which he enlivened with hilarious and uncannily accurate imitations of animal voices, and respected as a scientific zoologist, Seton always bedecked his writings with drawings: some witty and irreverent, others captivating for their fresh insights into nature or moving in their sympathy for animal suffering. Like Audubon Seton was master of the intimate study; both artists moved with a spontaneous flow of energy more like birds in flight than earthbound men. Conditioned to homelessness in his youth, Seton like Audubon learned the workings of nature on the fly and like Audubon despite a volatile temperament proved able to dedicate himself with heroic discipline to a major project, his *Lives of Game Animals* of 1909.

But in one important regard Seton differed from Audubon and the whole coterie of bird artists: an inherent but not a trained intellectual, he held a strong set of ideas on how nature works, and this viewpoint permeated his writings and drawings. The chapters above on nature fakery and on bird literature summarize the gist of Seton's concept of animal behavior, and how it put his thought well ahead of his time. As introductory to his art it is worth repeating that Seton was a pioneer in taking the animal's part, and as a thorough going Darwinian made his animals heroes but led them to bitter tragic ends. With these tenets he necessarily assumed that wild creatures could reason and feel in the manner, if not the degree, of humans. This point was so basic to his thinking that to support it Seton bent reality toward limited anthropomorphism—hence his brief penury as a nature faker.

A mercurial and flexible personality, Ernest Thompson Seton did not draw in any one technique but showed greater adaptability of means than most nature artists. Gouaches, grisailles and full-color wash drawings, pen and ink, chalk and charcoal occur; oil paintings are rare and outside his preferred range. Julia Moss Seton, his second wife, deposited the principal body of Seton's drawings in the Seton Memorial Library of the Philmont Scout Ranch in Cimarron, New Mexico. Here one learns that the type of drawing most fitted to Seton's personality was the simple pen and ink sketch, where swift execution permits directness of feeling and no second thoughts dilute the artist's rebellious effervescence or his funny asides on nature.

Two failures, both youthful false starts owed to inexperience, guided Seton toward his multiple career as illustrator, narrator, and naturalist. One concerns bird study; the other, oil painting. When he first lived on the frontier in Manitoba in 1882 at age twenty-two, Seton was entranced by the panoply of nature there, especially by the birds, which seemed the foremost actors on the scene. Soon, too soon, he undertook a scientific work on the birds of Manitoba, finally completed in 1890. Since Seton collected specimens for the Smithsonian Institution, his study went there to the bird curator Robert Ridgway, who found it amateurish and adolescent. Typically Seton had indulged his own feelings for nature and had set aside scientific objectivity in trying to enter the birds' lives. By nature proud and hypersensitive about his provincial origins, Seton reacted by abandoning bird study and turning to mammals instead, though he still produced a few bird stories and drawings.

The works that stand at the core of Seton's accomplishment are his animal stories, at once adult and juvenile in level. Seton did not turn to this genre until the late 1890s when he was nearly forty years old, and thereafter he steadily produced these stories for about twenty-five years until he became absorbed in revising the *Lives of Game Animals.* Bitterly realistic, harsher than the sweetened nature writings in vogue, fast-moving and laced with action, they brought Seton fame and wealth. Most were published first in magazines, then gathered in little books, which he generously illustrated. He started the series in 1894 with the most compelling of all the stories, "Lobo, the King of Currumpaw," curtain raiser of the first book, *Wild Animals I Have Known,* and continued with few pauses in seven other volumes.

Seton determined the formula for illustrating these works at the outset and varied it little. He played two contrasting kinds of art against each other: uncaptioned marginal pen sketches on nearly every page, flippant, swift, loose, and running from the ridiculous to the incisively interpretive; and less frequent, polished, full-page narrative scenes done in graded tones of gray wash in the convention of book illustration as practiced by Horsfall and the popular outdoor illustrator A. B. Frost. Seton both wrote and illustrated his volumes, impressing them in two ways with his sharply faceted personality.

The marginal sketches are so boldly personal that in one case the publisher tried to suppress them; the full-page illustrations are further linked to the text by captions quoting a phrase from it. These rounded drawings underscore Seton's narratives in moments chosen for vivid intensity, often providing a glimpse of ardent action or expressing an ideal of animal sentiment. Seton boldly induced his audience to see the animal world as he felt it was. His stories shine with wit, the drawings perhaps more than the text. Like Mark Twain's, Seton's wit was double-edged, drawing attention with an opening laugh before guiding the eye and mind through a veil to an abrupt shock of reality.

During his many-sided career Seton embraced another kind of drawing, quite different from the story illustrations. These were serious sketches for use in his scientific works, seen best in his first book, *The Art Anatomy of Animals,* an artist's guide to animal painting, and twenty years later in the *Lives of Game Animals.* These drawings were technical, illustrating parts of animals from many viewpoints, such as skulls from above and inside, even the variety of tracks on different surfaces and the scat. Yet Seton the artist did not retreat here, and even the most functional of these illustrations rings with the esthetic interest of his later style. On occasion Seton irritated his publisher by including racy

LEFT. Ernest Thompson Seton saw the bufflehead as abstract patterns in black and white.

BELOW. Seton depicted the downy woodpecker as more prominent than the boy who looks on.
Seton Memorial Library, Philmont Scout Ranch

pen sketches at chapter ends, a mischievous disruption in a scientific work.

*H*istorians have argued whether Audubon or Fuertes was America's first ranking bird artist, but there is a third candidate, Francis Lee Jaques (pronounced Jay-queeze), who merits consideration for his force of design and clarity of artistic conception. A midwesterner born in 1887 in Illinois and raised on a Kansas farm, Jaques had only an abbreviated formal education, but he drew competently from the age of seven. His father, a professional hunter and sports writer, taught him a love of the outdoors. Though without formal training in art, he invented his own striking style. While still young he left home for Minnesota to apprentice in his two passions, a taxidermy shop and the railroad. Railroading was for Jaques a love as strong as birds, as attested by some of his finest paintings and the artistry of the model railroad system he created. In 1924 Jaques determined to act on his dream of becoming a museum artist and, aiming as high as he could, he sent some drawings to Frank Chapman at the American Museum of Natural History who hired him forthwith.

Chapman was then undertaking the museum's ambitious series of bird habitat groups, and Jaques soon became the leading painter of their diorama backgrounds. He spent eighteen years at this work and completed as many scenes, their crisp mastery of space and fresh color spectrums in some cases still enjoyable today despite restorations. Jaques's approach to diorama painting, a challenging problem in design because of its irregularly curved surface, depended on common sense flexibility. Generally he painted his landscapes from the bottom up to assure their link to the three-dimensional foreground, and like Roger Tory Peterson he sometimes chose to do the bird inhabitants separately as cutouts, arranging them later in the whole. Since the dioramas were specifically topographical, Jacques traveled with Chapman and his crew to many bird sites, including Peru, the Bahamas, the Arctic and Alaska, the South Pacific, and his patron's beloved Barro Colorado in Panama. Jaques, always fascinated by transportation, developed affection for the schooners that took him to these romantic outposts, the *Morissey* in Alaska and the *Zaca* in the far Pacific, and his paintings of them catch the lure of far places. Word of the artist's expertise as a diorama painter spread, and today his backgrounds may be seen at the Peabody Museum of Yale

University, the Boston Museum of Science, the Bell Museum at the University of Minnesota, and elsewhere.

In time Jaques's service at the American Museum ran its course. Chapman's heavy-handed patronage fostered unnecessary competition among his artists, and Jaques, in some ways a virtuoso, felt he had received too little credit for his part in the diorama program. In 1942 he resigned from the museum but continued on in New York relishing the chance to work free-lance. New avenues soon opened to him as illustrator and brilliant practitioner of the scratchboard drawing. In 1927 he married Florence Page, a writer with a light touch, who moderated his intensity. They soon became inseparable camping partners and book collaborators, she as author and he as illustrator. The paradise they dreamed of from afar and then attained was the Quetico–Superior lake region, and their first joint book, *Canoe Country,* grew out of their honeymoon there. In 1952 they built a retirement house at North Oaks, Minnesota, near Duluth and within reach of the cherished canoe country.

Jaques's two masterpieces were the series of American Museum dioramas and the paintings he made for Robert Cushman Murphy's magnificent *Oceanic Birds of South America.* Critics have posed the question which of these two multiple works seems most worthy to crown his career. Both cycles are in oil, Jaques' preferred medium, because it allowed him a subtler modulation of colors. He worked only occasionally in watercolor or lithography. His scratchboard book illustrations came mostly after World War II, and he used careful, firmly outlined pencil sketches of details as preparation for works in any medium.

The dioramas and the oceanic bird paintings are not readily comparable, because they answer different functions in a way that reveals the flexible intelligence of the artist. The habitat settings define uncontained outdoor spaces where creatures move freely to reinforce the spatial illusion. For Murphy's volumes the artist grouped several species on each sheet, often in the textbook profile view and less visually related to the spatial sweep of the settings beyond. Inventive as he was, Jaques had to accept the conventions of formal bird portraiture for such a book, and did so again in Alexander Sprunt's books on South Carolina and Florida bird life.

Francis Lee Jaques's oil paintings have a defined place in American landscape art because their balance of reality and conceptual abstraction place them firmly in the modern era. But Jaques's claim to brilliance can also rely on his scratchboard drawings, done for book illustrations and recognized as among the most striking and inventive of the type. Jaques revived the scratchboard technique rather late in life, took it far ahead toward an innovative mastery and bequeathed it as a valued tool to younger nature artists like Roger Tory Peterson and Bob Hines. The

ABOVE. Jaques' dramatic scratchboard drawing of bald eagles and crows in winter. *Devin-Adair.*

RIGHT. Egret in a Florida pond by Jaques, circa 1935. *James Ford Bell Museum of Natural History, University of Minnesota.*

technique is simple and limited; its restraints challenge the artist to attain the fullest possible expression without the easy flow of oils and water-colors. The illustrator prepares a board covered first with a layer of black ink and over that a white layer. He then draws with a stylus or etching needle scratching through the white, representing highlights where un-touched, to the black beneath, giving shadows where revealed by the

stylus. The technique is starkly graphic; it deals in harsh chiaroscuro, though Jaques was adept at modulating contrast with subtly varied hatching lines.

Jaques illustrated more than two dozen books with scratchboard drawings, seven written by his wife. The scratchboard cuts in *Canoe Country* and in *John Burroughs' America,* edited by Farida Wiley, are perhaps the most arresting. Florence Jaques said Lee strove to paint more than is there, and this may be the clue to the scratchboard drawings' power to captivate the eye. They are abbreviatory but do more with less, consciously held back by a restricted technique; they are forcefully composed with aggressive lines and eye-stopping light–dark contrasts, yet they can encompass a fullness of space and add the implications of tonal gradation.

Francis Lee Jaques was much more than a portrayer of birds, for more than any other bird artist he showed sensitivity to place. Fuertes and his contemporaries focused on the foreground; and, while Audubon sometimes specified a topography, it was distant, often not connected to the birds depicted and generally painted by an assistant. For Jaques the animal lived in an appropriate locale in which it was deeply embedded. Sometimes it takes a second glance to find the bird or beast in his overpowering settings. The egrets among cypresses in the oil at the Burt Brent Collection float by, mist-colored like their native swamp and echoing the limb patterns above; and the scratchboard mink beneath winter trees is reduced to a dark, vulnerable patch.

Intellectually Jaques's viewpoint parallels the new behaviorism that turned around twentieth-century ornithology. Artistically Jaques is an American regionalist with links in style to Charles Sheeler's tightly delineated industrial scenes and to Edward Hopper's confident spatial designs with their large, strong color areas and abstract changes in light and shade. Jaques was intellectually aware, and more than others he worked in tune with his times. His style was conservative in holding forms within encasing lines, but in the disposition of forms in space and in color modulation it was advanced.

The art of Jaques, Fuertes, and Seton differs from most wildlife painting today because it always aspires to the level of fine art. The understanding of composition and draftsmanship these artists learned from tradition elevates their art above the merely illustrative. One has only to compare these painters' work with the standard black and white engravings which accompanied many ornithological treatises at the turn of the century or to Chester Reed's amateurish drawings to perceive the aesthetic superiority of their achievements.

*T*wentieth-century bird artists rarely attain this level of excellence. Frequently autodidacts, they derive their style not from an artistic heritage but from photography, which has recently dominated natural history illustration, forcing wildlife artists further and further away from artistic invention and closer and closer to the verisimilitude of the camera.

This prevailing cannon of realism has become a requirement for illustration of ornithological books. Artists are expected to create recognizable portraits of birds. Their aesthetics depend upon technical virtuosity rather than on expressive content. The best of these bird illustrators infuses standardized portraits with a flavoring of the bird's personality or arranges the frozen images stylishly. The techniques of realism become the painter's primary means. Even leading contemporary artists like Roger Tory Peterson or Robert Verity Clem are prisoners of their own illusionistic expertise.

Modern artists do not as often describe a dramatic event in bird life as their romantic predecessors did. Instead they design the bird like a sculptural image, with the profile silhouetted against the neutral background of the sheet. An object such as a clump of ferns or a dead tree near the bird may indicate a minimal setting. Paradoxically this realism is transcribed in an abstract way. The artist defines the bird as an organism tied only by inference to its ecological context. Modern bird art in this regard is opposed to behaviorism and committed to the goals of precise bird identification prevalent among many contemporary expert birdwatchers (see Chapter Fourteen).

George Miksch Sutton as both artist and ornithologist had a strong hand in directing bird art toward the new style of photographic realism. Born in 1902, Sutton served as curator of birds at the Carnegie Museum in Pittsburgh and later as a wildlife biologist for the state of Pennsylvania. In his late twenties he left Pittsburgh to attend graduate school in ornithology under Arthur Allen at Cornell, earning the Ph.D. in 1932. After a brief stint at the University of Michigan, Sutton found a permanent home at the University of Oklahoma, where he taught ornithology, supervised the research projects of his numerous graduate students, and established a study collection of bird skins for the museum. He died in 1982.

Sutton began drawing birds when he was in his teens. A letter to Frank Chapman resulted in an introduction to Fuertes who invited Sutton to study informally with him at Ithaca for a summer. This brief apprenticeship was Sutton's only artistic training. He became an adept watercolorist in the Fuertes manner but his lack of formal schooling led him to turn his back on landscape settings even more than his master did. Typically Sutton depicted the bird in profile against a plain background and often portrayed only the subject's head and neck, a device Fuertes also used. In the several scientific books he illustrated, such as W. E. Clyde Todd's *Birds of Western Pennsylvania* of 1940, Sutton kept to profile views of birds frozen in stiff poses against a rudimentary landscape backdrop. Sutton worked mostly from fresh specimens taken in the field. When he returned to base camp, he first rapidly brushed in a sketch of the bird's plumage. Sutton sought to document the variegation in the plumage of the species he drew, traveling as far as

George M. Sutton specialized in portraits of newborn chicks such as this golden plover.

Iceland or the Mexican rain forest to obtain subspecies for study purposes. Primarily concerned with appearance rather than behavior, he developed a delicate watercolor technique to capture the natal down of shorebird chicks in Iceland, for example, or plumage variations in subspecies of North American hawks in Mexico.

His perceptions and his art focused on the minute particulars of science. He rarely depicted the fanciful, dramatic, or humorous events in bird life. A much beloved man, Sutton, a bachelor, often traveled with ornithologist Olin Sewall Pettingill, director of the Cornell University Laboratory of Ornithology, and his wife Eleanor. Their expedition to Iceland was typical of their adventures. The Pettingills filmed wildlife while Sutton tried to draw a newborn chick of every species nesting there. The team made heroic efforts to locate nests which the Pettingills could film while Sutton captured live specimens.

Sutton frequently wrote books about his research travels and illustrated them with his own watercolors. For *Iceland Summer* of 1961 Sutton provided a chatty travelog of his birding missions with the Pettingills. Interlarding the pages are Sutton's watercolors of newborn chicks. Each portrait is isolated against the cream of the page. Sutton provided setting by including a selection of Pettingill's photographs of Iceland. In a similar book, *At a Bend in a Mexican River* of 1972, Sutton described his fieldwork with Pettingill and two other young ornithologists. In this later book his bird portraits were reproduced in color, allowing appreciation of his delicate brush. Sutton was an objective watercolorist, as specialized in technique as in subject. Occasionally he worked in pen and ink, providing standard anecdotal bird drawings for books such as Pettingill's *Guide to Bird Finding East of the Mississippi*. Because of his scientific training, he sought disciplined visual documentation as the goal of his art. Though often decorative, Sutton's drawings are somewhat dry and repetitive. These are the works of a technician who intentionally restricted his generous graphic talents to a focused purpose.

*R*oger Tory Peterson is the best-known bird illustrator of our time. He has achieved this fame through the popularity of his field guides, the first of which appeared in 1934. By 1939 when the second edition of the eastern bird guide appeared, Peterson had established himself as a nature educator and illustrator with the National Audubon Society, frequently designing spirited covers for *Bird-Lore*.

In Peterson's first independent commission, illustrations for Margaret Morse Nice's *Watcher at the Nest* of 1939, he drew in a lively but conservative style which he abandoned in subsequent work. His later black and white book illustrations are boldly rendered scratchboard drawings that owe much to the art of Lee Jaques.

In the years following his first field guide, Peterson worked in several styles. He made his most ambitious bird paintings for Alexander Sprunt's *South Carolina Bird Life* of 1949, a handsomely produced volume with full-page color paintings by Francis Lee Jaques, Edward von S. Dingle, John Henry Dick, and Peterson, who painted ten of the thirty-five plates. Jaques, the senior master for the project, determined the format for the plates. They are fully rendered landscape paintings in which the various species illustrated are artfully composed. These are among Jaques's most confident watercolors, and his accomplishment inspired Peterson to attain new heights in his own contributions to the volume.

In his "Shorebirds Along the Inland Waterway," Peterson depicted a setting familiar to all birdwatchers fond of salt marshes. He placed the birds mainly in the foreground and occasionally animated them with characteristic movements. Especially fine is a willet, shown as it lands in a way that demonstrates the artist's ability in foreshortening. But for the most part Peterson, despite the example of Jaques, does not effectively integrate his birds into the landscape setting. A certain naïveté in the construction of space permeates his art. He is more at ease with the genre of bird portraiture practiced by Fuertes and Sutton.

Peterson has frequently described his working method. He cuts out paper silhouettes of his bird subjects and moves them around on the sheet until he finds a pleasing composition. This method overlooks the need for a well conceived transition from picture plane to background. Peterson's birds rarely seem fully at home within nature, nor are they ever subordinate to their environment. Always correctly observed and drawn, his portraits are the products of an astute specialist, whose style was similar in some regards to Sutton's coeval work.

Peterson is a serious bird photographer, and his first major reworking of the *Field Guide* in 1947 shows the effects of this interest. Here the description of bird plumage becomes even more detailed and photographic realism begins to take hold. The resulting static quality dominates his mature scratchboard illustrations as well. The compositions are graphically bold and confident, yet seem to be collections of bird

These gyrfalcons demonstrate Roger Tory Peterson's
mature work. *Leigh Yawkey Woodson Art Museum.*

Peterson uses a formal composition for his color print
of bobwhites. *Mill Pond Press.*

portraits arranged self-consciously on the page. They are not noticeably freer from the constraints of formal portraiture than the earlier field guide illustrations.

Primarily a bird artist but also a working nature writer, Peterson has written about birds for the layman, illustrating the books with his art. Notable among these are his *Birdwatcher's Anthology* of 1959, in which his scratchboard illustrations complement the text. Peterson's art, unlike that of many bird illustrators, has developed and changed in style, but only within the limits of his chosen approach. This is particularly apparent in the plates for the 1982 edition of the *Field Guide* (Eastern Birds), where the photographic realism adumbrated in the earlier edition has become a firm aesthetic canon. Larger, bolder, and more sculptural than any of his previous portraits, the birds are meticulously rendered in exhaustive detail. The portraits, inanimate and objective, are even more abstract than their predecessors. Peterson derives all his precise aesthetic effects from the exquisite details of plumage, leg, and bill. For him, as for Sutton, the bird's appearance alone is the object of his draftsmanship.

Recently Peterson has been drawing large portraits of single species for reproduction as fine art prints. In such compositions as the "Bob-whites" of 1975 the covey of birds is arranged in a classic pyramid against a still life of leaves and flowers. A substantial portion of the sheet remains blank to highlight the birds in the center of the page. This means of expression is formal and static, almost in an academic mode. Even in the "Golden Eagle" of 1976, where the artist depicted the subject in profile against a panoramic mountain landscape, the design remains bird-centered. In neither print did Peterson introduce shadows cast by an actual light source, studiously depriving the portraits of local color and thus of a sense of time or real space. But Peterson's art is remarkable for its consistent high quality and integrity. The birds, which he knows intimately, are faithfully and honestly presented so as to enhance the minutiae of nature for any bird enthusiast who takes the trouble to study these careful portraits.

A single dominant exception to the exacting realism of modern bird portraiture is the art of Arthur Singer, who qualifies as today's most accomplished and sophisticated wildlife painter. Born in 1917, Singer is a trained artist who attended both Cooper Union and the Art Students' League. Singer's compositions are consciously varied and excite the eye with bright splashes of color.

The commission which brought Singer the most fame was the 1966 Golden Press's *Guide to Field Identification of the Birds of North America*. For 150 or so plates, Singer designed compositions of great variety and charm. Even in the tiny space allocated in the format for each species, he contrived to indicate habitat wherever possible. Ducks swim in ponds or lakes, nuthatches cling upside down to tree trunks, herons perch on snags in marshes. The artist consistently hinted at behavior and animating spirit in all his portraits. The clues to his sense of bird motivation come in part from the rudimentary settings or characteristic poses he chose for each species, but they also derive from Singer's brush strokes themselves. Much less calligraphic in technique than Peterson, Singer uses bold areas of color to enliven the portraits. He makes the bird's plumage and shape indications of personality.

Some of the success of Singer's illustrations lies in the artist's sheer graphic energy and innate talent for creating form, seen in how his birds dance across the pages. Color plays a large role in Singer's art. Although confined, like other bird illustrators, to a sunless world where local color has little place, Singer chooses a pure palette of strong primary hues to delineate his forms boldly. For Singer birds are exotic and gorgeous creatures, and he renders them with preternatural brightness and verve. It is noteworthy that this artist, who is free from the constraints of excessive realism, is not strongly influenced by color photography. He has solved the bird illustrator's dilemma: he clearly conveys his subjects' actuality while also raising their depiction to the realm of art.

For a more ambitious project, *The Birds of the World* with text by Oliver L. Austin, Jr., Singer took full advantage of a larger format and greater freedom to compose. The volume is one of the most splendid of modern bird books. The paintings are fully integrated with the text, often serving as bold marginal decorations as if in a modern bestiary. To browse through the book is to perceive Singer's vast knowledge of bird life and his protean creativity. Most pages contain one or more images, all ingeniously varied. He is an artist born to make fine designs and, although he rarely depicts a narrative event and primarily shows the bird in profile, he usually manages, with the empathy of a new Fuertes, to define its personality. As in the field guide, the chromatic brilliance of Singer's palette excites the eye, yet this exuberance does not distract from the accuracy of the portraits, which are always both recognizable and intensely alive.

Arthur Singer's illustration for *Birds of the World* shows the owls in correct relative proportions. *Western Publishing Company.*

*N*umerous bird artists today follow in the footsteps of Peterson and Sutton. The art of the Canadian painter James Fenwick Lansdowne, born in 1937, is a good example of fashionable contemporary bird painting. Lansdowne's commissions have been extensive, testifying to his liking for the current photographic realism. His most personal efforts are a series of books surveying the birds of Canada. His 1966 *Birds of the Northern Forest* with text by John A. Livingston serves as an exhibition catalog for Lansdowne's paintings. Each species is illustrated twice in full-page plates: first is the artist's working drawing, followed on the overleaf by a short biography of the bird and, facing the text, the full colored portrait itself. Lansdowne describes each bird, most often showing it in profile silhouetted against an abstract background. This format reveals his kinship to Roger Peterson. The artist renders the textures of feathers, bills, and feet superbly, and he is equally a master of pose. Although his birds are motionless, they are shown in their most characteristic postures, an artistic device that conveys their personalities.

King eider by William Zimmerman.
William Zimmerman.

Occasionally Lansdowne breaks with his own conventions and evokes Audubon's style. In his portrait of the white-winged scoter he shows the bird diving under water with feet turned up and head immersed as it reaches for some mussels at the bottom of the sea. This is an artist with considerable representational powers. He makes the most of the canon of realism, while producing some of the most creditable bird illustrations of our time.

Another able modern bird illustrator, William H. Zimmerman, is the same age as Lansdowne and studied at the Cincinnati Art Academy. His most impressive accomplishment and the one which demonstrates his mature style is the monumental 1984 *Birds of Indiana* with text by Russell E. Mumford and Charles E. Keller. Zimmerman works primarily in the tradition of the bird portraitist, rather than as a painter of landscape backgrounds. He contrives to integrate the illustrations, one to a page, to make an attractive ensemble. All of the plates for the *Birds of Indiana* are printed on a soft gray glazed paper that carries the suppleness of Zimmerman's brush gracefully. He renders the texture of

In Diane Pierce's watercolor of the horned grebe, its exotic silhouette is repeated on the water's surface. *Diane Pierce.*

plumage with subtle skill, but his drawing of branches, leaves, and flowers is stiff. Zimmerman's bird portraits are soft and gentle, evoking a benign but silent natural world. For example, he depicts his raptors without prey. And even though he silhouettes his birds in profile and isolates them from their environment, he animates them through the delicacy and empathy of his touch.

Numerous other competent bird artists, including Kenneth Carlson, Gary Low, and Robert Verity Clem, do not vary their style significantly from the naturalistic norms described here. Their bird portraits are realistic and attentive to detail. This homogeneity, as much the result of bird art's requirements as of photography's influence, is discernible in the plates for the 1983 National Geographic Society's *Field Guide to the Birds of North America,* painted by no fewer than thirteen different artists whose work is evenly competent and informal. The plates were particularly difficult to design. The artist had to illustrate several plumage variations for each species. Diane Pierce, for example, drew five versions of the common redpoll, three of the hoary redpoll, and eight of the rosy finch and laid them all out on one sheet. Her work stands out for its subtle textures and animation.

Like Lansdowne, Pierce has mastered the characteristic pose of a species which can convey behavior, even in the cramped format of the *Guide*'s pages. Her plates are thoughtfully varied, pleasing to look at, and instructive. She often manages to include an appropriate landscape setting such as in the drawing of the seaside sparrow where a salt marsh fades in the distance behind the five birds clinging to grasses in the foreground.

The quality of all the plates in the *National Geographic Guide* is remarkably high. It is as if the editors imposed a standard of virtuoso realism which all the artists met with ease. But proficiency does not make for art. The best bird artists of the past, such as Lee Jaques and above all John James Audubon, made bird portraiture a genuine art form inspired by the artist's whole vision of nature. If the future produces another revolutionary bird artist, he or she will be a figure with enough independence to break free of everyday realism and with enough insight to portray the essence of the bird and the drama of its life.

Chapter Fourteen

The Paraphernalia of Birding

An instructive indication of the growing popularity of birds with the community at large is supplied by the proprietors of a certain brand of chewing gum whose advertisement assures purchasers of their wares that they will find a colored picture-card of an American bird in every package. . . . Verily the ornithological millenium is approaching when we absorb bird-lore with chewing gum.
(*FRANK CHAPMAN*, *Bird-Lore*, 1912)

*B*ird designs, on everything from napkins and sugar packets to mailboxes are even more ubiquitous than they were in Chapman's time. Bird-watchers are bombarded with a vast selection of "birdiana," among which there is no larger category than books. Eighty years ago field guides, manuals, and bird encyclopedias appeared with as much regularity as they do today. Birders have always bought books promising them improvement of their identification skills, knowledge of bird behavior, and bird attraction programs for their yards. Publishers today, recognizing the buying power of the millions of birdwatchers in America, produce a stream of attractively illustrated books. Among these only a few survive a first printing to become popular successes. Roger Tory Peterson's *Field Guide to the Birds,* first published in 1934, is the most famous of these. It ushered in the era of the modern field guide and formed the birdwatching interests of a generation. But Peterson's *Guide* was not the first to be devised.

Two of the most prominent champions for the rights of birds, Frank Chapman and Mabel Osgood Wright, wrote the first inexpensive manuals for birders. Wright directed her considerable literary talents toward birdwatching in her first book, *Birdcraft: A Field Guide to 200 Common Birds of Eastern North America* of 1895. It was a brilliant effort. Illustrated generously but not completely with the earliest works of Louis Agassiz Fuertes, *Birdcraft* was an instant success. It was reprinted twelve times until finally eclipsed in the 1930s by Peterson's *Guide*. Frank Chapman's *Handbook of Birds of Eastern North America* appeared in the same year as Wright's book, which he intended to complement. The *Handbook* was reissued twenty-three times and became a standard reference work for the amateur bird student.

When Mabel Wright considered the format for an easy-to-use field guide, she found few models to aid her. Before her guide appeared, the birdwatcher had to take notes on an unfamiliar bird spotted in the field and then run home to look it up. If he was fortunate he owned a small edition of Audubon's *Birds of America* with its accompanying *Ornithological Biography,* which was dated by more than half a century and not up-to-date in nomenclature. He might also have Henry Nehrling's 1893 folio-sized *Our Native Birds of Song and Beauty,* which was fully illustrated by John L. Ridgway but was not arranged in any useful order. The birder interested in technical information might have acquired Elliott Coues's monumental *Key to North American Birds* of 1872 which was complete as to species and accurate for taxonomy, but was sparsely illustrated and contained no information about bird behavior. None of these reference volumes was cheap or portable. The persistent bird student could visit the local natural history museum, where cases of stuffed birds might lead to an identification but would offer no clues to the bird's behavior, habitat, or song.

An example of the difficulties birdwatchers encountered is provided by the transcendentalist poet Celia Thaxter. She was often frustrated by the dearth of reliable reference material about birds. So she began writing to New England nature writer Bradford Torrey. In her letters she included meticulous descriptions of the birds she had seen during migration on the Isles of Shoals near Portsmouth, New Hampshire, where she spent half the year. Torrey identified the species for her by

Celia Thaxter in her garden on Appledore
Island, painted by Childe Hassam.
*National Museum of American Art,
Smithsonian Institution, gift of John Gellatly.*

return mail. Thousands of backyard birders therefore greeted Mabel Wright's modest book with relief. By limiting her guide to birds of village and field she addressed the largest group of bird enthusiasts, those who encountered the common species in their yards, orchards, farms, or parks.

Wright's design was simple. The birds were arranged in taxonomic order but were labeled with their common names. After a pithy description of a species' appearance Wright provided the phrases of its song. For each bird she offered a substantial essay about its habits and haunts. These descriptive paragraphs were pleasant reading and contained sound ornithological observations. The literary quality of *Birdcraft* provided a clue to why the author did not illustrate each species. (Only ninety-eight or roughly half the birds were illustrated by Fuertes's masterful black and white wash drawings.) Early bird educators relied more on verbal description than they do today. Pictures were often somewhat misleading and color printing unreliable. A well-worded description of the bird avoided these difficulties.

This faith in communicating a bird's appearance waned a few years later when photographers began to specialize in nature studies and color printing improved. But Wright and Chapman, who later became a proficient photographer and a dedicated patron of bird artists, believed that a bird student could visualize a bird from written descriptions. Even the color key Wright and Chapman included at the ends of their volumes were verbal. In them the birds were arranged under color headings such as "primarily blue" or "primarily gray," and then under subheadings such as "primarily blue with white underparts." From the key the reader went to the pages indicated in the principal text.

Chapman adopted the predominantly literary tone of *Birdcraft* in his coeval but more ambitious *Handbook*. He hoped to reach serious students of natural history, especially teen-age boys, and to provide them with a home study manual of ornithology which covered all eastern North American species and served as a field guide as well. In the introductory chapters of the *Handbook,* Chapman supplied a complete text for beginning ornithological study, masterfully distilling a massive amount of information into a short space. His chapters on bird migration, song, and plumage, among others, are still a recommended introduction to the field.

At the heart of Chapman's *Handbook* are the more than 500 entries for individual species. His descriptions of the birds are more detailed than Wright's, and his bird biographies less discursive. His description of the blue jay explains why his *Handbook* needed few illustrations, only a few plates by Fuertes and a handful of line drawings of anatomical details interlarding the text:

354. Blue Jay. *Cyanocitta Cristate cristata*
(Fig. 102—shows only the wing)
Adults.—Upperparts grayish blue; underparts dusty whitish, whiter on the belly; forehead, and a band passing across the back of the head down the sides of the neck and across the breast, black; head crested; exposed surface of wings blue, the greater wing coverts and secondaries barred with black and tipped with white; tail blue barred with black, and all but the middle pair broadly tipped with white, this tip rarely less than 1:00 in width on the outer feather. . . .

In many ways Chapman's *Handbook* has never been matched. Its author placed complete faith in the ability of the observer to apply what he saw to the verbal descriptions provided in the text. Both the *Handbook* and Wright's *Birdcraft* set a high standard for the many books by other writers which followed. Three years later Florence Merriam Bailey published her popular *Birds of Village and Field, a Bird Book for Beginners*. After a brief introduction to birdlife and birdwatching and the now obligatory color key, Bailey catalogued eighty-six common birds, with black and white wash drawings illustrating about one-fourth of these. Small line drawings were scattered throughout.

Other early efforts to win a piece of the birdwatching market included several books by Neltje Blanchan Doubleday, which resembled Wright's and Bailey's. Another style of handbook, the state or area study, also became popular. Typical of the genre was Ora Knight's *Birds of Maine* of 1908 which follows the arrangement invented by Chapman for his *Handbook,* or Ralph Hoffmann's *Bird Guide to Massachusetts and New England,* which took *Birdcraft* as a model.

In 1902 Florence Merriam Bailey produced *The Handbook of Birds of the Western United States,* intended as a pendant to Chapman's *Handbook.* Written with the assistance of her husband, Vernon Bailey, and her brother, C. Hart Merriam, both scientists with the Biological Survey, the book was full of previously unavailable information. Bird students using the two handbooks could find reliable information on any birds in North America.

Only one other kind of bird guide emanated from this early period and it was a lasting success. In 1905 a young naturalist-artist from Worchester, Massachusetts, Chester A. Reed, brought out Part I of his series of guides covering land birds east of the Rockies. In 1909, the second volume for water and game birds and birds of prey appeared, followed in 1913 by the posthumous final volume for birds west of the Rockies and the Pacific Coast. Reed was not much of an artist, although he knew his birds. He pared down the verbose field guide, distilling the information it normally contained. His guide was tiny, smaller even than today's paperbacks, and only one bird appears on each page. Each bird was crudely illustrated in profile but is fully colored. A short description accompanies each picture. Reed's guides, unscientific and journalistic, were mistrusted by the Audubonists, Chapman included. His review of the revolutionary little guide was lukewarm:

Seton's least flycatcher for Florence Merriam Bailey's *Birds of Village and Field.* Seton Memorial Library, Philmont Scout Ranch.

In this attractive little volume Mr. Reed has succeeded in storing a large amount of information, together with colored figures which should prove of great assistance in identifying birds in life. Under each species is given a brief description of its principal color, characters, haunt, song, nest and eggs and range. The omission of the authority for matter not based on personal observation renders it impossible to determine just what is original and what is not, thereby decreasing the quotable value of this very convenient pocket manual.

Chapman apparently failed to grasp the appeal of Reed's guides. Their very simplicity made them popular. With *Birdcraft* and Chapman's *Handbook* the birdwatcher had to read and to think, while the birder using Reed's guides needed only to flip through the brightly colored pages, like flashcards. Cheaply produced, poorly drawn, and simply written, Reed's guides can be used by any child with greater success than *Birdcraft*. But Chapman's caution was justified, for Reed had ushered in the era of laconic, fully illustrated guides which aimed

ED-SHAFTED FLICKER *Colaptes cafer* **13 inches**

The linings of the wings and tail in this species are salmon red instead of golden yellow as with the Yellow-shafted Flicker, and the mustache marks of the male are red instead of black. The red crescent is usually lacking on the nape but is sometimes present in individuals. Red-shafted and Yellow-shafted Flickers interbreed in the overlap of their ranges and there are innumerable variations in their markings. Birds have been reported with one side of the mustache red, the other black. The two species are practically identical in habit.
Voice: Similar to that of the Yellow-shafted Flicker. **Nest:** Undistinguishable from that of the Yellow-shafted Flicker. **Range:** Breeds along the Pacific Coast from southeast Alaska to southern Mexico, east to South Dakota, Nebraska, Kansas, and eastern Texas; northernmost birds retire southward in winter.

Family Picidae: Woodpeckers 50

A page from one of Chester A. Reed's popular and portable guides.

exclusively at species identification. The little books encouraged bird listing at the expense of nature study. Reed's guides remained popular for decades. After their publication it was hard to imagine a field guide without an illustration for every species. Not until 1934, when Roger Tory Peterson published his guide, was Reed's design replaced by another concept still more appealing to the public.

One further landmark in bird books appeared before Peterson's guide. *Birds of North America,* an encyclopedia edited by Audubon Association's secretary T. Gilbert Pearson, came out in 1917. Written by a team of authorities, the encyclopedia aimed to provide the recreational birder with a home reference tool. Arranged taxonomically, the book thoroughly catalogued each species, outlining nesting habits, food preferences and other behavior in an anecdotal style. Each bird was illustrated but in groups with related species on the several dozen colored plates by Louis Agassiz Fuertes. Although large and attractive, the book was inexpensive and could be read by the whole family.

By 1920, then, the birdwatcher could have acquired several useful tools for a small sum. He could turn to Chapman's *Handbook* for an introduction to ornithology, Wright's *Birdcraft* for birding around home, Reed's guides for quick spots during excursions farther afield, and to Pearson's encyclopedia for informative home browsing. These books accomplished a great deal over a short period.

Chapman's *Bird-Lore* also responded to the need for better bird identification tools. As early as 1903 *Bird-Lore* began to publish a detachable educational leaflet with each issue of the magazine. The pamphlets consisted of full-page illustrations of a species followed by a discursive essay on appearance, habits, and the bird's value to man. Intended for school children, the leaflets were often written by distinguished experts, and the illustrations by such artists as Louis Agassiz Fuertes, Bruce Horsfall, and Allan Brooks far surpassed Reed's. *Bird-Lore* sold extra copies of the leaflets to schools and libraries for a negligible sum.

Ernest Thompson Seton, artist-naturalist, took a further step toward Peterson's method of bird identification when in 1897 he published a drawing in the *Auk,* republished in *Bird-Lore* in 1901. This drawing illustrated a note about raptor identification and depicted hawk silhouettes as seen by an observer looking up at the soaring bird. Seton demonstrated that each species displayed a key shape as well as one or more diagnostic colors or points of outline that were unique to that species. He called his drawing "Directive Marks of Hawks and Owls." This invention provided a clear precedent to Peterson's plates for his 1934 *Guide*. In it Seton abstracted the shapes of raptors so that they could be memorized by the birdwatcher as a primer of forms. Seton carefully indicated in his text accompanying the drawing that behavioral characteristics such as flight rhythms and perching preferences are crucial for the correct identification of raptors in the field. Examples from his own experience demonstrated how the birdwatcher can combine knowledge of "directive marks" with observations of behavior: "A long reddish bird darted past me to alight in a tree that almost concealed him. I thought it a thrasher, but the deliberate pumping of his tail (another recognition mark), taken with his size and color, told me at once that it was a Sparrowhawk (Kestrel). . . ."

Seton acknowledged two basic principles with this device. The first exhorts the observer to train his eye to perceive general traits of a bird rather than chaotic details. The second asserts that a bird's characteristic behavior is a field mark as good as its shape, color, or size. Seton was profoundly interested in animal psychology, which led him to believe that a bird's behavioral traits could serve as points for identification. Chapman welcomed Seton's invention for its emphasis on natural history as fundamental in acquiring birdwatching skills. The raptor drawing itself is ingenious, serving as a visual glossary of terms for bird identification.

In 1903 Seton pursued this invention in his famous book for boys, *Two Little Savages*. As an aid to duck identification, he drew a diagrammatic rendering of floating ducks, showing their characteristic profiles and color markings. By studying the drawing the birdwatcher could easily identify the swimming duck at a distance without field glasses.

Had Seton felt inclined to write a field guide to the birds of North America employing his revolutionary system of identification, Roger Tory Peterson would not have needed to devise his guide. But Seton's interests lay elsewhere, and his ingeniously simple invention had to wait thirty years for full articulation.

Peterson's great achievement immediately overshadowed earlier field guides. The authority of his comprehensive visual system has sometimes been challenged but never undercut. Though today's birders use the *Golden Guide* and the more recent *National Geographic Guide* with equal frequency, the formats of these two challengers to Peterson are *variants* of the design he invented in 1934.

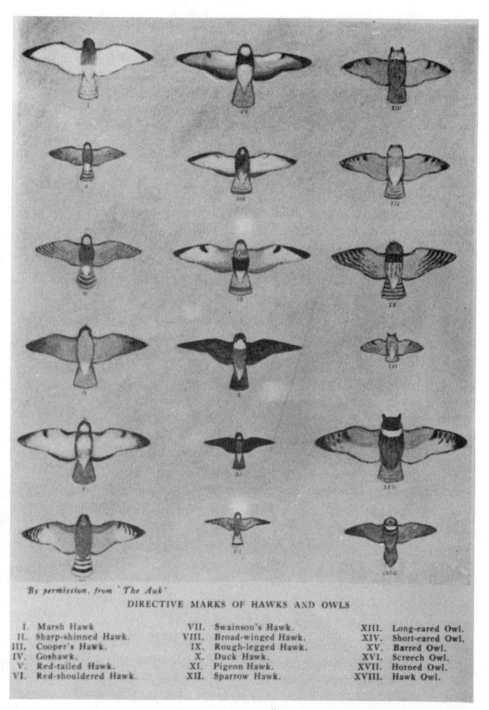

DIRECTIVE MARKS OF HAWKS AND OWLS

I.	Marsh Hawk	VII.	Swainson's Hawk.	XIII.	Long-eared Owl.
II.	Sharp-shinned Hawk.	VIII.	Broad-winged Hawk.	XIV.	Short-eared Owl.
III.	Cooper's Hawk.	IX.	Rough-legged Hawk.	XV.	Barred Owl.
IV.	Goshawk.	X.	Duck Hawk.	XVI.	Screech Owl.
V.	Red-tailed Hawk.	XI.	Pigeon Hawk.	XVII.	Horned Owl.
VI.	Red-shouldered Hawk.	XII.	Sparrow Hawk.	XVIII.	Hawk Owl.

"Directive marks" of hawks and owls by
Ernest Thompson Seton. From *Bird-Lore*.

Hawks in Flight by Roger Tory Peterson from *Field Guide to the Birds of Eastern North America. Houghton Mifflin.*

The underlying principle of Peterson's *Guide* was Seton's invention. Groups of related birds possess characteristic outlines which, when abstracted, can aid the student in developing a vocabulary of recognizable shapes and markings. Peterson elaborated on this idea by introducing lines outside a bird's outline that point to descriptive marks distinguishing one species of a family from another. These marks might be the white eyebrow of the red-eyed vireo or the black tip of the common tern's red bill. In the text for each bird, Peterson also described these fine points. The printed matter is terse, limited to a delineation of the points of difference among closely related birds. The book is slim, portable and inexpensive.

Peterson's commitment to his visual identification system was wholehearted. His text in the 1934 edition rarely included descriptions of song or behavior, and primarily supplied information about size and appearance of the bird, along with probable range. For Peterson, birding is a field sport with listing as its purpose. The popularity of Peterson's original *Guide* is difficult to understand, for it is not easy to use, especially for the beginner. The abstract shapes of birds are confusing to anyone accustomed to outdoor realities, and their applicability to everyday birding experience requires an unnatural mental leap. The text abounds with descriptions of minutiae:

> Black-Poll Warbler. *Dendroica striata.* Descr. 5–5½. Male in Spring:—A striped gray Warbler with a solid black cap; reminds the beginner of a Chickadee, but lacks the black throat. The Black and White Warbler, the only other species with which it might be confused, has a striped crown. Female in spring:—Less heavily streaked, lacking the black crown-patch; a plain black-streaked Warbler, greenish-gray above, white below; may be known from the Black and White by the lack of contrasting head stripings and from the female Myrtle by the absence of yellow in the plumage. Autumn birds:—Olive-green above, with two white wing-bars; dingy yellow below, faintly streaked. This is the common greenish-looking fall Warbler with white wing-bars, the one which causes the field student so much trouble. (See Bay-breasted Warbler [fall] and Pine Warbler.)

For the inexperienced birder these subtle differences are daunting. The experienced birder can sort out such meticulously described variants, and they often lead him to successful identification of a puzzling bird.

The original plates for Peterson's two early editions are pleasingly arranged and stylistically consistent. Hand lettering and penciled outlines of the bird forms impart to the plates a casualness fresh from the studio. The black and white patterns of forms in simple poses against the uniform gray sheets introduce a stylish art deco flavor.

Chapman warmly reviewed Peterson's *Guide* for *Bird-Lore,* perceiving at once the innovative nature of the book's approach and calling it "thoroughly modernistic." The *Guide,* he found, was indispensable for all birdwatchers, and he offered Peterson his "hearty congratulations on his success in blazing this new trail to bird-lore." Five years later Peterson revised the *Guide,* adding several new plates and introducing bird songs in the text, which now included a verbal description of the call notes and songs of most wood birds. These descriptions are somewhat subjective, but the attempt was important for it stressed the need to take song into account for field identification.

Chapman's review of the revised edition was even more cordial than his original remarks, and he quickly grasped the system's impact on birders:

> It truly turns the identification of birds in nature into a sport. In emphasizing this 'sport' or 'game' side of the kind of bird study that his work promotes we feel that Mr. Peterson underrates the value of his achievement. . . . The success of *Bird-Lore*'s Christmas Bird Census may be attributed, in no small measure, to love of the sport, which is common to most of us, and to that spirit of competition which is the mainspring of human endeavor.

Peterson's visual identification system dominates the birder using the *Guide* in the field. E. B. White wittily bemoaned his loss of innocence when he reviewed Peterson's *Guide.* Writing from Maine in 1942, he said:

> I say they [the song birds] have to be identified—we never used to identify songbirds, we used to lump them and listen to them sing. But my wife, through a stroke of ill fortune, somehow got hold of a book called *A Field Guide to the Birds . . .* by Roger Tory Peterson and now we can't settle down to any piece of work without being interrupted by a warbler trying to look like another warbler and succeeding admirably. . . . Our home roars and boils and seethes with activity. . . . On top of everything there are these indistinguishable little birds crying for our attention, flaunting an olive-green spot that looks yellow, a yellow stripe that looks gray, a gray breast that looks cinnamon, a cinnamon tail that looks brown.

Before being exposed to Peterson's system, birdwatchers could enjoy the charming behavior of backyard birds without feeling compelled to identify them. Thus the robin was potentially as exciting as the yellow warbler. But Peterson had invented an obsessive game. He supplied the player with neat bundles of clarified information about the differences among species, and the participant after sufficient observation identified a bird and so added it to his life list. The game, packaged by Peterson to be played by all comers, has become more and more popular ever since.

Peterson undertook a major revision of his *Guide* in 1947 and again in 1982. The 1947 edition is far more elaborate than its predecessors of 1934 and 1939, with completely redesigned plates in a more painterly style. A page facing each plate gives a brief summary of the bird's descriptive points and refers the birder to the appropriate page of text. Size relationships are still maintained but the informality of the original plates is lost. The charming hand printing has given way to bland typeface. In the new edition Peterson introduced a handful of useful comparative study plates, such as "Confusing Fall Warblers" and "Small Flycatchers," the last including where the species prefers to live as an aid for identification.

Peterson argues for the principle of paired comparisons of similar species for identification more strongly in the 1947 edition than in the prewar versions, adding in his text the category of similar species. For example, in the 1947 text for the gull-billed tern he states under "Similar Species" that the "young birds with their dusky head markings and short stubby bills look for all the world like very small Gulls (actually suggest winter European Little Gull but lack dusky wing-linings). Unless very young, the slightly notched tail gives away their identity." The revision, however much it varied from the original format, did not substantially alter the system of visual identification invented in the first edition. It merely made the rules of the game clearer and added some ingenious new comparisons. The success of Peterson's system has been phenomenal. By 1979 the *Guide* for eastern birds had sold more than two million copies, and the western volume, completed in 1941 and revised in 1961, more than one million.

This is not to say that the marketplace has been without competing bird guides. In the late 1940s the National Audubon Society sponsored a series of three guides written by Richard Pough and illustrated by Donald Eckelsberry. Pough's *Guides* differ strongly from Peterson's, with livelier illustrations that attempt to animate the birds in characteristic poses often lacking in Peterson's intentionally abstract portraits. Pough's text is more literary than Peterson's and includes more biographical information on individual species. As a result his *Guide* for eastern birds is bound in two volumes, a disadvantage over Peterson's one, and a third volume for the West includes complete entries only for birds not in the eastern volumes. Pough's intention was to return birdwatching to a more contemplative mode, echoing the studious flavor of earlier guides. But Pough's *Guides* seem to have had limited appeal for birdwatchers, and Peterson's *Guides* remained the popular choice for many years.

Peterson himself supplemented his guides in 1949 by writing *How to Know Birds,* a first-rate primer in which the principles of bird identification were patiently outlined in well illustrated chapters. Peterson stressed habit and behavior in this slim volume. From a study of *How to Know the Birds* the beginner can move on to field identification using the compact *Guide.* Joseph Hickey took a similar approach to the problem of teaching identification skills in his 1943 *Guide to Birdwatching,* a handbook that became authoritative and recalls Chapman's introductory chapters of the *Handbook.* But among books on birdwatching the field guide continues to sell at a lively pace. In 1978, for example, both Peterson's *Guides* together sold around 120,000 copies. In the same year a newcomer, the *Golden Guide to Field Identification of the Birds of North America,* sold a remarkable 300,000 copies, making it the best selling guide ever. Published originally in 1966, the *Golden Guide,* written by Chandler S. Robbins, Bertel Bruun, and Herbert S. Zim and illustrated by Arthur Singer, had actually outsold Peterson's *Guide.*

The Golden Guide adheres strictly to the dichotomous or paired visual identification system invented by Seton and developed fully by Peterson. It is by no means a groundbreaking volume. But several clever design elements make the *Golden Guide* easier to use and more attractive to the birdwatcher. These innovations were enough to guarantee it commercial success. Birdwatchers have grown in number—some say there are more than 10 million in America—and they buy bird guides, especially when no new one has appeared for over twenty years.

The authors of the *Golden Guide* managed to include all North American species, not just those east or west of the Rockies. The success of this plan depended on the skills of Arthur Singer, whose plates are crowded yet clear and attractive. Another advantage the *Golden Guide* has over Peterson's *Guide* derives from its format. The text for each species always faces its illustration. The birder using Peterson's 1947 edition had to locate the bird in the index, find the plate on which it is illustrated and, keeping a finger in that place, turn to another page for the text providing information on range, size, and song. The *Golden Guide*'s authors simplified this process. Beside the text for each bird the authors supply a range map shaded to indicate breeding, wintering, and migration habits. Each bird's measurements accompany its name on the plate. Sonograms, baffling and illegible, provide little clue to the song of each species, which the authors frequently describe.

Interlarded at suitable points are study plates, similar to Peterson's, comparing immature gulls or confusing fall warblers or hawks in flight. There is little to fault in Singer's plates, which surpass Peterson's in presenting the living bird. The woodpecker plates are particularly delightful. A slim birch tree slants across the page to which cling the various species. To the left the birds take flight and above and below a few more species perch on a rotting stump. Singer depicted the behavior of all birds *visually,* showing flycatchers perched on the outer branches of trees, bluejays frisking in pine trees, nuthatches descending conifers, vireos extending on branches, warblers among leafy twigs, scoters on cold green waves, and ovenbirds on the rock-strewn floor of a wooded glen. Less particularized than Peterson's portraits, Singer's plates, for all their painterly charm and compositional virtuosity, are meticulously correct.

The text accompanying the illustrations is laconic since the plates communicate so much information visually. Each entry begins logically by describing the bird's frequency of appearance in its habitat. The least tern is "common along sandy beaches, rare inland," the common tern "abundant coastally." Peterson rarely includes this category of occurrence in his *Guide.*

The *Golden Guide* in many respects is even more visually oriented than Peterson's *Guide.* The text is so laconic that subtle variations among immatures, males, and females are often obscure. The experienced birder frequently needs to turn again to Peterson's texts for more detailed descriptions of puzzling individuals, such as immature warblers and sparrows. But for the beginner the *Golden Guide* is less confusing.

Peterson's response to the *Golden Guide* was heroic. At the age of seventy-four he completed a definitive revision of his guide for birds east of the Rockies that was meant to challenge the *Golden Guide.*

Woodpeckers by Arthur Singer from *Golden Guide to Field Identification of the Birds of North America.* Western Publishing Company.

Peterson redrew all his plates in a more painterly style but adhered to his concept of clarifying abstractions. These new plates, less behaviorally communicative than Singer's, are more enlivened than the earlier portrayals. The text for each bird appears opposite its illustration, but the measurements still appear in the text, now shortened and less useful than in the 1947 edition. The range maps, drawn by Virginia Marie Peterson, are relegated to the back of the book so the birder still has to search in two places for information about a species. Map numbers appear in the text but not on the plates.

Many birders prefer Peterson's older editions of the *Guide* for their detailed descriptions of subtle variations among species, but the *Golden Guide* is unsurpassed for clarity and convenience and continues its remarkable sales record, outstripping Peterson's guide two to one in 1978.

Two additional new guides have won their share of supporters among birdwatchers. In 1977 the National Audubon Society sponsored the *Audubon Society Field Guide to North American Birds* (one volume each for eastern and western regions). Team-written by John Bull and John Farrand, Jr., these volumes are novel in many ways. Each bird is illustrated by a small color photograph—some useful and others much less so—grouped in the front of the guide by type rather than families and then within this category by color. This arrangement reverts to Chapman's and Wright's color keys and has some advantages for the beginner. A birder seeing a yellow bird in a tree, for example, can seek it among the photographs of predominantly yellow birds.

The text in the second half of the volume is arranged by habitat and does not adhere to the order in which the pictures appear. The birder finds the text page from the photo caption or the index. This text is the most comprehensive and useful of any guide. The description for each bird is not written as a comparison with similar species but stands alone. The voice descriptions are useful and range is indicated briefly. The authors end each entry with an excellent paragraph or two outlining key behavioral traits or habitat choices. For example, the authors tell their readers that the American redstart

> . . . is one of the most abundant birds in North America, because its favored habitat, second-growth woodland, covers such vast areas of the continent. It has a distinctive habit of dropping down suddenly in pursuit of a flying insect, then fanning its brightly marked tail from side to side. It takes a full

year for the males to acquire the black and orange adult plumage, so it is not unusual to find what appears to be a female singing and displaying like a male.

For the first time the text of a guide consistently adds the category of behavior as a field identification point, as Seton had suggested decades earlier. It is too bad that the text, so rich in information and insights, is wedded to photographs that are often unclear. Had Singer illustrated this text, an ideal guide would have resulted.

In 1983 the National Geographic Society entered the field guide contest. Team-written and with plates drawn by thirteen different artists, the guide includes all North American species. Its format is similar to the *Golden Guide,* but its goals are more allied to Peterson's. The National Geographic *Guide* is particularly concerned with visual identification of puzzling species. The plates often include five or more drawings of the same species, each illustrating a variant which might confuse the birdwatcher. The text opposite each bird's picture is full of descriptive detail, often containing eye-opening distinctions among confusing species. This precision derives from the specialized expertise of its various authors.

The National Geographic *Guide* is the finest one based on the Peterson model. Its technical virtuosity may make for dull reading and the plates though homely are useful. But the experienced birder who is a dedicated lister can find no equal. The authors rarely include descriptions of behavior and the bird songs are only summarily noted. It is not a guide for the beginner. But if the distinction between the perched female sharp-shinned hawk and the female Cooper's hawk has been elusive, the National Geographic *Guide* will set it straight. The sharpy's head is smaller in proportion to body length than the Cooper's. No other guide tells you that.

The birdwatcher today is likely to own many if not all of these field guides. They are inexpensive and do not share weaknesses. By consulting three or four guides, the puzzled observer can usually identify a confusing bird. He will probably learn little more than the bird's name using Peterson, the *Golden Guide,* or the *National Geographic Society Guide.* For information about the bird's life history he can start with the *Audubon Society Guide* but will soon have to move on to the two best sources for bird information, John Terres's *Audubon Society Encyclopedia of North American Birds* which replaces the outdated T. Gilbert Pearson

Encyclopedia of 1917 and Arthur Bent's multivolume *Life Histories of North American Birds* produced at the Smithsonian Institute from 1919–1958 and still the best source for detailed, clearly written expositions of what each species does and how it appears. The full set, available in paperback, is without equal.

In addition to the guides or handbooks on bird behavior, bird enthusiasts may subscribe to such attractive magazines as *Bird Watcher's Digest, Audubon* or *The Living Bird.* Here they might learn a bit more about native birds, pick up ideas for field trips, and gaze at startlingly beautiful photographs of birds. None of these books and magazines is a substitute for field instruction. Field identification is a skill which takes years of practice to perfect, but going birding with an expert instructor facilitates the process.

Today most state and local Audubon societies sponsor field trips and instruction for their members. By participating in these groups the birdwatcher learns techniques from experts who lead the sessions. As a result of the recent birding boom with its emphasis on listing, field trips have become a commercial venture. Top-ranking birders support themselves by offering trips to exotic bird paradises. This travel is not cheap but the birder is guaranteed new life species. Advertisements for these expeditions fill the pages of birding magazines. They are part of the new business of birding.

Guides to birding areas are the logical outgrowth of the emphasis on peripatetic bird-listing. The first such comprehensive guide, now a classic, was published in 1951. Olin Sewall Pettingill's *Guide to Bird Finding East of the Mississippi* and its sequel, *Guide to Bird Finding West of the Mississippi,* aim to guide the birder to wilderness areas outside his personal territory. Both volumes are clearly organized by state and attraction, including useful descriptions of flora and fauna as well as detailed driving or walking instructions for each center recommended. Tantalizing lists of likely species lure the birder into little known corners of nature. Most of the lists of available species Pettingill claims for his birding spots are accurate, given migratory variations.

Pettingill's *Guides* gave rise to numerous spinoffs, among them Susan Drennan's *Where to Find Birds in New York State,* a thick manual with explicit detail. With guides such as this in hand the birder who is eager for new species can strike out hopefully into fresh territory. It is understood that these books are addressed to the birdwatcher with an automobile. They reflect the widening gap between contemplative bird study and the listing compulsion which started as early as 1905 with the publication of Reed's *Guides*. The birdwatcher using these where-to books and armed with his field guides can dash around the countryside making quick stops here and there to log yet another life species.

Another sort of manual speaks to the backyard birdwatcher. Books such as John Terres's *Song Birds in Your Garden* of 1954 or more recently Alan Pistorius's 1981 *Country Journal Book of Birding and Bird Attraction* appear regularly. Intended to stimulate an interest in the ecology of the suburban plot, these guides seem to be all of a piece, similar in aim and content. Books on this theme appeared as early as 1910 and included, as they do today, designs for homemade feeding stations, bird baths, and houses. None pretends to the depth of Chapman's *Handbook* or the literacy of Wright's *Birdcraft*.

Today's technological enthusiasm has brought some high-tech birding aids. Birders can purchase videotapes through mail order houses. Peterson, for example, has starred in a videotape intended to accompany his *Guides* and demonstrate their use with footage of birds in nature. There is even a program to be used with a personal computer which stores the birder's life list and sorts it out in different categories, such as location of citing and date.

Technology has also contributed to recordings of bird songs. Albert Brand, a retired stockbroker turned sound ornithologist, who became interested in techniques for recording bird songs, devised some of the first examples of these. In 1934 he published his book *Songs of Wild Birds*, which came equipped with two phonograph records of bird songs. From this modest beginning, technicians have perfected the art of reproducing bird songs and today for a modest sum the birder can buy cassette tapes which follow the arrangement of Peterson's *Guides*. They are the best tools for learning the sounds of birds heard only fleetingly in nature.

No survey of birding tools would be complete without a mention of optical equipment. Before World War I most birders used opera glasses, which were no more than two spy glasses mounted together. Although they could be focused, they magnified poorly and were not of much use in identifying birds. Prism binoculars were invented in Germany in the 1890s. They could magnify images more times than opera glasses through the use of reflecting lenses. At first too expensive for general use, they were all manufactured in Germany until after

World War I, when American optical companies learned the technology. Quickly, prism binoculars became inexpensive standard equipment for birders, especially in the current birding boom as they have grown progressively lighter and cheaper. Birders may own several pairs of differing powers for various conditions. Spotting scopes, once an instrument mainly for field biologists, are now standard equipment for serious birdwatchers. Costing anywhere from $200 to $800, scopes are essential for observing far-off oceanic and shorebirds in open spaces.

Books, magazines, cassettes, video tapes, binoculars, scopes, feeders, bird fountains and travel all cost money, and the serving of birders has become a multimillion dollar business. As with any hobby, the apparatus mounts up, becoming a collection in itself. If the birdwatcher has also taken up bird photography, his opportunities for amassing cameras,

Albert Brand recording bird song with a parabolic microphone. *Department of Manuscripts and University Archives, Cornell University Libraries.*

lenses, and filters are unlimited. One hundred years ago Celia Thaxter watched birds with her naked eyes and identified them by writing descriptions of them to Bradford Torrey. Today the birder is overwhelmed with apparatus which threatens to take over the sport.

Chapter Fifteen

The Sport Today

*T*he earnest men and women who went "a-birding" with Mabel Osgood Wright's *Birdcraft* and opera glasses eighty years ago would hardly recognize today's sport. The pace of everyday life has quickened and birding has kept up with it. Automobile travel on superhighways and detailed guide books showing where birds can be found have transformed birding from a backyard idyll to a complex sport involving expeditions to remote places in search of rare species.

Roger Tory Peterson divides today's enthusiasts into two groups, "birders," whom he defines as listers, and "birdwatchers," a term he reserves for feeder aficionados and backyard watchers. But modern birders all seek to add to their life list, which frequently began modestly enough in their yard or on vacations, using the checklist provided in the front of Peterson's guides. The few birders who can boast of a life list of over 600 North American species are only more intensely involved in an activity shared by all bird enthusiasts. In practice birders and birdwatchers are the same.

The lure of the list is universal. As with collecting stamps, more is inevitably better. Today's most avid listers are not a separate species of birders but are instead a subspecies with a more highly developed instinct for collecting. They are the gatherers who get more berries than anyone else. Members of this subspecies, "birder-lister," are competitive with themselves as well as with others. They want their berries counted and a winner publicly declared.

In 1969 James Tucker founded the American Birding Association, dedicated to promoting this sport of listing. Tucker explained his hopes for the ABA in the first issue of *Birding,* the association's quarterly journal.

> With this, the first official issue of *Birding,* a new era has begun in the lives of many birders. It is an era of systematic and organized cooperation with other birdwatchers across the country. It is an era during which birding is destined to come into its own as a well-known sport, as well as a hobby. It is inevitable that this will happen, and this journal, rather than representing the cause, is only a strand in the interwoven complexity of the movement.

Although it has only a few thousand members, compared with the National Audubon Society's half a million or more, the ABA has earned widespread influence and respect. It publishes and frequently updates a checklist of North American birds for contestants to consult during Big Day and Big Year contests, the activities most encouraged by the organization and most enthusiastically embraced by the greatest listers today.

The Big Day Count is one of the ABA's favorite competitions. The ABA defines the Big Day as a single-team effort in which the objectives are to identify as many bird species as possible during a single day in a defined geographic area and to try to have all the members of a Big Day team identify all the species recorded. The ABA provides an elaborate set of rules governing this official contest and coordinates the event every year, publishing the results in a special issue of *Birding.* There is little new about the ABA's Big Day. Its origins can be found in the Christmas Bird Count (hereafter the CBC), an annual census coordinated by the National Audubon Society, enjoying a long and illustrious history beginning early in this century.

Like so many of birdwatching's finest institutions, the CBS was invented by Frank Chapman. In 1900 he initiated a Christmas count to challenge the tradition of the Christmas Day side hunts, whereby hunters customarily went out after Christmas dinner to shoot any bird that crossed their paths. Chapman reasoned that a hunt without guns for birds wintering over in one location might provide an alternative to the excitement of the side hunt. He believed that birdwatching could be enjoyed as a sport, and that the competitive aspects of the count could satisfy even the avid sportsman. And history has proved him right, for the side hunt is a thing of the past while the CBC is a thriving national institution.

In the first years of the Christmas count only a handful of reports were filed with *Bird-Lore,* but today almost 40,000 birders can be expected to participate, reporting from over 1500 locations, compared to the twenty-seven counting teams of the original 1901 CBC. There are no limits to the number of participants allowed on each count, but teams must elect a day between December 14 and January 5 and must count birds in a circle with no more than a fifteen-mile radius.

The Christmas Bird Count is perhaps the sport's most respected track meet and one of the few activities the National Audubon Society sponsors, in part because it generates useful information about the fluctuations of bird populations nationwide. Data gathered in the CBC are effective indicators of a decline in population vigor or an improvement over time. But many sightings during CBCs are haphazard, depending on weather conditions, the vagaries of migration, expertise, and luck. The CBC is championed by the Audubon Society for a more sentimental reason as well. It is an event steeped in tradition, an annual moment in birding when history seems close and records are broken, when memories of famous CBC teams of the past return to inspire the modern birder.

The Bronx County Bird Club was easily the most famous early CBC group. Boasting as members the young Roger Tory Peterson and Allan Cruickshank, the great bird photographer, the group purchased an old car and raced around the boroughs of New York in pursuit of ever more species. But they were not the first to break one hundred species for a CBC. That honor went to the Santa Barbara team, one of the most fruitful CBCs, which cracked one hundred in 1911 with only two observers.

Allan Cruickshank ran a particularly famous CBC in Titusville, Florida. In 1955 he gathered together a team of forty-two experts, including Roger Tory Peterson. The team netted a phenomenal total of 184 species. *Sports Illustrated* reported the event:

> All day long Cruickshank had been barking orders like a general dispatching crucial missions—"Get the old squaw"—"Honk up some fat

geese"—"Tie down the avocets." And when his crew assembled at his home at Rockledge that night, his eyes were still bright with the eagerness of the chase. Party leaders phoned in their tallies and the totals mounted. By 10 P.M. it became evident that their group had broken all Christmas Count records, and Cruickshank's grin was wider than ever.

Today intense rivalries have developed. Freeport, Texas, and Santa Barbara, two of the most successful CBCs, have set up an informal contest for the longest list of species. With expert listers dominating both counts, the totals keep climbing. Freeport currently holds the United States record with 226 species, and Santa Barbara vows to break that number. But what has happened to the less expert birders there? Knowledge of bird populations will hardly profit from the competition. Most of the species sighted above a certain predictable number are bound to be rare vagrants, telling little about general population trends. The CBC was designed to document the *numbers* of individuals in each species as well as their presence. Susan Drennan, editor of Audubon Society's *American Birds,* recently pointed out that the National Audubon Society treasures reports from observers confined to their backyard feeders (10% of the counters) as highly as sightings from roaming field observers. The most modest CBCs, Drennan reported with pride, were still of value. The single member of Bethel, Alaska's, CBC team in 1985 reported only two species in dense frozen mist. In contrast, the CBC team in Oakland, California, was 150 strong. This diversity is the animating spirit of the Christmas count.

But technology has begun to affect the CBC's original personality. The computer is now its chief record-keeping tool, and the issue of *American Birds* devoted to reporting the CBC is an impenetrable mass of data. It is becoming an event for highly skilled, almost professional birders, where expertise is more valued than enthusiasm. The quiet ramble to digest the Christmas pudding has become fast-paced, high-tech, and competitive.

Although the Christmas Bird Count closely resembles the American Birding Association's Big Day Contest, it is obviously more serious in purpose and less competitive. Another source in history for this modern olympics of birding can be found in the pages of *Bird-Lore.* In 1915 Waldron DeWitt Miller, a substitute editor for the magazine, suggested an official Big Day for spring migrations. He reported that the practice had existed informally for years, but he wished to make it an official activity sanctioned by the state Audubon societies. To date, Miller reported, the record for a one-day list was held by an Ohio State University professor in 1907 who, with two assistants, had recorded 144 species. Miller himself modestly recalled that in 1913 in New York City he had logged ninety-five species on a warm May day.

A decade later two men of exceptional personality who set an unrivaled standard for style in birding dominated the Big Day counts and the related Big Year lists. Ludlow Griscom, a 1912 graduate of Columbia University, was a trained ornithologist with a Ph.D. from Cornell University. He enjoyed a distinguished career, first as an assistant curator of ornithology under Chapman at the American Museum of Natural History and later until retirement at Harvard's Museum of Comparative Zoology. An occasional member of the Bronx County Bird Club, Griscom impressed Roger Peterson and others with his extraordinary identification skills. He knew hundreds of species by their flight pattern alone and could recognize 500 or more by song. At his death he had accumulated over 2500 species for his life list. After he moved to Cambridge Griscom initiated an annual list of species seen each year in the state, compared competitively to prior years. He was

Ludlow Griscom at sea, in search of birds. *Massachusetts Audubon Society.*

a natural leader with considerable charm and before long had established a network of informants who kept his yearly lists growing. By 1947 Griscom listed 318 species for one year in Massachusetts.

But Griscom was a scientist and disliked the publicity his listing feats received. He considered his Big Year and Big Day efforts a personal hobby with little importance for science. Yet the birding confraternity, like all groups, always longs for a hero, and his achievements continued to be famous. Every May he felt compelled to stride forth for a Big Day Count, inviting a group of fellow birders to come along. Griscom was one of the most talented birdwatchers of all time, a hero to today's listers. The ABA annually awards the Griscom Medal to a top birder.

Maunsell Shieffelin Crosby, the second listing luminary, was born into a family of wealth and culture in 1887. Crosby led the life of a dilettante. After graduation from Harvard in 1908 he settled down to a bachelor's life at his estate in Rhinebeck, New York. His greatest interest was in natural history exploration, and he sponsored several collecting trips undertaken by the American Museum of National History, and joined them himself, as did his friend Ludlow Griscom. At the time of his early death in 1931 Crosby had counted over 1000 species for his life list.

When in residence at Rhinebeck he often invited expert birdwatchers to participate in a Big Day in Dutchess County. These weekends became something of an institution and invitations were highly coveted. Like Griscom, Crosby had an uncanny talent for bird identification and an especially good ear for warbler songs. Florence Page Jaques accompanied her husband, bird artist Lee Jaques, on one of Crosby's Big Days. She later told of the weekend in a humorous essay. Her husband Lee took the whole thing seriously, but Florence saw the absurdity of rising at 2:30 A.M. to drive around the countryside madly seeking elusive birds. Late in the afternoon, after sixteen hours of nonstop birding, Florence complained:

> Now we were boarding the car again. All day we had been darting out of that car like imps out of hell; I did not want to do it *any more*. And I had seen so many birds they had mobbed my mind. I could remember no individual. Even without those incoherent warblers, there were veeries and vireos, nuthatches and sapsuckers, killdeers and redstarts—I couldn't remember which was where or what. Even hawks; I had thought a hawk was a hawk. But no, it had to be a sharp-shin or a red-tail or a Cooper's —Maunsell interrupted my brooding.

"We've time for this one more pasture and the wood," he reassured us, "before we meet the others at Brickyard Swamp."

Until 1971 there were no coordinated national contests. The Big Day remained for over fifty years a kind of birder's calisthenics intended to sharpen the participant's identification skills. Through the efforts of the ABA the event has become an organized contest, the most visible vehicle for today's style of birding for birding's sake.

And the ABA Big Day Count is popular. In 1984 fifty-six American teams comprising anywhere from two to six friendly birders entered the contest and nine more from foreign countries. Many of the participants were members of the new class of professional birders—men and a few women who earn their living by birding, teaching bird identification, leading tours for birders, and writing about birdwatching. The Big Day Count serves indirectly to advertise their expertise to the thousands of birdwatchers who enroll in the expensive field trips to exotic places packaged by these birders.

A major event in Big Day history occurred in 1984. Pete Dunne, a professional birder wanted to raise money for conservation. Dunne and his friends developed the concept of the Biggest Day (aka the World Series of Birding), a team contest for the State of New Jersey, and sought out the support of the ABA. The young organization had already become synonymous with sporting events in the birding community. Dunne agreed to use most of the ABA rules and their checklist. But Dunne's teams had to stay out of airplanes (the ABA allows air travel) and could not use tapes of calls to entice birds out of hiding (allowed by the ABA). A specific day in May was chosen when teams from all over the country were to converge on New Jersey. Dunne's most significant modification was the provision that any entering team had to be sponsored by an organization concerned with conservation. Members of supporting organizations could pledge a chosen amount for each species their team spotted. The Biggest Day, unlike ABA's Big Day Count, is a competition with a higher purpose, since winning is not the only motive. Every year the event raises thousands of dollars for research and nature education. Since these listing contests seem here to stay, linking them to fund raising and publicity for conservation gives them immense value to wildlife.

The ABA's even more prestigious contest is the Big Year, a listing contest involving complex itineraries to places where emigrating and

LEFT. Pete Dunne, ringleader of the World Series of Birding. *Pete Dunne.*

BELOW. Sweet victory! Bill Thompson and Susan Drennan presenting the Ed Stearns Award to the National Geographic Biggest Day team. *Pete Dunne.*

wandering birds are found. For this contest, the ABA has developed a wide network of bird spotters so that participants in a Big Year can reach rare birds before they leave for another place. Unlike the Big Day, the Big Year is a one-man effort. Each entrant tries to see as many species as possible in one twelve-month period in North America. The first recorded Big Year was probably undertaken by Guy Emerson, a former president of the National Audubon Society, who totaled 497 species in 1939. The most famous Big Year starred Roger Tory Peterson and British ornithologist James Fisher, who spent several months on the road together touring wildlife refuges in the national system and visiting other bird spots as well. They recorded their experiences in a book, *Wild America,* a jointly written travelog which did much to popularize birdwatching and to call attention to the wonders of American wildlife refuges.

Today's Big Year efforts are keyed to the competitive sport. The ABA publishes annual lists of bird totals submitted by contestants as well as endless computer-generated life lists for participating members. This publicity is in part a response to the needs of a small group of birders who have turned professional in attitude. Their success as birding leaders depends in part upon their accomplishments as listers. These aspiring professionals are committed to the sport to such an extent that their livelihood has become dependent upon it. Their point of view has begun to influence casual birders so that rules honored by the big listers are applied to everyday birdwatching as well.

A typical all-out Big Year effort, such as the one undertaken by businessman James Vardaman in 1979, first sets a goal, in this case to see 700 of the 840 species on the ABA's checklist. Vardaman actually listed 698 and the method of his sightings was remarkable. He located common species himself but relied upon a network of local experts to call him when an uncommon bird for his list was in their area. He would then drop everything and fly to the area where his informant, often meeting him at the airport, drove him to where the bird was last spotted.

Many birders find the joy of personal discovery more important than listing a new bird with outside help. But the ABA is committed to locating accidental species. The North American Rare Bird Alert (hereafter NARBA) is an independent company founded by ABA members. Its network of reliable birders all over the nation report rare birds and are paid a fee for each. NARBA puts together a telephone tape, and for an annual fee a member seeking to add to his life list calls an 800 number and then speeds to the location of the rarity he wishes to see. Or, for a larger fee, this same ambitious birder submits to NARBA a roster of the species he most wants to find. NARBA will call him when one of these shows up. At the end of each year NARBA awards $1000 to the birder who spots the rarest bird.

To the average birdwatcher these measures may seem extreme, but the enthusiasm of ABA's membership indicates that this is a genuine trend in birdwatching today. And the ABA's influence is significant. *American Birds,* the journal of the National Audubon Society devoted to recording bird populations, the Christmas Count, and migrations, has recently become more concerned with rare bird sightings. The ABA has noticeably influenced *American Birds* to take a greater interest in the finer points of bird identification. A recent issue featured a detailed analysis of the plumage variations in subspecies of the red-tailed hawk. The ABA has encouraged this kind of technical birding information, much of which can help the average birder identify confusing species more easily.

The extraordinary popularity of birding tours corroborates this trend. These packages are mostly offered by professional birders, some of whom view the ABA as an organization somewhat like a ski club that offers its membership arranged trips. The allure of these trips is expansion of the life list. The professional knows just where to find new species for his client in exotic places such as China or Attu. For example, one bird tour agent offers eighty trips a year, serving over 1,000 birders who pay an average of $1,500 a tour. Birding ABA-style is big business.

The ABA is sensitive to frequent criticism about emphasis on listing and bird identification. Its activities, it maintains, enhance one kind of birding without minimizing others. ABA members love the out-of-doors and support conservation but also want the extra spice of competition. But some deeply committed birders feel uneasy about the sporting aspects of modern birding. Terry Clark, a dedicated birdwatcher and journalist from California, recently spoke of "gestalt" birding (in England called "jizz") as the process of getting to know as much as one can about every species. Clark's ultimate goal is to know the bird rather than to list it. "To me," she said in a recent interview for *Bird Watcher's Digest,* "identifying a bird on 'gestalt'—being in touch with a whole that is greater than the sum of its parts—is the highest of the high. I think of birding as good mental hygiene, for even if I miss the bird, I will have had the pleasure of anticipation. . . . Birding creates healthy tensions, . . . helps me keep a perspective on the rest of my life."

This style of birding recalls Ernest Thompson Seton's recommendation to combine observations of the physical appearance of a species with knowledge of what that bird does—where it perches, how it flies, how it catches its prey, how it lands on a branch. The "high" that Terry Clark describes, an intense aesthetic pleasure stimulated by familiarity with birds, may for some begin with the detailed knowledge of species' appearance that the ABA encourages. Once a birder has named the species in his binoculars, he can put aside the minutiae of the identification process and begin to take in the "gestalt" of the actual bird, perhaps achieving that aesthetic "high" Terry Clark described.

But the style of birding the ABA advocates is unlikely to foster contemplative study, since it emphasizes technology, high speed travel, and quantitative success. One is tempted to call this type of birding materialistic, as compared to the transcendental values embraced one hundred years ago.

The ABA's influence is in many respects positive. The members' enthusiasm for the finer points of bird identification has elevated the level of knowledge, and the average birder today is more adept at field identification than a Victorian bird lover. Modern birders find reward in unraveling subtle differences among similar species. The improvement of bird identification skills benefits scientific research as well. The Migratory Bird Populations Office of the Fish and Wildlife Service, for example, sponsors an annual breeding bird survey undertaken with the help of birders nationwide. The 1,200 amateur birders who manned 1,800 fact-gathering routes in 1979 were good enough at identifying birds to undertake this difficult task. Each team had to stop fifty times at half-mile intervals on a twenty-five mile route near their home and list all birds seen or heard during each three minute stop. This technique yielded a rich body of information about bird populations.

But not all birders today find birding, ABA-style, to their tastes and prefer the less rushed stroll in the woods after Sunday lunch. For those aficionados, by far the majority, William and Elsa Thompson of Marietta, Ohio, founded a charming little magazine which they called *Bird Watcher's Digest*. The couple sought to change their lifestyle to include their fondness for birds. William Thompson, vice president of a small college, wanted to work at home with his wife and growing family. In the magazine's first years the family produced every issue out of their home, including layout and mailing.

From a modest compendium of regional articles about local bird-watching events, *Bird Watcher's Digest* has grown to take the place of

Bird-Lore as an informal, friendly voice for today's average birder. With a circulation in 1987 in excess of 50,000, every issue of the magazine contains a potpourri of articles, interviews, and features. Regular features include a column by Roger Tory Peterson, an essay on behavior by Donald and Lillian Stokes, a question and answer box for backyard birders, and book reviews. Central to each issue are the short articles by regional nature writers on a great variety of topics. Readers of *Bird Watcher's Digest* can thus communicate with other fellow nature lovers. They learn a bit of natural history, get ideas for bird-finding trips, and

Cover of *Bird Watcher's Digest* with ruby-crowned kinglet.

find out about conservation projects such as the California condor breeding program. They can work the *BWD* crossword and enjoy cartoons about birds and birdwatchers. The *Bird Watcher's Digest* is a journal for the hobbyists among birdwatchers, amateurs who love their home bird life and rarely go birding far afield.

The editors of *Bird Watcher's Digest* have reinvented the personal charm of *Bird-Lore* in its early years when the pace of the hobby was slow and contemplative. They assume that the preservation and encouragement of bird populations is the ultimate goal of nature education, a movement closely associated with birdwatching. The magazine demonstrates that birding with a purpose is not dead. Birding for birding's sake fostered by the American Bird Association is a game peripheral to the real rewards of birding—to explore the world of nature through birds, and to learn to preserve their beauties for our children. Will they hear a woodthrush sing or see an eagle soar?

Arctic tern chicks on binoculars, by Allan
Cruickshank. *National Audubon Society,*
courtesy of Helen Cruickshank.

Chapter Sixteen

From Guns to Binoculars

In March 1853, Henry David Thoreau wondered in his journal "if it would not be well to carry a spy-glass in order to watch these shy birds such as ducks and hawks? In some respects, me thinks, it would be better than a gun. The latter brings them nearer dead but the former alive. You can identify the species better by killing the bird because it was a dead specimen that was so minutely described, but you can study the habits and appearance best in a living specimen." A few weeks later Thoreau bought a spy-glass in Boston for eight dollars, a large sum of money for him. He justified the expenditure with these words: "I buy but few things and those not till long after I begin to want them, so that when I do get them I am prepared to make perfect use of them and extract their whole sweet."

Thoreau might not have been the first American to watch birds with a telescope or spy-glass, an instrument then used primarily for military purposes, but he may have been the first to purchase one specifically to watch birds. During sea voyages to gather specimens of pelagic birds, Audubon probably borrowed the captain's glass but there is no record of his owning one. He relied on his own vision and his remarkable patience to study birds in the wild. His knowledge of marsh and pelagic birds was consequently more detailed than his grasp of small woodland species, as he demonstrated in the bird biographies he prepared to accompany *The Birds of America*. Alexander Wilson was too poor to own an optical instrument; William Bartram, like Audubon, observed nature with his naked eye.

But when Thoreau purchased his spy-glass—still extant and difficult to use—he was only underlining the differences between his attitude about nature and that of the early naturalist-explorers, who thought nothing of procuring dozens of bird skins for study and seemed as pleased with a fine dead specimen shot after hours of stalking as with a fleeting glimpse of the same species sailing from tree to tree.

A year after he bought his spy-glass Thoreau remarked in his journal that "in Boston yesterday an ornithologist said significantly, 'If you held the bird in your hand—'; but I would rather hold it in my affections." A few years later he elaborated on this pithy remark in his journal entry for October 9, 1860: "This haste to kill a bird or quadruped and make a skeleton of it, which many young men and some old ones exhibit,

Henry David Thoreau
by Samuel W. Rowse.
*Concord Free Public
Library.*

Thoreau disliked displays of stuffed birds like this didactic
arrangement of domestic fowl. *Department of Library Services,
American Museum of Natural History.*

reminds me of the fable of the man who killed the hen that laid the golden eggs, and so got no more gold. It is a perfectly parallel case. Such is the knowledge you get from the living creature. Every fowl lays golden eggs for him who can find them or can detect alloy and base metal."

Thoreau's concern was an outgrowth of methods customarily used by ornithologists. Shortly after the discovery of North America early explorers perceived that the flora and fauna of the new continent were related to but bafflingly different from European species. Naturalists from the other side of the Atlantic were eager to procure specimens to begin classification. An early trade in bird skins expanded in the second half of the nineteenth century, as morphologists struggled with the reclassification tasks set by the discovery of common descent outlined by Darwin in *The Origin of Species.* As urban life expanded in the newly industrialized United States, cultural institutions were established. In many cities natural history museums opened with collections of bird skins, some of which were mounted and displayed for amateur naturalists and college students. These museums, often attached to universities, competed with each other for comprehensiveness of collections. Dead birds, properly skinned after being shot, often brought high prices.

Classification became an absorbing game for amateur naturalists. Throughout the nineteenth century the pressing issues of biology centered around the arrangement of species in a family tree. Comparative morphology could be undertaken only with dead specimens. Opera glasses might have been available to birdwatchers as early as the civil war, but prism binoculars, the only effective tool for field observation, were not invented until the turn of the century and remained expensive until after World War I, when they no longer had to be imported from Germany.

Thoreau was years ahead of his contemporaries. Natural historians continued to study dead specimens well into the present century. Even when bird study became popular outside scientific circles, hobbyists continued to collect specimens. Only a few exceptionally aware conservationists watched birds in the field without a shotgun, and those few who did—among them Bradford Torrey, Celia Thaxter, and John Burroughs—were the intellectual offspring of Emerson and Thoreau.

Bird students were collecting skins, eggs, and nests well into the present century, and the activity had even become a hobby in its own right during the Victorian era. Collecting was a suitable amusement for boys on summer holidays in the country. By shooting at birds boys learned gunning skills, which as men they could apply to hunting. In his autobiography ornithologist-illustrator George M. Sutton describes his passion for bird collecting as a young man; like many others he stuffed specimens for his own private museum. He fleshed out his collection with eggs and nests. Sutton later applied these skills professionally when employed by the Carnegie Institute in Pittsburgh, procuring skins of Pennsylvania birds for the museum's collections. But more often a youthful collecting hobby did not lead to serious adult research.

A more typical collector was Manly Hardy, a fur trader from Brewer, Maine. A recognized expert on the flora and fauna of the Penobscot region, Hardy purchased specimens from all over North America. He formed his collection of 3,300 bird skins with the help of his daughter, Fannie Hardy Eckstorm, who became a capable taxidermist while still a teenager. Eckstorm continued her interest in ornithology after graduation from Smith College, contributing two books and numerous articles to the literature of bird study. Her father collected, not to advance science, but to amass as complete a sampling of North American birds as possible. At his death he lacked only twenty-two species.

Sarah Orne Jewett attacked this destructive hobby in her polemical 1886 short story, "A White Heron." In it a young bird collector searches for a snowy egret in the marshes near the Maine coast. A girl, living with her grandmother on a small freehold, knows where to find the egret's nest but refuses to tell the collector. She is baffled by the senselessness of the young man's hobby and he departs empty-handed. Jewett shared with other early conservationists an abhorrence for bird slaughter. But this dislike of collecting was slow to spread, especially among ornithologists who regarded specimen collecting as their most fundamental tool.

Frank M. Chapman collected birds for much of his career as curator at the American Museum of Natural History. Under his guidance the museum built up a major collection of bird skins with good scientific justification. Less understandable was Chapman's enthusiasm for museum displays of stuffed birds. He promoted the idea of the diorama, a glass-enclosed environmental *tableau vivant* filled with stuffed birds, their young and nests. The museum sponsored annual collecting expeditions, during which Chapman and his colleagues shot thousands of birds. His enthusiasm for collecting was so great that his honeymoon was a combined holiday and collecting expedition. The young Mrs. Chapman skinned her first specimen as a bride and worked as a taxidermist on many of her husband's trips.

Chapman did not caution against gratuitous specimen gathering until he prepared the second edition of his popular *Handbook of Birds of Eastern North America* in 1912. In an extensive introduction to amateur bird study Chapman suggested that collecting was only warranted in new territories, untouched by previous ornithologists. He concluded somewhat ambiguously that "the student with some definite problem in view is always justified in taking the specimens which are required to aid in prosecuting his researches, nor can there be any reasonable objection to collecting for purposes of identification; but there can be no doubt that throughout the greater part of eastern North America there is no longer need for general, indiscriminate collecting." He included a detailed description of skinning for students who took specimens.

The bridge between Henry Thoreau, the transcendentalist nature enthusiast, and the modern birdwatcher could not be constructed overnight. Resistance to Thoreau's point of view was due to the split personalities of the early conservationists. Frank Chapman embodies this confusion. He never studied ornithology formally, but was committed to his work as a morphologist at the American Museum. Chapman loved birds and spent his entire life among them (dead or alive), but viewed the undirected nature worship of Thoreau and Burroughs with suspicion. Wholeheartedly behind an orchestrated effort to stimulate bird appreciation, he felt that people should watch birds with a definite purpose in mind—the gathering of knowledge about bird appearance and behavior.

Chapman's *Handbook of Birds of Eastern North America,* published in 1895, reflects this point of view. The first 140 pages are an introduction to the study of birds. Intended for the amateur bird student, and in this group he included backyard birders, these pages introduce the reader to avian biology as well as to finding birds, identifying them and recording observations of their behavior.

This seriousness is also embodied in Anna Comstock's *Handbook of Nature Study* of 1911. Comstock wrote her definitive tome as a lesson book to guide public school teachers' presentations of nature study to children. The lessons are all oriented toward serious study. Bird biology, nesting and identification were recommended topics for children culminating in an appreciation of the value of birds.

Popular nature essayists brought a more humanistic viewpoint to birding literature. Writers like John Burroughs and Bradford Torrey preached nature appreciation for its own sake, reinvoking the voice of Henry Thoreau. Burroughs and Torrey sold well, but so did Chapman's *Handbook* and the many field guides and manuals published between 1885 and about 1920. Mabel Wright's *Birdcraft,* an early guide for backyard birders, was reissued eleven times, and Neltje Blanchan Doubleday's guides sold well over 100,000 copies. The well crafted essays of post-transcendentalists like Burroughs and Torrey in which the pleasures of birding were extolled were bought by readers everywhere, not necessarily only by bird lovers. The taste for pure nature appreciation appealed to a more refined social level than the taste for collecting bird nests and eggs.

The Birds of North America, the team-written encyclopedia which came out in 1917, was one of the first books written for bird watchers who between its covers could find *all* North American species illustrated, described and catalogued. The introduction eloquently addressed the two kinds of bird students who might purchase the book. The first group included professional ornithologists and amateur bird students who could consult the technical descriptions of the bird's size, shape, color, range, and eating habits. The second group were the bird lovers for whom the authors had provided anecdotal information about the birds' habits and personalities. The bird lover thus could perceive the kinship between himself and the birds. By 1917 the gap was widening between nature students and bird watchers who were watching birds for enjoyment.

In the entry for each bird in *The Birds of North America* the authors also included economic ornithology, an applied approach which developed in the nineteenth century to reconcile conservation and bird appreciation with scientific inquiry. Economic ornithology was taken up primarily by the Biological Survey in Washington, formerly in the Department of Agriculture but now the Sport Fisheries and Wildlife Service of the Department of the Interior, as well as by the state departments of agriculture at the end of the last century. Economic ornithologists analyzed the stomach contents of birds, by which they estimated the usefulness of a species as beneficial consumers of insects injurious to croplands or to evaluate the harm a species does to useful fruits, trees or crops. The discipline had its heyday in the first thirty years of this century, but was already popular in Henry Thoreau's time. Thoreau was the first critic of economic ornithology. In his journal entry for April 8, 1859, he mused:

When the question of the protection of birds comes up, the legislatures regard only a low use and never a high use; the best-disposed legislators employ one, perchance, only to examine their crops and see how many grubs or cherries they contain, and never to study their dispositions, or the beauty of their plumage, or listen and report on the sweetness of their song. The legislature will preserve a bird professedly not because it is a beautiful creature, but because it is a good scavenger or the like. . . . It is as if the question were whether some celebrated singer of the human race—some Jenny Lind or another—did more harm or good, should be destroyed, or not, and therefore a committee should be appointed, not to listen to her singing at all, but to examine the contents of her stomach and see if she devoured anything which was injurious to the farmers and gardeners, or which they cannot spare.

Thoreau's point of view was not taken up again until well after economic ornithology had become popular as an argument in support of bird conservation. Edward Forbush, leading Massachusetts ornithologist, was an enthusiastic practitioner of economic ornithology. In his *The Usefulness of Birds,* published in 1907 under the auspices of the Massachusetts Department of Agriculture, Forbush presented the economic case for the most common birds in the United States. Written for the legislator, farmer, bird hater, and bird lover, the book is materialistic in tone. In his introduction, Forbush explained in layman's terms the intricate relationship between species and the ecology, laying out simplistically the balance of nature. Forbush had been influenced by Darwin's analysis of the utility of species. By relating evolution to utilitarianism, Darwin used the theory of natural selection to argue for the moral perfection of species. A species with little moral worth could be viewed as imperfectly evolved, one with high utilitarian worth as completely evolved. Birds, argued Forbush, except for two or three species of raptors like the Cooper's hawk or the great horned owl which preyed on birds, were perfectly evolved for man's use. By analyzing the stomach contents of birds as well as by observing their feeding habits, Forbush proved with example after example the moral worth of birds in a man-dominated world. Robins destroyed caterpillars preying on fruit tree buds, field sparrows ate noxious weed seeds, and vultures consumed carrion which bred flies.

Forbush's point of view was widely shared by conservationists and bird students. It was useful in convincing farmers that the birds they shot as injurious to their crops were actually beneficial to agriculture. The widespread conviction that a bird's economic worth warranted its protection led some authors of popular bird guides to include economic ornithology in their texts. Neltje Blanchan Doubleday wrote an essay called "What Birds Do for Us" in her popular *The Book of Birds* of 1917 and Gene Stratton Porter in *Homing with the Birds* in 1919 wrote a prolonged polemic on the subject. Among Frank Chapman's listed reasons for bird study in the introduction to his *Handbook* was the economic usefulness of birds. "The claims of birds to our attention may then be formally summarized as follows," he wrote:

> *First,* because, as the natural enemies of harmful insects and rodents, as destroyers of weed seeds and as scavengers, birds are of inestimable value in the economics of nature.
>
> *Second,* because birds are sensitively organized creatures and respond so readily to the influences of their surroundings that in their structure, distribution, migration and habits, they convincingly demonstrate the creative and controlling forces of Nature.
>
> *Third,* because birds, more effectively than any other forms of life, arouse our inborn interest in animals, not only through their abundance and familiarity, but because their form, color, and power of flight stimulate our love of beauty and grace.. . . .

This hierarchy of goals was generally accepted by the conservation community. Contributors to *Bird-Lore* repeatedly stressed the economic value of birds, and the Audubon societies employed an economic ornithologist to supply the movement with further information to encourage bird conservation.

But even as early as 1910 there were rumblings of discontent with economic ornithology. Mabel Osgood Wright complained about its polemical nature in *Bird-Lore*. She wondered why farmers had to see the material worth of the bluebird or robin when its aesthetic and spiritual values were obviously superior. The patently materialistic bias implicit in economic ornithology undermined its future.

Another point of view about birdwatching was first put before American readers by Francis Herrick, best known for his biography of John James Audubon. Herrick taught zoology at Case Western Reserve, but his real passion was for bird studies with a camera. In 1901 he upset ornithologists with his book *The Home Life of the Wild Birds,* illustrated with over 100 of his own photographs from nature. In his text Herrick outlined an inventive methodology for observing nesting behavior of secretive woodland species. Instead of watching the birds at often inaccessible nests, Herrick moved them, tree limbs and all, to his yard or to a nearby lower perch where he reestablished the pair's territory. In most cases, he informed his readers, the birds took up where they had left off and Herrick could photograph nesting behavior.

Chapman and others were pleased with Herrick's results but uneasy about his methods. They feared that every backyard birder would disrupt nests in emulation of Herrick. Bird populations could decline if too many birders mismanaged the delicate operations Herrick described.

Herrick's methods reflected man's curiosity about what birds do and why they do it. Both amateur and professional bird students have become absorbed in the study of behavior. Famed ornithologist Marga-

A fashionable bird walk in Central Park during the 1940s. *Department of Library Services, American Museum of Natural History.*

ret Morse Nice first became obsessed in 1927 with the nesting activities of song sparrows occupying a forty-acre tangle of trees and vines behind her home in Columbus, Ohio. After a few hours of rapt absorption she was confused about which bird was doing what. She devised a method, now commonplace, to identify individuals with different colored bands. Ten years later Nice possessed minute data on song sparrows logged during thousands of hours with binoculars, pad and pencil. Cordelia Stanwood of Ellsworth, Maine, spent the forty years before her death in 1958 searching for warbler nests and photographing the young. Chapman considered her the authority on warbler nesting in North America. Nice and Stanwood were amateur students obsessed with birds who turned their obsession into a body of priceless information.

This kind of study became a scientific discipline called ethology through the work of Nobelists Konrad Lorenz and Niko Tinbergen, who studied avian behavior. Birds act in complex and obscure ways, serving as perfect subjects for a methodology based on observation with the eyes, binoculars, and notes.

Most observers cannot aspire to Lorenz's inventiveness nor to Nice's patience, but the effect of their work is felt by bird students on every level. Ethologists have convincingly linked behavior to taxonomy. How a bird sings may be just as good a clue to its place in evolution as the shape of its larynx. A birdwatcher can identify a species not just by its appearance but by what it does—how it flies, where it perches, how it sings. A birder develops identification skills that quickly take in shape of bill and color of plumage but also learns characteristic movements at length.

Birds, Henry Thoreau knew, are captivating creatures, exotically colored and shaped, often difficult to see and exasperating to study. It is small wonder that Audubon and Wilson, birding without field glasses, shot their subjects. But to hold a dead bird in the hand is a different experience from seeing an egret in breeding plumage, or a scarlet tanager drink at a spring, or even a starling attract its mate by ruffling its homely feathers. Before this panoply of color, form, and movement, the birds' usefulness seems less significant and its taxonomy secondary. We are well into an era of aesthetic birding. Birders today admit frankly that they watch birds because they are beautiful and fascinating creatures.

Bibliography

NOTE TO THE BIBLIOGRAPHIES

The publications included here comprise two kinds of material: books and articles the authors have used and found helpful as sources, and general works for those who want to read further about a particular topic. Sources for quotations to each chapter follow the selected readings. Only a few of the most important references are repeated in both sections.

ONE BIRD DISCOVERIES IN THE NEW WORLD

SELECTED READINGS

The best general account of early American bird study is Elsa Guerdrum Allen, "The History of American Ornithology before Audubon," *Transactions of the American Philosophical Society,* n.s. 41, 1951, 387–591.

Seventeenth and eighteenth centuries: John Josselyn's travel report is *An Account of Two Voyages to New England* (London, 1675), republished in *Collections of the Massachusetts Historical Society,* 3rd ser., 3, 1833, 211–354. An essential source on Catesby is John Reinhold Forster, *A Catalogue of the Animals of North America in Selected Works by Eighteenth Century Naturalists and Travelers,* 1771 (reprinted by Arno Press, New York, 1974), and a useful modern biography is George Frederick Frick and Raymond Phineas Stearns, *Mark Catesby, the Colonial Audubon* (Urbana, Illinois, 1961). The standard scholarly edition of Bartram's *Travels,* with good annotations and indices, is

The Travels of William Bartram (Naturalist Edition), ed. Francis Harper (New Haven, 1958); Bartram's nature drawings are handsomely reproduced and annotated in *William Bartram's Botanical and Zoological Drawings, 1756–1788*, ed. Joseph Ewan (Philadelphia, 1968). Little is available on Benjamin Barton beyond one sound article: Jeanette E. Graustein, "The Eminent Benjamin Smith Barton," *The Pennsylvania Magazine of History and Biography*, 85, 1961, 423–428.

Early nineteenth-century explorations: The primary sources are the travelers' own journals. Those consulted are: *Original Journals of the Lewis and Clark Expedition, 1804–1806*, ed. R. G. Thwaites, 5 vols. (New York, 1904–1905); *The Northern Expeditions of Stephen H. Long: The Journals of 1817 and 1823 and Related Documents*, ed. L. M. Kane, J. D. Holmquist, and C. Gilman (Minneapolis, 1978); *The Journal of Captain John R. Bell, Official Journalist for the Stephen H. Long Expedition to the Rocky Mountains, 1820*, ed. H. M. Fuller and L. H. Hafen (Glendale, 1967); John Kirk Townsend, *Narrative of a Journey across the Rocky Mountains to the Columbia River* (published with John B. Wyeth, *Oregon, or a Short History of a Long Journey*) (Fairfield, Wash., 1970), also in *Early Western Travels*, ed. R. G. Thwaites (Cleveland, 1905). On the wildlife observed by Lewis, Clark and company, see *The Natural History of the Lewis and Clark Expeditions*, ed. R. D. Burroughs (East Lansing, Michigan, 1961). Basic information on Say and Nuttall is found in Jeanette E. Graustein, *Thomas Nuttall, Naturalist: Explorations in America, 1808–1841* (Cambridge, Massachusetts, 1967), and Harry B. Weiss and Grace M. Zeigler, *Thomas Say, Early American Naturalist* (Springfield, Illinois, 1931).

SOURCES OF QUOTATIONS

26 "prospect is greatly beautified": *John and William Bartram's America, Selections from the Writings of the Philadelphia Naturalists*, ed. Helen Gere Cruickshank, New York, Devin-Adair, 1957, 278.

26 "This notion": *Bartram's America*, 1957, 302; *The Travels of William Bartram* (Naturalist Edition), ed. Francis Harper, New Haven, Yale University Press, 1958, 178–179.

28 "The bill or beak": *Bartram's America*, 1957, 291–292.

29 "doubtless many others": Thomas Jefferson, *Notes on the State of Virginia* (1785), New York, Evanston and London, Harper Torchbacks, 1964, 70.

TWO   ALEXANDER WILSON,
       PIONEER BIRD STUDENT

SELECTED READINGS

The first biography of Wilson is by his closest follower who added it to the final posthumous volume of Wilson's masterpiece, *American Ornithology;* it is also separately published as George Ord, *Sketch of the Life of Alexander Wilson, Author of the American Ornithology* (Philadelphia, 1828). Subsequent editions of Wilson's great book with information on him are: Alexander Wilson and Charles Lucien Bonaparte, *American Ornithology, or the Natural History of Birds of the United States*, ed.

Robert Jameson, 4 vols. (Edinburgh, 1831), with a memoir on Wilson by W. M. H[etherington]; also Wilson, *American Ornithology . . .* , continued by C. L. Bonaparte with notes and biography by Sir William Jardine, 3 vols. (London, 1832). Critical biographies of Wilson are: James Southall Wilson, *Alexander Wilson, Poet-Naturalist, A Study of his Life with Selected Poems* (New York and Washington, 1906); and, most recently and thoroughly, Robert Cantwell, *Alexander Wilson, Naturalist and Pioneer* (Philadelphia and New York, 1961). An article by Elsa G. Allen is also important: "The American Career of Alexander Wilson," *Atlantic Naturalists,* 8, 1952, 61–76. A recent and extensive compendium of source information on Wilson is now available: *The Life and Letters of Alexander Wilson,* ed. Clark Hunter (Philadelphia, 1983).

SOURCES OF QUOTATIONS

42 "All the stories": *Life and Letters of Wilson,* ed. Clark Hunter, Philadelphia, American Philosophical Society, 1983, 141–142.

43 "Yet I don't know but a description": *Life and Letters of Wilson,* 1983, 356.

43 "I started this morning": *Life and Letters of Wilson,* 1983, 261.

47 "the greatest number of descriptions" and "From these barren and musty records": Alexander B. Grosart, *The Poems and Literary Prose of Alexander Wilson,* Paisley, 1876, 1, 245 (from second prefatory essay, *American Ornithology,* Philadelphia, Bradford & Innskeep, 1808, 1) and 259 (from sixth prefatory essay, *American Ornithology,* 1812, 5).

48 "reverend doctors": "spacious sanctuary"; "didn't know a sparrow": *Life and Letters of Wilson,* 1983, 275–276.

49 "Science and literature": Alexander Wilson, *American Ornithology,* 1814, 9, ed. George Ord, xxxix; *Life and Letters of Wilson,* 1983, 93, 271.

53 "The appetite of the Bald Eagle": *American Ornithology,* 1811, 4, 93–94; *Wilson's American Ornithology,* ed. T. M. Brewster, 1840 (reprinted by Arno, New York, 1970), 330.

54 "overwhelms us with astonishment"; "leads us to the contemplation": *American Ornithology,* 1808, 1, 3; *Poems and Literary Prose of Wilson,* 1876, 1, 242.

56 "neither received one act of civility": *American Ornithology,* 1814, 9, xxxix; *Life and Letters of Wilson,* 1983, 93, 271.

THREE   JOHN JAMES AUDUBON,
        PIONEER BIRD ARTIST

SELECTED READINGS

Audubon's travel journals, a primary source, are available in part in Maria R. Audubon, *Audubon and His Journals,* 1900, 2 vols., with contribution by Elliott Coues (reprinted by Dover, New York, 1960) and *The Journal of John James Audubon Made during His Trip to New Orleans in 1820–21,* ed. Howard Corning (Boston, 1929). The standard biography of Audubon is Francis Hobart Herrick, *Audubon the Naturalist, a History of His Life and Times,* 2 vols. (New York and London, 1917); 2nd ed. (New

York, 1938). Other biographies are numerous; worthy of mention are Robert Buchanan, *The Life and Adventures of Audubon the Naturalist* (London and New York, 1864); Stanley Clisby Arthur, *Audubon, an Intimate Life of the American Woodsman* (New Orleans, 1937); Alexander B. Adams, *John James Audubon, a Biography* (New York, 1966). An eloquent article by Robert Cushman Murphy is "John James Audubon (1785–1851): An Evaluation of the Man and His Work," *The New York Historical Society Quarterly,* 40, 1956, 315–350. Roger Tory Peterson and Virginia Marie Peterson, *Audubon's Birds of America,* The Audubon Society Baby Elephant Folio (New York, 1981) is a recent deluxe edition of the artist's great book with annotations. The essential bibliographic and production information on it is in Waldemar H. Fries, *The Double Elephant Folio, the Story of Audubon's "Birds of America"* (Chicago, 1973). Mary Durant and Michael Harwood, *On the Road with John James Audubon* (New York, 1980) is a delightful description of journeying in Audubon's wandering footsteps. Some current views of the bird artist are found in Alton A. Lindsey, *The Bicentennial of John James Audubon* (Bloomington, Ind., 1985) with articles by five other authors.

NOTES ON QUOTATIONS

67–68   "Should one of the young feel fatigued": *The Bird Biographies of John James Audubon,* ed. Alice Ford, New York, Macmillan, 1957, 205.

68   "will alight on the highest branch"; "The hole is, I believe": *Bird Biographies of Audubon,* 1957, 96, 54.

68–69   "The Whip-Poor-Will": *Bird Biographies of Audubon,* 1957, 190.

69   "These notes seem pretty plainly": *Wilson's American Ornithology,* ed. T. B. Brewster, 1840 (reprinted by Arno, New York, 1970), 377.

72–73   "Persons unacquainted with these birds": *Bird Biographies of Audubon,* 1957, 161.

FOUR   JOHN BURROUGHS,
           HUDSON RIVER NATURALIST

SELECTED READINGS

The standard complete edition of Burroughs's essays is *The Writings of John Burroughs,* 23 vols. (Boston and New York, 1904–1923). Dr. Clara Barrus, a psychiatrist and Burroughs's literary executor, published studies of the naturalist based on intimate knowledge of sources about him, especially *The Life and Letters of John Burroughs,* 2 vols. (Boston and New York, 1925) and *John Burroughs, Boy and Man* (New York, 1926). There are several critical and biographical monographs on Burroughs, of which the best are: William Sloane Kennedy, *The Real John Burroughs* (New York and London, 1924); Elizabeth Burroughs Kelley, *John Burroughs Naturalist, the Story of His Work and Family by His Granddaughter* (New York, 1959); and Perry D. Westbrook, *John Burroughs* (New York, 1974). A recent anthology, *The Birds of John Burroughs, Keeping a Sharp Lookout,* ed. Jack Kligerman (New York, 1976) introduces and presents a selection of the author's bird writings. Burroughs's critique of Audubon is found in his book *John James Audubon* (Boston and New York, 1902).

SOURCES OF QUOTATIONS

81   "I detect this song rising": *The Writings of John Burroughs,* Boston and New York, Riverside Press, 1904–1923, 23 vols, 1, *Wake-Robin,* 1871, 51–52. *John Burroughs' America, Selections of the Writings of the Hudson River Naturalist,* ed. Farida Wiley, New York, Devon-Adair, 1951, 220.

83   "I want rather to feel the inspiration": *Writings of Burroughs,* 13, "Wildlife about My Cabin," in *Far and Near,* 1904, 155–156.

84   "Man can have but one": *Writings of Burroughs,* 7, "A Sharp Lookout," in *Signs and Seasons,* 1887, 37.

84   "If I name every bird": *Writings of Burroughs,* 1, *Wake-Robin,* 1871, xv–xvi.

84   "studied the birds?": *Writings of Burroughs,* 17, "The Summit of the Years," in *Summit of the Years,* 1913, 13.

85   "I killed it, little dreaming": *Writings of Burroughs,* 20, "The Spring Procession," in *Field and Study,* 1919, 4; *Burroughs' America,* 1951, 213.

85   "to see no more and no less": *Writings of Burroughs,* 14, "The Book of Nature," in *Ways of Nature,* 1905, 238.

90   "Don't forget I showed you": *Writings of Burroughs,* 22, *Under the Maples,* 1921, 109.

90   "One April I went to Yellowstone": *Theodore Roosevelt, an Autobiography,* New York, Scribners, 1927, 320–321.

90–91 "Throughout the trip": John Burroughs, *Camping and Tramping with Roosevelt,* Boston and New York, Houghton Mifflin, 1906, 40.

91   "I'm glad you've come, Chapman": Frank M. Chapman, *Autobiography of a Bird Lover,* New York and London, Appleton-Century, 1933, 29.

FIVE   JOHN MUIR, MOUNTAIN NATURALIST

SELECTED READINGS

The primary source on Muir, other than his own books, is found in his journals, published as *John of the Mountains, the Unpublished Journals of John Muir,* ed. Linnie Marsh Wolfe (Boston, 1938). The standard biography of Muir is by his literary executor, William Frederick Badè, *The Life and Letters of John Muir,* 2 vols. (Boston and New York, 1924). Another biography with much unpublished source material is Linnie Marsh Wolfe, *Son of the Wilderness, the Life of John Muir* (New York, 1945). Two modern biographies are also useful: Herbert F. Smith, *John Muir* (New York, 1965) and James Mitchell Clarke, *Life and Adventures of John Muir* (San Diego, c. 1979). On Muir in Yosemite and the Sierras see first of all John Muir, "Studies in the Sierra," *Overland Monthly,* 12–14, 1874–1875, reprinted in *Sierra Club Bulletin,* 9–11, 1913–1921, ed. William E. Colby, rev. eds. by Colby, San Francisco, 1950 and 1960, and summarized in John Muir, *The Yosemite* (New York, 1912), ch. 11; and also a recent selection of the mountaineer's writings, John Muir, *To Yosemite and Beyond, Writings from the Years 1883–1875,* ed. Robert Engberg and Donald Wesling, Madison, Wisconsin, 1980. Roderick Nash, *Wilderness and the American Mind* (New Haven, 1967, rev.

ed. 1973), ch. 8, discusses Muir's intellectual contributions to nature studies. Recently two scholarly books have assessed Muir's place in American natural history and the conservation movement: Stephen Fox, *John Muir and His Legacy* (Boston and Toronto, 1981) and Michael P. Cohen, *The Pathless Way, John Muir and the American Wilderness* (Madison, Wisconsin, 1984).

SOURCES OF QUOTATIONS

96   "chattered and scolded": John Muir, *A Thousand Mile Walk to the Gulf,* ed. W. F. Badè, Boston and New York, Houghton Mifflin, 1916, 78.

97   "Oh, no, not for me": John Muir, *To Yosemite and Beyond, Writings from the Years 1863–1875,* ed. Robert Engberg and Donald Wesling, Madison, University of Wisconsin Press, 1980, 43.

97   "I have crossed the Range": William Frederic Badè, *The Life and Letters of Muir,* Boston and New York, Houghton Mifflin, 1924, 1, 201; Linnie Marsh Wolfe, *Son of the Wilderness, the Life of John Muir,* New York, Knopf, 1945, 124.

97   "bewitched, enchanted": *Life and Letters of Muir,* 1924, 1, 202.

97–98   "tough old clothes": *John of the Mountains, the Unpublished Journals of John Muir,* ed. Linnie Marsh Wolfe, Boston, Houghton Mifflin, 1938, 35.

99   "There are no harsh": *John of the Mountains,* 1938, 82.

100   "Some smug practical old": John Muir, *The Story of My Boyhood and Youth,* Boston and New York, Houghton Mifflin, 1913, 161.

100–101 "Now it never seems to occur": *Thousand Mile Walk,* 1916, 138–139; *The Wilderness World of John Muir,* ed. E. W. Teale, Boston, Houghton Mifflin, 1954, 141–142.

101   "Any fool can destroy trees": *Our National Parks* [1901], Madison, University of Wisconsin Press, 1981, 364–365; *Wilderness World,* 1954, 231.

103   "I would gladly lie awake": *John of the Mountains,* 1938, 227.

103   "in one moment": *John of the Mountains,* 1938, 58.

103   "looking like a little clod": "the oddest daintiest": John Muir, *My First Summer in the Sierra,* Boston and New York, Houghton Mifflin, 1911, 87–89.

104   "No wonder he sings well": *Our National Parks,* 1981, 240.

104   "a bird is not feathers": *John of the Mountains,* 1938, 437–438.

SIX   THE FIRST FIFTY YEARS OF THE
        AUDUBON MOVEMENT

SELECTED READINGS

The history of the Audubon movement is mainly found in the serial publications of the national and state Audubon societies, especially in *Bird-Lore* and its predecessor and successors, *Audubon Magazine* and *Audubon.* George B. Grinnell's statement of purpose for the initial short-lived Audubon society is in his publication, *The Audubon Magazine,* 1, 1887–1888, 5. Later summaries of goals for the national Audubon association are by Frank M. Chapman, "The National Association, its Needs and Aims," and by William Dutcher, "History of the Audubon Movement," *Bird-Lore*, 7, 1905, 39–57. A joint statement by leading ornithologists and conservationists was an important opening for bird preservation: "The Present Wholesale Destruction of Bird Life in the United States," *Science*, 7, 1886, 191–205, with articles by Joel A. Allen, William Dutcher, George B. Sennett, et al. On Grinnell, the founder of the Audubon movement, see T. Gilbert Pearson, "Some Audubon Workers, IV: George Bird Grinnell," *Bird-Lore*, 14, 1912, 77–80. Some other indicative summaries of Audubon movement history are: T. Gilbert Pearson, "The Audubon Association and the Spirit of Cooperation," *Bird-Lore*, 31, 1929, 225–232; and Frank M. Chapman, "The Relation of *Bird-Lore* to the National Association of Audubon Societies," *Bird-Lore*, 34, 1932, 284–328.

SOURCES OF QUOTATIONS

111 "Miss Brady": William Dutcher, "The Destruction of Bird Life in the Vicinity of New York," *Science*, 7, 1886, 199, quoting *New York Sun*, December 13 and 20, 1885.

114 "I had expected to see some": Carl W. Buchheister and Frank Graham, Jr., "From the Swamps and Back, a Concise and Candid History of the Audubon Movement," *Audubon*, 75, 1973, 7.

115 "to discourage the buying and wearing": "Swamps and Back," 1973, 10.

118 "It is probable": Frank M. Chapman, *Autobiography of a Bird Lover*, New York and London, Appleton-Century, 1933, 38.

121 "scientifically correct": William Dutcher, "History of the Audubon Movement," *Bird-Lore*, 7, 1905, 43.

SEVEN   THE AUDUBON MOVEMENT
          FROM CRISIS TO MATURITY

SELECTED READINGS

The best overall history of the Audubon societies from the beginning to recent times is a long, readable article by Carl W. Buchheister and Frank Graham, Jr., "From the Swamps and Back, a Concise and Candid History of the Audubon Movement," *Audubon*, 75, 1973, 4–45. See also a speech of John H. Baker, president of the National Audubon Society, on its fiftieth anniversary, published as "Fifty Years of Progress in Furtherance of Audubon Objectives," *Audubon*, 57, 1955, 8–9. Roger Tory Peterson has told the story of Audubon society publications, to which he often contributed, in "The Evolution of a Magazine," *Audubon*, 75, 1973, 46–51.

SOURCES OF QUOTATIONS

139 "Beneath the tall white lighthouse": Celia Thaxter, "Under the Lighthouse," *Audubon Magazine*, 1, 1887, 211.

EIGHT   SAVING THE BIRDS

SELECTED READINGS

The pioneering essay on bird conservation is Joel A. Allen, "On the Decrease of Birds in the United States," *The Penn Monthly*, 7, 1876, 931–944. Also historically important are A. K. Fisher, *The Hawks and Owls of the United States in Relation to Agriculture* (Washington, 1893) and W. E. D. Scott, "The Present Condition of Some of the Bird Rookeries on the Gulf Coast of Florida," *The Auk*, 4, 1887, 135–144, 273–284. The earlier spread of sanctuaries is summarized by Robert P. Allen, "The Wildlife Sanctuary Movement in the United States," *Bird-Lore*, 36, 1934, 80–84, 269–272. The political and legal aspects of bird conservation have generated a number of good works, especially John C. Phillips, "Migratory Bird Protection in North America, the History of Control by the United States Federal Government and a Sketch of the Treaty with Great Britain" (Special Publication of the American Committee for International Wildlife Protection, 1, n.p., 1934); Whitney R. Cross, "Ideas in Politics: The Conservation Policies of the Two Roosevelts," *Journal of the History of Ideas*, 14, 1953, 421–438; William S. Boyd, "Federal Protection of Endangered Species," *Stanford Law Review*, 22, 1970, 1289–1309; and a book-length study, Donald C. Swain, *Federal Conservation Policy, 1921–1933* (University of California Publications in History 76, Berkeley, 1963). An essential general book on conservation is Samuel P. Hays, *Conservation and the Gospel of Efficiency, the Progressive Conservation Movement, 1890–1920* (Cambridge, Massachusetts, 1959), and an excellent overview of bird preservation and its bibliography is found in Robert Henry Welker, *Birds and Men, American Birds in Science, Art, Literature and Conservation, 1800–1900* (Cambridge, Massachusetts, 1955), ch. 12, 15, 16. For more bibliography see Thomas LeDuc, "The Historiography of Conservation," *Forest History*, 9, 1965, 23–28, and recently James A. Tober, *Who Owns the Wildlife? the Political Economy of Conservation in 19th Century America* (Westport, Connecticut, 1981), which is also informative on the political, legal, and economic background of the many-sided issues of conservation.

SOURCES OF QUOTATIONS

156   "There is a compensation": Theodore Whaley Cart, "The Lacey Act: America's First Nationwide Wildlife Statute," *Forest History*, 17, 1973, 4.

156   "an open season on migrant game": George Shiras 3rd, *Hunting Wildlife with Camera and Flashlight, a Record of Sixty-Five Years' Visits to the Woods and Waters of North America*, 2 vols., 1, Washington, National Geographic Society, 1935, 447.

158   "Here a national interest": Missouri vs. Holland, 252 U.S. Supreme Court 434 (1920).

158–159 "all our recommendations": Stephen Fox, *John Muir and His Legacy*, Boston and Toronto, 1981, 158.

160   "put the federal government": William T. Hornaday, *Thirty Years War for Wildlife, Gains and Losses in the Thankless Task*, 1931 (reprinted by Arno, New York, 1970), 236.

169   "sucked funds for wildlife": Ira N. Gabrielson, *Wildlife Refuges*, New York, Macmillan, 1943, 18.

NINE *WOMEN AND BIRD CONSERVATION*

SELECTED READINGS
For a survey of women in American science see Margaret Rossiter's excellent *Women Scientists in America, Struggles and Strategies to 1940* (Baltimore, 1982). Biographies of main protagonists can be found in Harvard University's *Notable American Women, 1607–1950* (Cambridge, Massachusetts, 1971). Accounts of some important figures are: Anna Botsford Comstock, *The Comstocks of Cornell* (New York, 1953); Margaret Morse Nice, *Research Is a Passion with Me* (Toronto, 1979); Jeanette Porter Meehan, *The Lady of the Limberlost* (Garden City, 1928) and Mabel Osgood Wright, *My New York* (New York, 1926).

SOURCES OF QUOTATIONS
177 "Whereas: the beautiful white herons": *Bird-Lore,* 9, 1907, 61.

179 "On May 16 came": George Miksch Sutton, *Bird Student, An Autobiography,* Austin, University of Texas Press, 1980, 36.

TEN *NATURE FAKERY AND CONCEALING COLORATION*

SELECTED READINGS
A good account of nature fakery can be found in John Henry Wadland, *Ernest Thompson Seton: Man in Nature and the Progressive Tradition* (New York, 1978). Intriguing is Seton's self-defense in Ernest Thompson Seton, *Trail of an Artist Naturalist* (New York, 1940). Another perspective is offered in Frank M. Chapman, *Autobiography of a Bird-Lover* (New York, 1933). For concealing coloration see the famous treatise by Gerald Thayer, *Concealing Coloration in the Animal Kingdom* (New York, 1918). A general account is offered by Ross Anderson, *Abbott Handerson Thayer* (Syracuse, 1982).

SOURCES OF QUOTATIONS
194   "He turned to a statue": Ernest Thompson Seton, *Wild Animals I Have Known,* New York, Scribners, 1898, 335 and 344.

194   "who can tell": *Wild Animals I Have Known,* 1898, 357.

194–95 "have the wild things": *Wild Animals I Have Known,* 1898, 360.

196   "of course it is": John Burroughs, "Real and Sham Natural History," *Atlantic Monthly,* 91, 1903, 299.

199   "That interesting little comedy": William J. Long, *School of the Woods,* Boston, Ginn and Company, 1903, 5.

200   "There is nothing": Burroughs, "Real and Sham Natural History," 305.

200–201 "Twenty years ago while": William J. Long, "Animal Surgery," *Outlook,* 75, 1903, 122.

201   "Are we to believe": Frank M. Chapman, "The Case of William J. Long," *Science,* 19, 1904, 387.

202   "It requires the briefest": "Case of William J. Long," 388.

202   "Men of this stamp": Theodore Roosevelt, "Nature Fakers," *Everybody's Magazine*, 17, 1907, 430.

206   "On former occasions": Frank M. Chapman, *Autobiography of a Bird-Lover*, New York, Appleton-Century, 1933, 80.

208   "In sufficiently thick cover": Theodore Roosevelt, *African Game Trails*, New York, Scribners, 1909, 643.

ELEVEN   CATS, STARLINGS, AND
                 ENGLISH SPARROWS

SELECTED READINGS

For a good overview on cats see Muriel Beadle, *The Cat, History, Biology, and Behavior* (New York, 1977). An amusing polemic is Edward Forbush's *The Domestic Cat: Birdkiller, Monster and Destroyer of Wildlife* (Massachusetts State Board of Agriculture Bulletin Number 2, 1916). On introduced species of birds two books stand out: John L. Long, *Introduced Birds of the World* (Sydney, Australia, 1981) and George Laycock, *The Alien Animals* (Garden City, 1966).

SOURCES OF QUOTATIONS

209   "from being originally": Mabel Osgood Wright, "Birds of My Garden," *Bird-Lore*, 13, 1911, 132.

212   "the association is not at this time": T. Gilbert Pearson, "Cats and Birds," *Bird-Lore*, 17, 1915, 408.

212   "One of the greatest menaces": T. Gilbert Pearson, "Birds and Cats," *Bird-Lore*, 20, 1918, 326.

213   "How did they get in?": Mabel Osgood Wright, "Birdcraft Sanctuary," *Bird-Lore*, 32, 1930, 401.

213   "Nowhere in the country": T. Gilbert Pearson, "Report of T. Gilbert Pearson, President," *Bird-Lore*, 25, 1933, 362.

213   "The problem of cat": Muriel Beadle, *The Cat: History, Biology, and Behavior*, New York, Simon and Schuster, 1977, 218. See also Walker Johnson, ed., *The Papers of Adlai Stevenson*, 3, *Governor of Illinois, 1949–1953*, Boston, Little Brown, 73–74.

TWELVE   THE LITERATURE OF BIRDING

SELECTED READINGS

The cornerstone of American nature and bird literature is the writing of Henry David Thoreau, whose central work by far is his journal, published with some omissions, as *The Journal of Henry D. Thoreau*, 14 vols. in 2 vols., ed. Bradford Torrey and Francis H. Allen, 1906 (reprinted by Dover, New York, 1962). Most but not all of Thoreau's remarks on birds are gathered and annotated in *Thoreau on Birds*, ed. Helen Gere Cruickshank (New York, Toronto and London, n.d.). Critical monographs on Thoreau are plentiful, but two may be recommended: Joseph Wood Krutch, *Henry David Thoreau*, 1948 (The American Men in Letters Series, reprinted by Greenwood Press, Westport, Connecticut, 1973) and recently Robert D. Richardson, *Henry Thoreau, a Life of the Mind* (Berkeley, 1986). General analyses of works by Thoreau and his successors include Henry Chester Tracy, *American Naturists* (New York, 1930) and Robert Henry Welker, *Birds and Men, American Birds in Science, Art, Literature, and Conservation, 1800–1900* (Cambridge, Massachusetts, 1955), ch. 7–11. Two good anthologies of bird literature are: Donald Culross Peattie, *A Gathering of Birds, an Anthology of the Best Ornithological Prose* (New York, 1939) and Roger Tory Peterson, *The Bird Watcher's Anthology* (New York, 1957). On major individual nature writers, for Burroughs see: Norman Foerster, *Nature in American Literature, Studies in the Modern View of Nature* (New York, 1923), ch. 9; and Philip Marshall Hicks, *The Development of Natural History in American Literature* (Philadelphia, 1924), ch. 4. On Ernest Thompson Seton: *Trail of an Artist Naturalist, the Autobiography of Ernest Thompson Seton* (New York, 1940); *Ernest Thompson Seton's America, Selections from the Writings of the Artist-Naturalist*, ed. Farida Wiley with a contribution by Julia Seton (New York, 1954); and the thoughtful analysis in John Henry Wadland, *Ernest Thompson Seton, Man in Nature and the Progressive Era, 1880–1915* (New York, 1978, reprint by Arno of doctoral dissertation at York University, Toronto). On Aldo Leopold: Susan Fleder, "Thinking Like a Mountain: a Biographical Study of Aldo Leopold," *Forest History*, 17, 1973, 14–28. For many of these writers and American bird students in general see: T. S. Palmer et al., *Biographies of Members of the American Ornithologists' Union*, ed. Paul H. Oehser, reprinted from *The Auk*, 1884–1954 (Washington, 1954).

SOURCES OF QUOTATIONS

222   "The change from storm and winter": Henry David Thoreau, *Walden, or Life in the Woods*, ed. E. W. Teale, New York, Dodd Mead, 1946, 347–348.

222   "A new bird, probably an eagle": *The Journal of Henry D. Thoreau*, ed. Bradford Torrey and Francis H. Allen [1906], 14 vols. in 2 vols. (reprinted by Dover, New York, 1962), I, 351 (entry for 26 March 1842).

222   "a very slight": *Walden*, 1946, 351.

222   "the night warbler: *Thoreau's Journal*, 2, 238 (11 June 1851), and introduction, xlvi; *Thoreau on Birds*, ed. Helen Gere Cruickshank, New York, Toronto and London, McGraw-Hill, n.d., 168.

223   "Now about the first of September": *Thoreau's Journal*, 2, 63 (31 August 1850).

223   "flew in their usual": *Thoreau's Journal*, 8, 262 (8 April 1856); *Thoreau on Birds*, 80.

223   "picking up the crumbs": *Walden*, 1946, 308.

224   "were adapted to their circumstances": Henry David Thoreau, *Cape Cod*, New York, Crowell, 1966, 81.

224   "I rejoice that there are owls": *Thoreau's Journal*, 3, 122–123 (16 November 1851).

224   "What a delicious sound": *Thoreau's Journal*, 7, 112–113 (11 January 1855): *Thoreau on Birds*, 135.

224–25 "Vegetation starts": *Thoreau's Journal*, 3, 459 (23 April 1952).

225   "You can study the habits": *Thoreau's Journal*, 5, 66 (29 March 1853).

225   "I cannot excuse myself": *Thoreau's Journal*, 6, 452 (18 August 1854).

225   "it was worth more to see them soar": *Thoreau's Journal*, 5, 246 (13 June 1853); *Thoreau on Birds*, 73–74.

225   "And is not that shell": *Thoreau's Journal*, 4, 269 (30 July 1852).

225   "Each town should have a park": *Thoreau's Journal*, 12, 387 (15 October 1859): *Walden*, 1946, 233.

227–28 "She is the parodist": *The Writings of John Burroughs*, Boston and New York, Riverside Press, 1905, 1, *Wake-Robin*, 1871, 30–31.

229   "Nature is not benevolent": *Writings of Burroughs*, 16, "The Gospel of Nature," in *Time and Change*, 1912, 271.

231   "From May to September": Dallas Lore Sharp, *Wild Life Near Home*, New York, Century, 1901, 134.

231   "Part of the answer": *Wild Life Near Home*, 1901, 261.

232   "It suggested the choking": Frank Bolles, *Land of the Lingering Snow, Chronicles of a Stroller in New England from January to June*, Boston and New York, Houghton Mifflin, 1893, 162–163.

233   "Particularly do I note": J. Hibbert Langille, *Our Birds in Their Haunts, a Popular Treatise on the Birds of Eastern North America*, New York, Judd, 1892, 5.

233   "Precious is the solitude": Mabel Osgood Wright, *The Friendship of Nature, a New England Chronicle of Birds and Flowers*, New York, Macmillan, 1894, 29.

235   "On April nights": Aldo Leopold, *A Sand County Almanac, and Sketches Here and There*, New York, Oxford University Press, 1949, 19.

236   "Sitting there in the twilight": Edwin Way Teale, *A Naturalist Buys an Old Farm*, New York, Dodd Mead, 1974, 16.

238   "I hate to say this": Robert Porter Allen, *On the Trail of Vanishing Birds*, New York, Toronto and London, McGraw-Hill, 1957, 48–49.

247   "[Rynchops] joined a flock of other skimmers": Rachel Carson, *Under the Sea Wind, a Naturalist's Picture of Ocean Life*, New York, Simon & Schuster, 1941, 8.

THIRTEEN   ARTISTS OF BIRD LIFE

SELECTED READINGS

On bird art in general see: Jean Anker, *Bird Books and Bird Art*, Copenhagen, 1938 (reprinted by Arno, New York, 1974); Robert Henry Welker, *Birds and Men, American Birds in Science, Art, Literature, and Conservation, 1800–1900* (Cambridge, 1955); *Animals in Art*, exhibition catalogue, Royal Ontario Museum (Ottawa, 1975). Some articles on bird art by, or in part by, America's senior bird artist are useful: Roger Tory Peterson, "Bird Painting in America," *Audubon Magazine*, 44, 1942, 166–176; Edwin Way Teale and Roger Tory Peterson, "Artist at Work," *Audubon Magazine*, 44, 1942,

350–359. Martina R. Norelli, *American Wildlife Painting,* New York, 1975, is an attractive visual anthology, and an article by Robert M. Mengel, "Beauty and the Beast: Natural History and Art," *Living Bird,* 18, 1979–1980, 27–70, is thoughtful and provocative. On individual bird artists, *Robert Bruce Horsfall (1868–1948), American Natural Science Illustrator,* exhibition catalogue, Rutgers and Morristown, New Jersey, Art Museums (New Brunswick, New Jersey, 1974). Hamilton M. Lain, *Allan Brooks, Artist Naturalist,* British Columbia Provincial Museum Special Publication no. 3 (Victoria, 1979); on Arthur Singer see *The Bird in Art,* exhibition catalogue, University of Arizona Gallery (Tucson, 1965); John Devlin and Grace Naismith, *The World of Roger Tory Peterson* (New York, 1977). Several of the leading American bird artists have extensive bibliographies, of which a few selections follow. Monographs on Louis Agassiz Fuertes: *Louis Agassiz Fuertes, His Life Briefly Told and His Correspondence,* ed. Mary Fuertes Boynton (New York, 1956); Frederick George Marcham, *Louis Agassiz Fuertes and the Singular Beauty of Birds* (New York, 1971); Robert M. Peck, *A Celebration of Birds: The Life and Art of Louis Agassiz Fuertes* (New York, 1982). A few of the more important articles on Fuertes: Frank M. Chapman, "In Memoriam: Louis Agassiz Fuertes," *The Auk,* 45, 1928, 1–27; Frank M. Chapman, "Fuertes and Audubon, a Comparison of the Work and Personalities of Two of the World's Great Bird Artists," *Natural History,* 39, 1937, 202–213; Roger Tory Peterson, "The Fuertes Legacy Will Never Die," *National Wildlife,* 10, 1972, 20–34. There are two recent books on Francis Lee Jaques: Florence Page Jaques, *Francis Lee Jaques, Artist of the Wilderness World* (New York, 1973) with contributions by Sigurd Olson and Harriet Buchheister; Donald T. Luce and Laura M. Andrews, *Francis Lee Jaques, Artist-Naturalist* (Minneapolis, 1982).

FOURTEEN   PARAPHERNALIA OF BIRDING

SELECTED READINGS

Celia Thaxter's letters to Bradford Torrey are published in *Letters of Celia Thaxter* (Boston, 1895). A good example of an early field guide is Mabel Osgood Wright's *Birdcraft* (New York, 1895). For an account of Peterson's methods see John Devlin and Grace Naismith, *The World of Roger Tory Peterson* (New York, 1977). Olin Sewall Pettingill's *Guide to Bird Finding, East of the Mississippi* (New York, 1951 and 1977) and *Guide to Bird Finding West of the Mississippi* (New York, 1953 and 1981) are models for most other regional guides.

SOURCES OF QUOTATIONS

287   "An instructive indication": Frank M. Chapman, "Editorial," *Bird-Lore,* 14, 1912, 237.

291   "354. Blue Jay": Frank M. Chapman, *Handbook of Birds of Eastern North America,* New York, Appleton, 1895, 388.

293   "In this attractive": Frank M. Chapman, "Book Notes and Reviews," *Bird-Lore,* 8, 1906, 30.

295   "A long reddish bird": Ernest Thompson Seton, "Recognition Marks of Hawks," *Bird-Lore,* 3, 1901, 187.

298   "Black-Poll Warbler": Roger Tory Peterson, *A Field Guide to the Birds*, Boston, Houghton Mifflin, 1939, 130.

299   "It truly turns on": Frank M. Chapman, "Book News and Reviews," *Bird-Lore*, 41, 1939, 177.

299   "I say they (the song birds)": E. B. White, "Song Birds," in *One Man's Meat* (Personal Library Edition), New York, Harper and Row, 1966, 248.

300   "Young birds with their": Roger Tory Peterson, *Field Guide to the Birds*, 1947, 85.

304–05 "is one of the most": John Bull and John Farrand, Jr., *The Audubon Society Field Guide to North American Birds, Eastern Region*, New York, Knopf (A Borzoi Book), 1977, 575.

FIFTEEN   THE SPORT TODAY

SELECTED READINGS

An anecdotal account of birding history is found in Joseph Kastner, *A World of Watchers* (New York, 1986). Roger Tory Peterson's *Bird Watcher's Anthology* (New York, 1957) contains accounts of birding adventures. Two books describe Big Year efforts: Roger Tory Peterson and James Fisher, *Wild America* (Boston, 1955) and James Vardaman, *Call Collect, Ask for Birdman* (New York, 1980). Mary Beacom Mower's *Stories about Birds and Bird Watchers from "Bird Watcher's Digest"* (New York, 1981) provides samples of this popular magazine's style.

SOURCES OF QUOTATIONS

312   "With this, the first": James Tucker, "Editorial," *Birding*, 1, 1969, 3.

313–14 "All day long Cruickshank": John O. Reilly, "The Biggest Bird Watch," reprinted in Roger Tory Peterson, *The Bird Watcher's Anthology*, New York, Harcourt Brace, 1957, 63.

316–17 "Now we were boarding": Florence Page Jaques, "The Big Day," reprinted in Roger Tory Peterson, *The Bird Watcher's Anthology*, New York, Harcourt Brace, 1957, 57.

320   "Identifying a bird": Ron Naveen, "Birding California Style," reprinted in Mary Beacom Mowers, *Stories about Birds and Bird Watchers from "Bird Watcher's Digest,"* New York, Atheneum, 1981, 81.

SIXTEEN   FROM GUNS TO BINOCULARS

SELECTED READINGS

A primer on economic ornithology is Edward H. Forbush's *Useful Birds and Their Protection* (Boston, 1907). Margaret Morse Nice described her methods in *The Watcher at the Nest* (New York, 1939). For an account of Cordelia Stanwood's work see Chandler S. Richmond, *Beyond the Spring, Cordelia Stanwood of Birdsacre* (Lamoine,

Maine, 1978). Methods of behavioral research are outlined by Konrad Lorenz in *The Foundations of Ethology* (New York, 1981).

SOURCES OF QUOTATIONS

325   "if it would not": *The Journal of Henry D. Thoreau,* ed. Bradford Torrey and Francis H. Allen, Boston, Houghton Mifflin, 1906, 5, 65 (29 March 1853).

325   "I buy but few": *Thoreau's Journal,* 6, 192 (9 April 1854).

326–28 "This haste to kill": *Thoreau's Journal,* 14, 109 (9 October 1860).

330   "the student with": Frank M. Chapman, *Handbook of Birds of Eastern North America,* New York, Appleton, 1912, 16.

332   "When the question of": *Thoreau's Journal,* 12, 124 (8 April 1858).

333   *"First,* because as the": *Handbook of Birds,* 1912, 2.

Index